LOVE,

The Bond of Perfection

An Extensive Study of Biblical
Passages Pertaining to Marriage
and Marriage-related issues

By

Tom Caldwell

WESTBOW
PRESS®
A DIVISION OF THOMAS NELSON
& ZONDERVAN

WestBow Press books may be ordered through booksellers or by contacting:

WestBow Press
A Division of Thomas Nelson & Zondervan
1663 Liberty Drive
Bloomington, IN 47403
www.westbowpress.com
1 (866) 928-1240

ISBN: 978-1-4497-4808-1 (sc)
ISBN: 978-1-4497-4792-3 (hc)
ISBN: 978-1-4497-4793-0 (e)

Library of Congress Control Number: 2012906736

Print information available on the last page.

WestBow Press rev. date: 11/15/2018

Tom Caldwell is an ordained Assemblies of God minister and has served as a full-time prison chaplain in Kentucky since 1998. Tom and Kim have been married since 2001; they have two daughters, Emma, born in 2005, and Anna, born in 2007. Tom Caldwell has also written a book entitled *Jesus Heals Today*.

Contents

Introduction and Acknowledgments

Just after the creation of the first woman, God says in Genesis 2:24, "Therefore a man shall leave his father and mother and be joined to his wife, and they shall become one flesh." Marriage is the first human institution in the Bible. And the institution of marriage is the foundational human relationship in the family unit. So strong marriages are necessary for strong families. And strong families are necessary for a strong society. But it is difficult to have strong families and a strong society when the divorce rate is as high as it is in our country.[1] I have heard people say that marriage is the most difficult part of their lives. This is understandable because each marriage partner is responsible, not only for his or her own level of contentment and peace, but also for meeting certain needs that his or her spouse may have, as well as those of the children. And the difficulties of marriage are compounded if husband and wife are not Christians, or if they are not trained from the Word of God in how to have a loving, victorious marriage and family life. God says in Hosea 4:6a: "My people are destroyed for lack of knowledge." The destruction that has befallen a high percentage of marriages is due mainly to biblical ignorance and a lack of biblical application. For the married person and for the person anticipating the prospect of marriage in the future, a thorough study of the Word of God pertaining to marriage and related issues is vitally important. That is the purpose of this book. Important topics that are discussed include: What is love, and how does love require sacrifice? How can one sustain

---

[1] "It is estimated that 40% of all (American) marriages have ended in divorce as of 2008." (source: *Divorce*, Wikipedia).

positive, romantic feelings for one's spouse year after year? How is meeting certain expectations of one's spouse important to the marriage relationship, and what does God's love require of a spouse if or when certain expectations are not met? What are the purposes and roles of man and woman, and of husband and wife? What are the main points of *Song of Solomon* and other biblical passages that focus on marriage, love, parenting, and sexuality? What should singles know about the prospect of marriage? (This includes choosing the right spouse, expectations in marriage, appropriate boundaries with the opposite sex both before and after marriage, and the responsibilities of raising children [note Dt. 6:4; Eph. 6:4]). What does the Word of God say about sexual immorality (including lust, pornography, fornication, adultery, and homosexuality), and how can one avoid these sins?

Marriage is the context for many things, including an intimate male-female relationship, procreation and sexual pleasure within that relationship, the raising of children in the training and admonition of the Lord (Eph. 6:4), faith enhancement, and kingdom-of-God building through corporate Bible study, prayer, ministry, and service (Dt. 6:4-9; Mt. 18:19-20). Moreover, earthly marriage is a type of, or picture of, the ultimate and eternal marriage—that of Christ the Bridegroom to the church, His spotless, beloved bride. Many marriage books deal with just one or a few aspects of marriage. One book might focus on communication, another on honoring one's spouse, and another on meeting the needs of one's spouse. Each of these is an important aspect of marriage, and the advice found in such books, if it agrees with the biblical perspective, can be helpful to any marriage. But the purpose of this book is to be biblically comprehensive when it comes to marriage— to offer exposure to a large number and great variety of verses from the Old Testament and New Testament about love, marriage, and related topics. After all, the Bible is God's holy, inerrant Word for mankind, and it is authoritative and sufficient for the equipping of man and woman to live victoriously in all aspects of life, including marriage. I know this to be true, for I have been a Christian since 1992, when at the age of twenty-four I received Jesus as my Lord and Savior by personal faith in His shed blood on the cross of Calvary and in His bodily resurrection three days later. In this book I have tried to give you, the reader, exposure to and insight on many verses and passages related to marriage and love, and to make them handy for your own further study and frequent review.

I began this writing around June 2010 at the prompting of the Lord. This was not my plan; I was writing on evangelism at the time. So when the Lord impressed this project upon me, my initial vision was to write a booklet, perhaps fifty pages in length, and my initial motive was to obey the Lord as well as to strengthen my own marriage. That initial motive is still the main motive, and my wife, Kim, and I often read portions of this book together as part of our joint devotion time. As I studied and wrote about various passages on love and marriage, more and more passages came to mind. Also, I became even more convinced that I need to pursue expertise on all that the Bible says concerning how to be a godly husband and father, and I need to be a doer of the Word in these matters and not just a hearer (James 1:22). It is my conviction that, in regard to whatever responsibilities and talents the Lord gives a person, that person should pursue excellence. In other words, bloom where you are planted. Colossians 3:23 says it this way: "And whatever you do, do it heartily, as to the Lord and not to men." So if you are married, be married with all your heart! Give your marriage your wholehearted, best effort. And do so as to the Lord, to whom we all must give account.

I do hope the Lord continues to bless my ministry to the body of Christ—through my current position as a prison chaplain, through various preaching and evangelistic opportunities, and perhaps through a future pastorate. But I cannot build a solid ministry on a shaky foundation. Christ is my ultimate foundation. And my marriage and household are also foundational for any ministry the Lord may graciously give me. Paul wrote, "For if a man does not know how to rule his own house, how will he take care of the church of God?" (1 Tim. 3:5). It is my hope that you, the reader, will also be equipped and inspired through this writing to wholeheartedly pursue excellence in your present or future prospective role as a spouse and parent. To God be all glory! May we who are Christians and are married, or perhaps will one day be married, always glorify God with our attitude and conduct within our homes!

I want to take a moment to acknowledge my wife, Kim. She said yes to my marriage proposal on October 20, 2001; we were married December 15, 2001. God has given her to me as my helpmate, soul mate, and best friend. I commit to being an excellent husband to you, Kim, for the rest of my life. God has also given us two beautiful children so far, Emma (born in 2005) and Anna (born in 2007). I also commit to being an excellent father to you, Emma and Anna, for the rest of my life. Concerning my role as husband and father (as well as concerning my salvation), I claim Philippians 1:6—"being confident of this very thing, that He who has begun a good work in you will complete it until the day of Jesus Christ." As God gives us the desires of our hearts when we delight in Him (Ps. 37:4), I desire excellence in my marriage and family life, knowing this can only come as I delight in God the Father through Jesus Christ my Lord.

Thank you, Tom and Janet Caldwell (my parents), for supporting me in all my endeavors, for demonstrating great love to Kim, Emma, Anna, and myself, and for raising me in church! Thank you, Carole and Don Carman (Kim's mother and stepfather), for your tremendous help with our children and around our house, and for your love. I am thankful you are my parents-in-law! Thank you, Don and Pam Mayberry (Kim's father and step-mother), for your love and support of our family, and for your visits. I am thankful you are my parents-in-law! Thank you, Tim and Sara, for being a great brother and sister-in-law! May the Lord bless you and your four beautiful children.

I want to acknowledge a good friend of mine, James Grant, who at this time is working on his doctoral dissertation at the Southern Baptist Theological Seminary. Through the years, James, you have shared with me, at my request, many insights pertaining to the Word of God. You have been very gracious to me in this matter, and I greatly appreciate that. Many of your insights are reflected in this book, and I thank you for editing a significant portion of this book. Thank you especially, James, for your valued friendship.

Chapter 1

Facets of Love–Part 1

A cut and polished diamond is a gem very precious to almost any woman. It is often the gem used in wedding rings, and it can represent the great value of the one whose finger is receiving it to the one who is putting it on, as well as the great value of the commitment in marriage the two are making. The blue diamond ring is perhaps the most expensive of all rings. A 6.04 carat blue diamond ring once sold at an auction in Hong Kong for $7.98 million. Hopefully, whoever receives such an engagement ring would place even more value in the marriage vows to be taken at the wedding ceremony than in the ring itself.

A wedding ring's diamond is multifaceted. The most popular diamond cut—"the modern round brilliant cut"—consists of fifty-eight facets (or polished plane surfaces). The crown of the diamond (which is the top half and most visible part of the diamond) consists of thirty-three cuts, and the pavilion of the diamond (the bottom half which is embedded in the ring) consists of twenty-five cuts. The cutting of the diamond is the procedure that changes the rough diamond stone into a faceted diamond gem; it's a procedure that obviously takes much knowledge and skill. Each facet of the diamond adds character, beauty, and value to the diamond.

As a diamond is perhaps the most precious of all gems, *agape* love is the most precious of all Christian virtues (1 Cor. 13:13). Though we will deal with the definition of *agape* love in Chapter 9, we can now view love as having many facets (e.g., self-sacrifice, forgiveness, patience, generosity, and hope), and each facet makes a significant contribution to the overall makeup of the spiritual gem that love is. This chapter and Chapter 11 will explore some of the facets of love, reflected in verses typically pertaining to love, in order to help carve, shape, and sculpt the attitudes and motives of our hearts as we relate to our spouse, so that we will best reflect the heart of our God, who is the embodiment and source of love.

"Now Jacob *loved* Rachel; so he said, 'I will serve you (Laban) seven years for Rachel your younger daughter. (20) So Jacob served seven years for Rachel, and they seemed only a few days to him because of the *love* he had for her" (Genesis 29:18, 20).

Glynn Wolfe of Blythe, California holds the record for being married (monogamously) the most times—twenty-nine times! His longest marriage lasted seven years and his shortest marriage lasted nineteen days. Twenty-four of the marriages reportedly ended in divorce and the other five ended due to death. Wolfe married his last wife, Linda Essox-Wolfe, after having known her for only one week. He died in 1997 at age eighty-eight while married to her, but she could not afford to fly to his funeral.[2]

What a contrast—the quick-committing but easily disillusioned Glynn Wolfe to the patient and devoted husband-to-be, Jacob. As love requires sacrifice, Jacob was willing to sacrifice seven years of his life in order to marry Rachel. He exercised great patience, seeing Rachel daily but not being able to have her as his bride until the seven years were completed. His love for Rachel was so great that the seven-year wait was not a burden to him; it seemed like only a few days. Furthermore, at the end of the seven years, because of the deceitfulness of Rachel's father, Laban, he also had to take her older sister, Leah, as his wife and then work for Laban seven additional

---

[2] *Glynn Wolfe*—Wikipedia.

years (though he did have Rachel, as well as Leah, as his wife during these next seven years).

Many people in their marriages could use a dose of such patience and endurance as Jacob displayed in his marriage. It takes patience to wait on God for the right person to come along, and it takes endurance when trials beset one's marriage. But through the strengthening of Christ and the renewing of your mind by the Word of God, you can walk in patience and endurance as a spouse. What would it take for you and your spouse to maintain the type of love, patience, and endurance that Jacob displayed in his relationship with Rachel?

Jacob knew he wanted to marry Rachel after he had known her for only one month (verse 14). This is probably the closest biblical story to love at first sight. Why did Jacob so love Rachel?[3] The only hint given by Scripture was that "Rachel was beautiful of form and appearance" (verse 17). Her physical attractiveness was a large part of the reason. Physical attractiveness is a big deal to many, if not most, men. If a man falls in love because the woman is physically attractive, then it stands to reason that what helps the man remain in love is the continued physical attractiveness of his wife. Over the long term, as Proverbs 31:30 says, "beauty is passing." With aging can come wrinkles, aches, and pains in a spouse. Nevertheless, remaining in physical shape and looking good is typically an important aspect in meeting the desires of your spouse. I encourage you to ask your spouse how you can meet his or her desires, including in terms of your physical appearance, and then make the necessary changes, as painful as it may initially seem, in order to meet those desires.

"*love* is as strong as death" (Song of Solomon 8:6).

On August 17, 2010, the *New York Times* contained an article by Rod Nordland, entitled "In Bold Display, Taliban Order Stoning Death." The article reported that in Kabul, Afghanistan, the Taliban ordered the first public stoning in nine years, killing a young couple who had eloped. Family members, as well as hundreds of neighbors, were involved in the stoning, and family had reportedly even tricked the couple to return home after they had fled. The victims, Khayyam (twenty-five years old) and Siddiqa (nineteen years old) confessed in

---

[3] James Grant, in conversation with me.

public to their relationship. Siddiqa's family had arranged for her to marry someone else. Her unwilling to do so, but instead elope with Khayyam was the cause for the stoning. It was reported that Khayyam and Siddiqa said before their accusers, "We love each other no matter what happens."[4]

As Khayyam and Siddiqa began their marriage with great love in their hearts for each other, hopefully most, if not all, of us also had great love in our hearts for our spouse on our wedding day. Would it not be wonderful if husband and wife would keep that first love they had for each other on their wedding day alive day by day and year by year, and even cause that love to grow? However, that first love often diminishes as spouses fail in their efforts to meet each other's expectations. But God calls the husband and wife to cultivate a love for each other that "is as strong as death" (Song 8:6). First, this means that love necessitates death to self. Death to self is for the purpose of complete devotion to Christ as well as blessing and devotion to the spouse. In John 15:13, Jesus said, "Greater love has no one than this, than to lay down one's life for his friends." You should demonstrate the greatest love possible toward your spouse by laying down your life for the godly edification and benefit of your spouse. Do not permit selfishness and sinfulness to take root in your marriage. And do not seek to save your life in the midst of your marriage, but instead lose your life for the sake of Jesus (Mt. 10:39) and lose your life for the sake of serving and blessing your spouse. Second, "love is as strong as death" means that love overcomes death.[5] Through knowing Christ, one is entitled, on account of Christ's redeeming love, to life beyond the grave—eternal life! So if the Christian husband or wife is required to literally lay down his or her life, then that is not loss but rather gain. Paul said, "For to me, to live is Christ, and to die is gain" (Phil. 1:21). So do not fear death, but rather fear Him who has the keys of Death and Hades—Christ. Why have a struggling, mediocre marriage when you can have an excellent marriage? Die to selfish ways in order to love your spouse. What self-gratifying attitudes or practices might you need to lay down in order to demonstrate love for your spouse?

---

[4] *In Bold Display, Taliban Order Stoning Death*, by Rod Nordland, (The New York Times, Aug. 17, 2010).

[5] James Grant, in conversation with me.

"Love does no harm to a neighbor" (Romans 13:10).

To love a person and to harm that person are absolutely contrary to one another. Certainly, no one should ever harm his or her spouse physically. That's called domestic violence, which is a felony. Do not remain in the house with someone who is a threat to your physical safety. If your spouse is a physical threat to you, then your spouse needs to submit to some sort of professional help such as counseling. And you should keep your distance.

Romans 13:10 includes the need to be harmless toward your spouse (and all other neighbors) with your thoughts, words, and actions. Speak wholesome words to your spouse as well as about your spouse—words which edify and impart grace. Furthermore, unfaithful or rebellious thoughts about your spouse, even if you keep such thoughts to yourself, are contrary to love. As a married person, it is sinful to entertain longing, lustful, or fantasizing thoughts about others to whom you are not married. Proverbs 12:5a says, "The thoughts of the righteous are right." Again, 2 Corinthians 10:5 says you are to bring "every thought into captivity to the obedience of Christ." To lust is to commit adultery (Mt. 5:28). To hate is to commit murder (1 Jn. 3:15). You must think good thoughts in your heart about your spouse. Kiss, don't curse. Hug, don't hit. Bless, don't blame. Forgive, don't fight. Help, don't harm your spouse. Encourage, don't exasperate your spouse. Pray for godly character to develop within your spouse. Make sure your attitudes and actions foster your spouse's growth in Christ.

"Live peaceably with all men" (Romans 12:18).

In 2008, Herbert and Zelmyra Fisher, from North Carolina, set the Guinness Record for being the world's longest-married living couple. They were married in 1924. In February 2010, Herbert was 104 years old and Zelmyra was 102. In Zelmyra's interview with the *New Bern Sun Journal*, she said when they married, "He was not mean; he was not a fighter. He was quiet and kind. He was not much to look at, but he was sweet." They claim to never fight. Zelmyra also said that she is happy to yield the television to her husband whenever baseball comes on.[6]

---

[6] By Kathryn Hawkins. *Gimundo, Good News…*served daily, posted on Feb. 11, 2010.

The word "peace" comes to mind when I think of the Fishers. Webster's defines peace as "a state of harmony between people…freedom from dissension…freedom from anxiety."[7] The most important type of peace is having vertical peace—peace with God, which stands in contrast to one's being an enemy of God because of one's unrepentant, depraved core self from which emanate wicked works. Such peace with our Maker occurs only through our having personal faith in Christ Jesus, the Prince of Peace (Rom. 5:1; Isa. 9:6), who died on Calvary's cross to redeem mankind from sin. Once we have achieved peace with God through faith in our Lord Jesus Christ, then we are equipped to be peacemakers. Matthew 5:9 says, "Blessed are the peacemakers, for they shall be called sons of God." Again, Hebrews 12:14 says, "Pursue peace with all people, and holiness, without which no one will see the Lord." Are you a peacemaker with your spouse, or are you a source of strife and stress with your spouse? Even if your spouse says or does something that initiates strife and stress, you are not to retaliate or feed into such strife, but rather you should defuse the strife with a peaceable reaction and a forgiving heart. If you find yourself spiritually "in the flesh," I recommend that you not say a word. Rather, retreat and get "in the Spirit." Speaking your mind when you are "in the flesh" will likely make the problem worse. Instead, draw near to God and be a peacemaker. Will you determine to become a peacemaker in your home? "Now may the God of *peace* Himself sanctify you completely" (1 Thess. 5:23a)!

"Greet one another with a kiss of *love*" (1 Peter 5:14a).

In a Middle School in Oregon, a trend developed among the female students that irritated the principal. After the girls would put their lipstick on in the girls' bathroom, they would press their lips to the mirrors to leave their lip prints. So one day, the principal called a handful of girls into the bathroom to show them how he had instructed the custodian to clean the mirrors. The custodian dipped a brush into the toilet water and then thoroughly wiping the mirrors clean, thus removing the lip prints. That was enough to end the lip print trend.

As the girls' pressing of their lips against the school bathroom mirrors was off-limits, I believe that Christians' pressing their lips together—

[7] *Webster's American Dictionary*, Second College Edition, (Random House, Inc. 2000), 581.

6

kissing—when they are dating, courting, or engaged should likewise be off-limits. I see no provision in the Bible for a man and woman who are not yet married to stir up passions in each other through intimate physical contact such as kissing. Colossians 3:5 says, "Therefore put to death your members which are on the earth: fornication, uncleanness, *passion*, evil desire, and covetousness, which is idolatry." I do support holding of hands, which can be an acceptable way to show affection to the Christian person you are courting or to whom you are engaged without stirring up passions.

The excitement of the wedding day and honeymoon could be so much greater if the husband and wife would reserve their expressions of physical intimacy toward each other for that special wedding day. Furthermore, being willing to exercise such physical restraint can make for shorter engagements! Kim and I did this. We were only engaged for about three months, and we first kissed each other on the day we were married.

As husband and wife continue to cultivate and maintain hearts of love for each other, intimate expressions such as kissing should naturally flow out of that and should continue throughout marriage. So let husband and wife maintain the passion we see in the newlywed Shulamite when she said of her husband, "Let him kiss me with the kisses of his mouth" (Song 1:2).

"Let each of us please his neighbor for his good, leading to edification" (Romans 15:2).

Willard Harley, a clinical psychologist, has written numerous marriage books. From two of these in particular, *His Needs, Her Needs*[8] and *Mom's Needs, Dad's Needs*,[9] I have benefited. He says that each spouse has emotional needs: The husband has certain emotional needs that the wife should meet, and the wife has certain emotional needs that the husband should meet. Furthermore, the emotional needs of the husband are often different from the emotional needs of his wife. Harley says it is very important that the husband learn the top emotional

[8] Willard F. Harley, Jr. *His Needs, Her Needs, Building an Affair-Proof Marriage*, (Fleming H. Revell. 1984, 1994, 2001).
[9] Willard F. Harley, Jr. *Mom's Needs, Dad's Needs, Keeping Romance Alive Even After the Kids Arrive*, (Fleming H. Revell. 2003).

needs of his wife and that he should make any adjustments which are necessary in order to meet her needs. Likewise, the wife ought to learn the top emotional needs of her husband, and she should make any necessary adjustments in order to meet those needs of her husband. I have found it helpful on occasion to ask my wife, "Kim, what are your top needs from me these days and how am I doing in meeting them?" Kim seems to always appreciate this question. It is important to strive to meet your spouse's needs (or expectations). To do so is an act of love. A failure to meet the needs of your spouse will likely reduce the quality of your marriage. If your spouse continuously fails to meet one of your emotional needs, then you must be patient with your spouse, remembering that our Lord is patient with us. You may need to die to that desire in order to prevent a root of bitterness from developing in you toward your spouse who has failed to meet one of your needs. You will also likely need to spend significantly more time focusing on Scriptures related to walking in love and patience toward your spouse.

Romans 15:2 should be applied to your marriage (your spouse being seen as your neighbor), and the verse exhorts you to please your spouse. The verse indicates you are to please your spouse for his or her good, which includes helping your spouse become more like Christ. Adam pleased his wife when he ate of the forbidden fruit, but in doing so he sinned and got this world into a huge mess. But if your spouse requests something of you that is not sinful, and if it is within your power to do so, then you probably should do it. Please your spouse! If your spouse wants you to help with the kids more, do it. If your spouse wants you to help keep the house clean, do it. If your spouse wants you to get in better shape, do it. When your spouse has a need he or she wants you to meet, if you are able to meet that need but you are not willing to do so, then you are failing to fully love your spouse. Jesus did not say, "If you love Me, you will have positive feelings." Jesus did say, "If you love Me, keep My commandments" (Jn. 14:15). Love is not merely a sentiment; love requires sacrifice. Any ongoing demonstration of wonderful, Christ-like love toward your spouse will include making sacrifices to meet the needs of your spouse. An excellent marriage occurs when the husband and wife consistently demonstrate to each other the greatest love possible. The greatest love requires the greatest sacrifice—sacrifice of self. Jesus said, "Greater love has no one than this, than to lay down one's life for his friends" (Jn. 15:13). To lay down your life, which includes making changes within your life that your spouse requests, is sacrifice (again, it must be in accordance with the will of God); and sacrifice is a necessary aspect of love.

One of my top needs is for Kim and me to spend quality time together. Just as I need regular quality time with my heavenly Father, I also need regular quality time with my wife. Our time together should include Scripture reading and prayer. It may also include our playing games together such as Rummikub, Skip-Bo, Monopoly, or cards. It may also include sharing a meal at a restaurant together, going on a vacation together, or taking walks together. I believe every husband and wife ought to pursue having fun together. You cannot have an enjoyable relationship if you don't take time to relate in enjoyable ways.

"How can you say, 'I *love* you,' when your heart is not with me?" (Judges 16:15)

These words were spoken by Delilah to Samson because he would not divulge to her the secret of his God-given great strength. However, because of her continual nagging, Samson finally yielded to her demands and revealed the secret of his strength; thus, Sampson transgressed the command of God (Judg. 13:5). This sin cost Samson his eyes and eventually his life, and it also cost Israel a major force in their security against their national enemy, the Philistines. All this occurred because Samson became unequally yoked by romantically attaching himself to Delilah, one who did not follow the God of Israel. Second Corinthians 6:14 says, "Do not be unequally yoked together with unbelievers." Christians should marry only Christians. Nevertheless, the words of Delilah to Samson in Judges 16:15 get to the heart of the matter of love.

Colossians 3:23 says, "Whatever you do, do it *heartily*, as to the Lord and not to men." "Heartily" means with all your heart. If you are married, then I encourage you to give yourself to your marriage with all your heart. Seek to be an excellent spouse, and do so as to the Lord. I wish that when I first became engaged I had spent more time studying biblical passages on love and marriage. Such preparation would have likely spared Kim and me some of the mistakes I made early on.

Matthew 6:21 says, "For where your treasure is, there your *heart* will be also." Your treasure is your investment—your time, energy, and resources. Investing in your marriage will help incline your heart *toward* your spouse. I have heard at least one husband say, "I no longer feel anything for my wife. There's nothing there." In reaction to that sad admission, I point out that right feelings follow right actions. If you, by faith, will latch on to the abundance of Scriptures about love— including putting your spouse ahead of yourself, and looking out for your spouse's interests over your own, and if you will wholeheartedly serve your spouse in obedience to such Scriptures, then feelings of love toward your spouse will likely return to you. This concept applies to many other areas of life—that if you will line up your investment with your lot in life then you can develop a love for your lot in life, and with that can come contentment and peace. Paul wrote from a prison cell, "I have learned in whatever state I am, to be content" (Phil. 4:11). This concept of right feelings following right actions was demonstrated in the excellent movie, *Fireproof,* which was produced for the purpose of strengthening marriages through Christ.[10] One character wisely advised another who was struggling in his marriage that he ought not follow his heart, but rather he should lead his heart. This is because the natural inclination of one's heart, without the Word of God hidden within, is deceitful above all things and desperately wicked (Jer. 17:9). But through consistently hiding God's Word in your heart and through investing in your spouse, you can lead your heart to the place that you will be able to say, "I love you" and sincerely mean it. What are some specific steps you should take in order to invest more strongly in your marriage?

"I will walk within my house with a perfect heart" (Psalm 101:2b).

The word "heart" means the core you, your control center, your inner man including your inmost desires; it means deep down who you really are. Proverbs 23:7 says, "As a man thinks in his heart, so is he." So you are what is in your heart. Therefore, in the greatest commandment of the Bible, Matthew 22:37: "You shall love the Lord your God with all your heart, with all your soul, and with all your mind," loving God "with all your heart" is mentioned first.

---

[10] *Fireproof* (movie), By Affirm Films, Samuel Goldwyn Films, Sherwood Pictures in association with Provident Films and Carmel Entertainment (A Kendrick Brothers Production. 2008).

David, the writer of Psalm 101, showed an admirable determination to cultivate and maintain a right heart within his house: he said, "I *will* walk...." David did not want to settle for an above-average heart. He wanted "a perfect heart" because he knew that the God whom he served, and the One he was to emulate, is perfect! Jesus said, "You shall be perfect, just as your Father in heaven is perfect" (Mt. 5:48). Sometimes people get their priorities backwards and place too much emphasis on building up their professions, such as their ministry or business, and do not place sufficient attention on cultivating a solid home life. But a solid home life is foundational to having a solid professional life, and one should not build a profession on a faulty foundation. So David's pursuit of perfection in the attitude of his heart within his house and amongst his family ought to be emulated by each of us today. What would you need to do to "perfect" your heart and attitude toward those within your household?

"He who covers a transgression seeks *love*, but he who repeats a matter separates friends" (Proverbs 17:9).

The story is told of an elderly man who became very fond of an elderly woman in their retirement home. So one day he asked her to marry him. The next morning when he woke up, he couldn't remember what her answer was to his proposal. So he admitted to her, "I know I proposed to you yesterday, but I cannot recall your answer." She replied, "Oh, praise the Lord! I knew I said 'yes' to someone, but I couldn't remember who it was."

Though forgetfulness can be a sobering reality for an elderly couple, forgetfulness can be an asset in marriage in terms of being willing to forgive and forget the transgressions of your spouse. For husbands to love their wives as Christ loved the church, and for wives to also walk in a spirit of Christian love, husbands and wives must thoroughly forgive each other for past hurts and offenses inflicted upon each other and not dredge them up again in later conversation. It is amazing that, for us as Christians, our holy heavenly Father has forgiven us of the infinite degree of sins we have committed against Him and has even forgotten those sins, according to Isaiah 43:25, "I, even I, am He who blots out your transgressions for My own sake; and I will not remember your sins." (Jeremiah 31:34 speaks to the same effect.) Who are we, then, to bring up the past failures and offenses of our spouse? We are to forgive and exercise patience toward our spouse even if our spouse's shortcomings have been numerous and have continued for a long time. Peter said to Jesus, "'Lord, how often shall my brother sin against me, and I forgive him? Up to seven times?' Jesus said to him, 'I do not say to you, up to seven times, but up to seventy times seven'" (Mt. 18:21-22). One aspect of Christian love that is essential for a strong marriage is a willingness to forgive and overlook transgressions. Proverbs 19:11 states, "The discretion of a man makes him slow to anger, and his glory is to *overlook a transgression*." This does not negate the fact that if a spouse is "overtaken in any trespass," then the marriage partner, in a spirit of gentleness, ought to help bring restoration (Gal. 6:1). That also is an aspect of walking in love.

"You are all fair, my *love*, and there is no spot in you" (Song of Solomon 4:7).

Christ loves the church even though the church, consisting of its individual members, is not perfect. In marriage, though each spouse is an imperfect person, husband and wife should not focus on the imperfections of the other. James Grant once said, "Does God focus on our imperfections, or does He see us in a higher way?" He sees His children in a higher way![11] Romans 8:33 expresses this, "Who shall bring any charge against God's elect? It is God who justifies." Again, Romans 5:20b says, "Where sin abounded, grace abounded all the more." (See also 2 Cor. 5:21.) Despite our imperfections, God has shown us amazing grace, especially seen in His justifying those of us who believe in His Son even though we have all sinned infinitely against Him. And if we want God to continually lavish His love, kindness, mercy, and favor upon us, then we should continuously lavish love, kindness, mercy, and favor on our spouse. We should view our spouse in the manner that God views us. Song 4:7 reveals that King Solomon saw his wife as all fair, not ninety-five percent fair. It's not that his wife had no sin, for we have all sinned (Rom. 3:23). But Solomon looked at her through the eyes of love.

---

[11] James Grant, in conversation with me.

"Can two walk together, unless they are agreed?" (Amos 3:3).

The story has been told of a young couple who were about to get married. The young man went to his dad and said, "I'm a bit apprehensive about getting married, Dad." The dad replied, "Why, son?" "Well, I have terribly smelly feet, Dad, and it will be very embarrassing when my wife finds out." The dad replied, "Don't worry about it, son. Just go to bed with your socks on and she will never notice the smell. You'll be fine." Meanwhile, the young lady goes to her mother and says to her, "I'm a bit worried about getting married, Mom, because I have terrible breath in the mornings and it will be very embarrassing when my husband finds out." The mom replied, "Don't worry, dear. All you need to do is not to open your mouth first thing in the morning. Don't say a single word until you've brushed your teeth." The wedding occurs, and for the next six months the newlyweds each manage to keep their secrets safe. Then one morning at about 5:00 a.m., the young husband wakes up and suddenly realizes one of his socks has come off in bed. He frantically rummages around under the sheets trying to find the elusive sock so he can put it back on his smelly foot when suddenly the wife wakes up. As he pops his head out from under the blankets, she says to him, "What are you doing?" He replies, "Oh my goodness; you've eaten one of my socks!"

Husbands and wives need to pursue a relationship of honesty and openness with each other. Hidden secrets are a bad idea. However, make sure that when you speak the truth, you do so in love (Eph. 4:15). Philippians 2:2 encourages believers to be "likeminded" and "of one accord." This is achieved as both husband and wife pursue the mind of Christ (Phil. 2:5) by meditating upon the Word of God, together as well as individually, throughout the day (Joshua 1:8; Psalm 119:97). Then they can walk together in agreement, and in paths of righteousness. Furthermore, an aspect of love is to overlook the shortcomings of your spouse, and to pray for your spouse to be an overcomer. Also, maturity requires putting forth serious effort to personally grow up in the areas of your own shortcomings.

"Her sins, which are many, are forgiven, for she *loved* much. But to whom little is forgiven, the same *loves* little" (Luke 7:47).

In Luke 7, while Jesus was dining at the house of Simon, a Pharisee, a woman who was a sinner, likely a prostitute, came and ministered to Jesus. (It may seem inappropriate to even mention a prostitute in a marriage book, but there is a spiritual lesson here I don't want us to miss.) She washed Jesus' feet with her tears, wiped His feet with her hair, kissed His feet, and anointed His feet with fragrant oil. Consequently, Simon's thoughts were condemning toward Jesus because Jesus let a woman with such a sinful past touch Him. But Jesus commended the woman's extravagant demonstration of love toward Him. Also, Jesus pointed out to Simon that her actions stood in contrast to the lack of a demonstration of love toward Jesus exhibited by Simon. Therefore, Jesus said, "her sins, which are many, are forgiven, for she loved much. But to whom little is forgiven, the same loves little" (verse 47).

This is a reminder that Jesus can forgive us of tremendously bad sins. In marriage, any sort of infidelity (unfaithfulness to one's spouse) is tremendously bad! So no matter what sin one has committed in one's past, whereby one offended God as well as one's spouse, one can repent and receive forgiveness (1 Jn. 1:9). Just as Jesus forgave this woman, we are required to forgive all humans no matter what their transgressions against us have been (See also Mt. 18:21-35). Since our holy God was willing to demonstrate extravagant love toward us by sending His Son to die for us (and all of us are undeserving of such divine love as we have all sinned infinitely against God), then who are we to think of ourselves as above God and not forgive our fellow man, or even our spouse? *There is no place for bitterness or resentment in marriage.* The Spirit of God, working through the Word of God, can drive bitterness out of any heart.

Do you want to experience God's forgiveness? Then, like this woman, demonstrate great love for God. Seek His face, read and obey His Word, love and serve His people. This woman spared no expense in lavishing great love upon her Savior, for the fragrant oil with which she anointed Him was likely very costly. Do you need more love, and perhaps forgiveness, in your marriage? Then show your spouse great love. Don't hold back in your demonstration of love toward your spouse, but demonstrate lavish love. Pour it on! Some ideas are: surprise your spouse with a bouquet of roses, provide a candlelight dinner, give a lengthy back-rub or foot-rub for consecutive nights, and/or take your spouse for a weekend getaway. Ask your spouse to tell you a particular marital desire he or she may have that you can meet. Then go the extra mile to meet your spouse's desire. Your efforts will be worthwhile because "love never fails" (1 Cor. 13:8a)!

"Let *love* be without hypocrisy" (Romans 12:9).

Nancy Shulins of *Journal News*, Nyack, N.Y., reported the following story. Bob wanted to be a weather man. He had attended three different colleges and studied courses relevant to weather, but he never earned a degree. Nevertheless, he chose ambition over integrity as he contacted WCBS-TV, introducing himself as a Ph.D. in geophysics from Columbia University. After a two-month tryout, Bob was hired as an off-camera forecaster. He performed well at his new job and was promoted. Later, the *New York Times* hired him as a consulting meteorologist. Also, Long Island Railroad as well as Baseball Commissioner Bowie Kuhn hired him. He was known as "Dr. Bob," and his vocational dream was being fulfilled. But then an anonymous letter was sent to WCBS urging them to investigate Dr. Bob's credentials. As a result of the investigation, he was fired by WCBS and the *New York Times*. He has since publicly apologized for his dishonesty.[12]

What is your definition of a hypocrite? In Jesus' day, the Pharisees were religious leaders who showed great concern for their own ritualistic cleanness according to the tradition of men but little concern for purity of heart according to the standard of God's Word. In Matthew 23, Jesus said of the Pharisees, "whatever they tell you to observe, that observe and do, but do not do according to their works; for they say, and do not do" (verse 3). Therefore, Jesus called them "hypocrites" (verse 27), as well as "serpents, brood of vipers" (verse 33), "fools" (verse 19), "blind guides" (verse 24), and "sons of hell" (verse 15) who will receive "the condemnation of hell" (verse 33). A hypocrite is someone who proclaims that one ought to adhere to certain moral standards but simultaneously lives contrary to the very moral standards he proclaims. In Matthew 7:21, Jesus said, "Not everyone who says to Me, 'Lord,

---

[12] LIE—Sermon Illustrations, Nancy Shulins, *Journal News*, (Nyack, New York).

Lord,' shall enter the kingdom of heaven, but he who does the will of My Father in heaven." So one can say, "Hallelujah," "God bless you," and "Jesus is Lord," but if that person never receives from God a new heart of obedience to the Lord, then Jesus will declare, "I never knew you; depart from Me, you who practice lawlessness" (verse 23)! The bottom line is: we must do the will of God! James 1:22 says, "But be doers of the word, and not hearers only, deceiving yourselves." What might you need to change about your life in order to be a doer of the Word of God?

Being a doer of the Word of God applies not only to whether or not you love God, but also to whether or not you genuinely love your spouse. *Do you maintain love in your heart for your spouse?* For example, it is hypocritical to say to your spouse "I love you" while you maintain resentment toward your spouse. Another example of hypocrisy is that you say "I love you" to your spouse, but you consistently focus your attention and desires elsewhere because you have allowed your spouse to become a low priority to you, though your spouse has pointed this problem out to you. If you cannot be genuine and truthful when you say "I love you," then you need to take inventory of your marriage and invest more in it. Where you invest, that is where your heart is (Mt. 6:21). The proper order in terms of priority for the investments of one's heart is as follows: first, the Lord Jesus Christ and obedience to Him and His Word; second, your spouse (spending quality time with your spouse and meeting your spouse's needs); third, your children ("bring them up in the training and admonition of the Lord"—Eph. 6:4b—and spending quality time with them); fourth, others (loving and serving others, including through your occupation and your church-related ministry activities). Selfishness appears when any aspect of your life has not been consecrated to Christ and His kingdom purposes. I do not want to be a hypocrite in any area of my life. As an ordained minister, it is especially important that I remain a humble, genuine man of God, and a loving husband and father. After all, we who are teachers will receive a stricter judgment (James 3:1). Let love be genuine, coming from the heart.

"Yet if your brother is grieved because of your food, you are no longer walking in *love*. Do not destroy with your food the one for whom Christ died" (Romans 14:15).

If your choice of food (content and quantity) grieves your spouse, then you are no longer walking in love. If, for instance, your spouse is grieved because you eat too many sweets, carbohydrates, and fatty foods, then you should honor your spouse's concern and reduce such food intake. If your spouse wants you to eat less and lose weight (and if doing so would not be unhealthy to you), then honor your spouse's desire. You do not have authority over your own body, but your spouse does (1 Cor. 7:4). If your spouse wants you to be fit and maintain an attractive figure, then lay down your life (including any lifestyle element which prevents your having the fitness and attractiveness your spouse wants), put your spouse ahead of yourself, and meet your spouse's desire. Again, it gets back to 1 John 3:16, which I consider to be one of the ultimate verses for determining whether or not one walks in love: "By this we know love, because He laid down His life for us. And we also ought to lay down our lives for the brethren." If you are not willing to lay down your life for your spouse (and this includes any poor eating choices), then you are not walking in love toward your spouse.

However, if your spouse is not pleasing you in one of these or other areas, you also are expected by God to lay down your life concerning your attitude toward your spouse and any perceived shortcomings in which your spouse may persist. James Grant has said:

Marriage is not a 50%-50% proposition; it is a 100%-100% proposition. One can't die 50% and ask the spouse to meet one half-way. One must believe the Lord to empower oneself to die to self, so that what one had desired in the past, what had caused one to have negative emotions at times, will not continue to do so—so there will always be peace in one's heart toward one's spouse.[13]

You must die 100% to anything that would prevent you from continually walking in love and edification toward your spouse. It is never appropriate for you to allow continued resentment in your heart toward your spouse for your spouse's failure to meet your expectations.

---

[13] James Grant, in conversation with me.

James 1:2-4 says, "My brethren, count it all joy when you fall into various trials, knowing that the testing of your faith produces patience. But let patience have its perfect work, that you may be perfect and complete, lacking nothing." Whenever you are going through a trial in your marriage (perhaps your spouse is falling short in some area), you should rejoice that there is divine purpose in your trial. It is a test from the Lord for the purpose of your learning to be patient, which is in emulation of the Lord who is patient with each of us. Pass your test. Allow the Lord to work patience and perfection into your heart. And as you rejoice in your trial and grow in patience, remember that God "will fulfill the desire of those who fear Him" (Ps. 145:19a). Walking in patience, love, and forgiveness toward your spouse will grant greater freedom to your spouse, and this in turn may give your spouse the victory in the particular areas of his or her life that you have desired.

My wife shared with me that after three weeks of being on a diet, she was frustrated because she still had not lost any weight. To inspire my wife, I offered to take her to her favorite vacation place, Whitestone Country Inn, near Kingston, Tennessee, if she would diligently stick with a particular diet program for three months. Kim was elated at this incentive, and she began to steadily lose weight. This is an example of what I call an *extravagant positive incentive*. You can motivate your spouse to make positive changes by offering extravagant positive incentives, whether the incentives come in the form of gifts, vacations, nice dinners, backrubs, or more help with household chores. Extravagant positive incentives are certainly more effective in motivating a spouse to make a change than being critical, making accusations, or griping at one's spouse. "Love never fails" (1 Cor. 13:8).

"Better is a dinner of herbs where *love* is, than a fatted calf with hatred" (Proverbs 15:17).

Sometimes, a spouse may consider taking a second job to increase income. If the extra income is necessary, that is fine for the time being. But if the desire for extra income is simply to increase unnecessary material possessions for oneself or for the family (seeking to be rich), then that second job is likely a bad move. The "fatted calf" dinner of Proverbs 15:17 may indicate the unnecessary material possessions a spouse may pursue, which comes at the expense of quality family fellowship. The "dinner of herbs where love is" may indicate a simpler, less expensive meal or lifestyle, but a time rich in family fellowship. Husband and wife should spend much quality time together in order to maintain a solid, loving marriage, even if the family's financial net worth is lower than it otherwise would be.

"Be kindly affectionate to one another with brotherly *love*, in honor giving preference to one another" (Romans 12:10).

Let's look at some key words in this verse. "Kindness" refers to the desire in your heart to do good to someone. Diane Cornelius, a Christian who lives in Lexington, Kentucky, had the desire to provide wedding dresses for brides in Haiti since most brides there could not afford their own. Since 2009, Diane has made many trips to Haiti and has provided bridal gowns for over 120 brides.[14] Such consistent kindness comes from abiding in Christ who is the embodiment of kindness, as Psalm 117:2 says, "His merciful kindness is great toward us...." Could your spouse generally describe you as being kind to him or her? Do you maintain a desire in your heart to bless your spouse with gracious words, thoughtful gestures, acts of service, and perhaps an occasional gift such as flowers?

Norma and Gordon Yeager, ages ninety and ninety-four respectively, had been married for seventy-two years when they were both hospitalized after a car wreck in Iowa in October 2011. They shared a room in ICU and held hands in adjacent beds. On October 12th at 3:38 p.m., Gordon died. However, his heart monitor continued to register a beat. The nurse explained the phenomenon saying, "because they're holding hands, and (Norma's heart beat) is going through them." Norma died at 4:38 p.m., exactly one hour later. Their son, Dennis, said, "They just loved being together. He always said, 'I can't go until she does because I gotta stay here for her.' And she would say the same thing.'"[15] What an example of loving affection! Would your spouse consider you *affectionate*, meaning your spouse feels that you are lovingly fond of him or her, and tender in your dealings with him or her?

[14] *Is Her Mission*, by Katya Cengel. Lexington Herald Leader, Jan. 12, 2012.
[15] *Long-Married Couple Gordon Yeager and Norma Yeager Die Holding Hands*, www.huffingtonpost.com /2011/10/19.

"Honor" means to highly respect; to show courteous regard. King Ahasuerus honored Mordecai who had saved his life by adorning Mordecai with a royal robe and crown while Mordecai was paraded through the city square on the king's horse and while the one parading him proclaimed, "Thus shall it be done to the man whom the king delights to honor!" If you own a horse, perhaps you could do this for your spouse. Seriously though, you can honor your spouse in the way you treat your spouse in front of others. You can show respect for the comments and ideas expressed by your spouse, especially in company. When preaching, on occasion I will make a comment or use an illustration that honors Kim, which she appreciates. The husband can open the door for his wife and pull out his wife's chair for her. She will feel honored by these thoughtful acts. The wife will honor the husband when she shows respect for, rather than reacting negatively to, his comments, ideas, and ambitions. How could you improve in demonstrating honor to your spouse?

Love also includes *giving preference to* your spouse. Do you consider your spouses' feelings and desires, or do you satisfy your own feelings and desires ahead of your spouse? Preferring someone else over oneself is not the natural inclination of man; rather catering to oneself is natural, but it is sinful. However, through consistent meditation on the Word of God, especially verses pertaining to love, and by being filled and empowered by the Holy Spirit, each of us can genuinely prefer his spouse ahead of himself.

"Nevertheless I have this against you, that you have left your first *love*. Remember therefore from where you have fallen; repent and do the first works..." (Revelation 2:4).

Jesus speaks these words to the church of Ephesus after affirming several positive things about them such as their labor, patience, perseverance, not growing weary, and refusing to tolerate evildoers and liars who had tried to infiltrate their church. But in verse 4, Jesus reminds them of their failure to maintain obedience to the greatest commandment of the Bible, which is Matthew 22:37: "You shall love the LORD your God with all your heart, with all your soul, and with all your mind." A brand new convert to Christ loves God more than all else. But as time passes, many Christians backslide to some degree and allow other things to vie for their attention and become the desires of their hearts. The Ephesian church did this. They still labored for Christ, they did not love Christ to the degree that they initially had. Therefore, Jesus commanded the Ephesian church to do two things: *remember* and *repent*.

Obviously, one's marriage can have the same outcome. You hopefully married because you loved your spouse with all your heart. But as time has passed, it could be that the initial love, which was of a great magnitude, has waned. That initial love has perhaps waned to the point where your marriage is in trouble. Or, perhaps it has waned to a lesser degree—you are still committed to your spouse, but the feeling of love has decreased. Maybe your marriage has gone from excellence to mediocrity, or from thriving to surviving. (Speaking for myself, I do not want anything less than an excellent marriage, and I am willing to make whatever changes I must make in order for my marriage to be sustained at the excellent level. This is the main reason I have written this book—to pursue an excellent marriage.) Whichever case describes the quality of your marriage, Jesus' words to the Ephesian church are applicable to you. *You need to remember and repent.* Remember all the things that caused you to initially fall in love with your spouse. It is wise for each spouse to ask the other, "Why did you marry me? What was it about me that caused you to fall in love with me?" (Be wise and tender in the wording of these questions so as not to offend.) Then each spouse ought to make whatever changes are necessary in order to be the type of marriage partner that initially attracted the other to him or her. If, for instance, your wife said she fell in love with you because she felt that you sincerely loved God and that you would always treat her right, then have you *continued* to love God and treat your wife right? If you have not, then you must repent. Make the changes necessary to meet the particular needs that your wife has listed. If, for instance, your husband said he fell in love with you because you loved God and looked great, then have you *continued* to love God and look great? If not, then you must repent. Make the changes necessary to meet the needs that your husband has listed. If you or your spouse resists the idea of repenting and meeting these needs for each other, then you or your spouse is failing to love. First John 3:16 says, "By this we know love, because He laid down His life for us. And we also ought to lay down our lives for the brethren." To not repent in order to meet the needs of your spouse is to not lay down your life for your spouse, which is to not love your spouse. As much as is possible, whatever caused love to be felt initially ought to be maintained. Jesus commanded: "Do the first works." Husband and wife: Do the first works. If you submit yourselves unreservedly to Christ and return to doing those first works, the feelings of that initial great love can fully return. Right feelings follow right actions. May the Lord bless you as you lay down your life in order to meet the needs of your spouse!

"That if you confess with your mouth the Lord Jesus and believe in your heart that God has raised Him from the dead, you will be saved" (Romans 10:9).

Usually, when a couple gets married, they vow to stay together until death do them part. But in France, you don't even have to let death get in the way of marriage. On April 22, 2004, Cox News Service reported the following unusual article: In France, under a law enacted during World War I, people can apply to marry dead people. (There are some stipulations that prevent getting the inheritance unless it was already allowed for in the will.) And people are doing it. For instance, Christelle was engaged to a man who was later killed by a drunken driver. But long after his death she said her feelings for him had not subsided. Therefore, about two years later, she married the dead man. The wedding ceremony, which was followed by a champagne reception, was attended by about forty friends and family members; then Christelle and the mother-in-law went together on a "honeymoon" in Paris. How bizarre is that—for a person to cling to that degree to something or someone who is lifeless?

I have shared this story to illustrate something that affects, in a profoundly horrible way, many people throughout the world, both single and married—the futility of dead religion. Many people are deceived and persist in spiritual deadness due to their commitment to false religious institutions, ritualistic practices, and man-made idols. For example, in the Philippines, people annually scourge (whip) themselves to the point of bloodshed—an attempt at self-atonement (but this is futile, since the blood of Jesus is the only atonement for sin—Rom. 3:23-25). In India, thousands annually bathe in the Ganges River believing that the water of that particular river washes away their sins (again, only faith in the blood of Jesus washes away one's sins). Other religions engage in repetitious, ritualistic chanting, falsely believing that such chanting produces a spiritual cleansing. Others pray to man-made idols and altars as if such things that they make with their hands can divinely intervene into their lives and help them. All of these attempts to get right with the God of the universe, as well as be helped by Him, are as futile as the "marriage relationship" into which Christelle entered.

Many biblical passages teach us that we are called to an abiding relationship with the living God. For example, Jeremiah 2:11-13 says, "My people have exchanged their Glory for what does not profit... They have forsaken Me, the fountain of living waters, and hewn for themselves cisterns—broken cisterns that can hold no water." Here, God is likened to a fountain of living water—one that produces clear, clean water that brings life-sustaining nourishment and freshness. This is contrasted with a cistern, which is a receptacle for holding, at best, stagnant water. Furthermore, the cistern spoken of is broken, meaning it holds nothing. Through the prophet Jeremiah, God was saying to His people that they had forsaken Him who is the source of abundant and eternal life (Ps. 16:11; Jn. 10:10; Rom. 14:17) and replaced His presence and provision with the comparatively dead and empty traditions and rituals of men. If your life, and consequently your marriage, seem stale, stagnant, or dead, remember that "God is not the God of the dead, but of the living" (Mt. 22:32b). And as God raised the Lord Jesus Christ from the dead, God can likewise raise you and your marriage up from a state of stagnancy and deadness and give you new life.

Note how Jesus Christ, His Spirit, and His words constitute one's true life source, as the following verses in John's gospel testify: "In Him was *life*, and the *life* was the light of men" (1:4); "I have come that they may have *life*, and that they may have it more abundantly" (10:10); "I am the resurrection and the *life*" (11:25); "I am the way, the truth, and the *life*" (14:6); "It is the Spirit who gives *life*; the flesh profits nothing. The words that I speak to you are spirit, and they are *life*" (6:63); "And this is eternal *life*, that they may know You, the only true God, and Jesus Christ whom You have sent" (17:3). Therefore, I advise you (if you are not already trusting in Jesus as your Lord and Savior) to put your complete faith in Him and the words of the Bible for spiritual life. Colossians 1:17b says, "in Him (Christ) all things consist (or hold together)." Christ can hold your life together as well as hold your marriage together if you, individually and as a couple, will wholeheartedly trust and obey Him.

Step one is that you must realize that you are a sinner, as all people are sinners. Romans 3:23 says, "For *all have sinned* and fall short of the glory of God." Let's look at the Ten Commandments (Exod. 20:1-17) to see how we have done in obeying God. Have you ever coveted your neighbor's belongings? If you have, then you are guilty of violating the Tenth Commandment—"You shall not covet...." Have you ever broken the Ninth Commandment? It says, "You shall not bear false witness against your neighbor." If you have told a lie against your neighbor, then you are guilty of bearing false witness. Revelation 21:8 says, "all *liars* shall have their part in the lake which burns with fire and brimstone, which is the second death." Have you ever broken the Eighth Commandment? It says, "You shall not steal." Have you ever broken the Seventh Commandment? It says, "You shall not commit adultery?" Jesus narrows the Old Testament definition of adultery by saying, "whoever looks at a woman to lust for her has already committed adultery with her in his heart" (Mt. 5:28). So if you have ever lusted, then you have broken the Seventh Commandment. Have you ever broken the Sixth Commandment? It says, "You shall not murder." First John 3:15 says, "Whoever hates his brother is a murderer, and you know that no murderer has eternal life abiding in him." So if you have hated your brother, you are guilty of murder in God's eyes. If you have ever dishonored your parents, then you are guilty of breaking the Fifth Commandment: "Honor your father and your mother." If you have ever failed to keep the Sabbath Day holy, then you are guilty of violating the Fourth Commandment. If you have ever taken God's name in vain, then you are guilty of breaking the Third Commandment. If you have worshipped carved images rather than the invisible God who alone is worthy of worship, then you are guilty of violating the Second Commandment. And if you have loved anything in your life (whether money or other possessions, prestige, other persons, yourself, etc.) more than you have loved God, then you have violated the First Commandment which says, "You shall have no other gods before Me." There are many other commandments in the Old and New Testament that each of us has likely violated at one time or another, but I have used the well-known Ten Commandments to show that each of us has sinned against our holy God. James 2:10 says,

"For whoever shall keep the whole law, and yet stumble in one point, he is guilty of all." We have all stumbled in obeying the Law of God at many points, and we are all guilty as sinners. No one can be justified in God's sight by obeying His Law.

If a car has a bad transmission, then a good paint job just won't compensate. Surface solutions do not fix root problems. Every person's root problem is sin. If one does not know Christ, then one is a sinner by nature, and sin is all that one can do. In order to begin living a life pleasing to God, one cannot simply repair one's old heart. The natural man's deceitful and desperately wicked heart (Jer. 17:9) must be completely replaced by a new and pure heart (Mt. 5:8). Ezekiel prophesies of God's willingness to do this for you—"I will give you a new heart and put a new spirit within you; I will take the heart of stone out of your flesh and give you a heart of flesh. I will put My Spirit within you and cause you to walk in My statutes, and you will keep My judgments and do them" (Ezek. 36:26-27). To receive this new heart from God, one must put one's entire faith in the Lord Jesus Christ. Jesus said in John 3:7, "You must be born again." This is the moment that God the Holy Spirit comes into the life of a person and changes his (or her) heart, or core being. And God promises to give the Holy Spirit to those who obey Him (Acts 5:32). Romans 10:9 is perhaps the number one verse used for praying to receive Jesus Christ as one's Savior. It says, "That if you confess with your *mouth* the Lord Jesus and believe in your *heart* that God has raised Him from the dead, *you will be saved*." Please be mindful that saying pious words does not necessarily save a person. *Having faith in Jesus Christ within one's heart* is what saves a person, as Romans 10:9 specifies. Furthermore, remember that if one seeks God with one's whole heart, then one will find God (Jer. 29:13). Making Jesus Christ the Lord of one's life is the most important thing one can do. If you want to receive Jesus Christ into your heart to be your personal Savior, I urge you to read through and then say out loud the following prayer:

> Father, I confess with my mouth that Jesus is Lord. Jesus is Lord of all there is, and I invite Jesus right now to be the Lord of my life. I turn away from my sin and rebellion against You, Lord, and I now turn to You, Lord, to obey You in all that I do. I believe in my heart, God, that you raised Jesus from the dead. Please take control of my life and lead me. Thank You, Lord! In Jesus' name, Amen.

If you just prayed this, congratulations! I recommend you share your commitment (or recommitment) to Jesus Christ with a local pastor or Christian friend. Now comes the joyous opportunity for you to cultivate a relationship with Jesus, which includes hiding the Word of God (the Bible) in your heart, and obeying that Word. Jesus expresses this in John 15:7, "If you abide in Me, and My words abide in you, you will ask what you desire, and it shall be done for you." This same principle appears again in John 8:31-32, "Then Jesus said…'If you abide in My word, you are My disciples indeed. And you shall know the truth, and the truth shall make you free.'" Each Christian should become a life-long student of the Word of God (the Bible), because God's Word is "spirit" and "life" to you (Jn. 6:63); it is a lamp unto your feet and a light unto your path (Ps. 119:105. See also Ps. 119:11 and James 1:22.) I recommend that you be immersed in water baptism, and that you get involved in a Bible-based church where you can surround yourself with a community of Christian believers and where you can use your gifts to serve God and others. God bless you!

"Love never fails" (1 Corinthians 13:8)

In 1998, not long after I began as a staff chaplain at the first prison where I served, I visited our psychiatric lockdown unit. It was two tiers high, and it served as the residence for about fifty inmates, each of which were living in individual cells. Each cell door was steel, with a thick glass window at eye level and a tray slot through which to deliver the inmate his meals. As I was distributing Bibles and other literature to the men through the tray slots, one man, Lenny, began tapping on the glass and motioning for me to come to him. Lenny appeared to be in his forties; thin, but wiry, and hyperactive. He began talking to me rapidly and loudly about alleged injustices that were befalling him. After listening for several minutes, I said, "How can I help you?" Lenny replied, "I want you to get me out of here!" I said, "I don't think I can do that." Lenny replied, "Then go get Chaplain Jackson (not her real name); she can get me out of here." I said, "She's likely gone home for the day; I can call her in the morning about your request." Lenny replied, "This ain't no nine-to-five job; you get me out of here!" Then Lenny began cursing and yelling at me, so I began to walk away. Lenny yelled, "Chaplain!" I turned to face him. He yelled, "Come pray for me!" At this point, I made my first major mistake as a chaplain. I should have humbled myself, walked over to Lenny, and prayed for him, just as Scripture says to "give to everyone who asks of you" (Luke 6:30), and "overcome evil with good" (Rom. 12:21). But I was angry that he had cursed me, so I said, "I'll come back in a little while and pray for you." When I put Lenny off with that statement, he exploded in anger. He began pounding the cell door with his fists, continuously shouting, "Punk you up! Punk you up!" The officers ran to his cell and ordered Lenny to shut up, but he yelled all the more, "Punk you up! Chaplain, when you hit the yard, you're dead meat!" This commotion brought all the inmates in that wing to their cell windows, peering out at this new, boyish-looking chaplain who was at the center of the disruptive situation. The officers eventually calmed Lenny down. Meanwhile, I was pacing in the wing and saying to myself, "What have I gotten myself into? It is feasible for Lenny to get word to the yard for inmates to assault me." But then I determined I would stand on God's Word! God had called me to prison chaplaincy just months earlier and God had allowed me to be selected for this position. Psalm 23:4 says, "Yea, though I walk through the valley of the shadow of death, I will fear no evil; for You are with me...." (See also Psalm 121:7, all of Psalm 91, and Luke 10:19 for promises of protection from evil.) So I decided not to exit that wing until I had spoken to every inmate in there to make the point that I was not going to be chased away from God's assignment for me. I remained about two more hours in that wing, and I think spoke to every awake inmate. One man even prayed with me to receive Christ as his Savior! When I arrived home, my brother and another friend prayed for me about Lenny's threat because I was still concerned about it. The next morning, I went to Lenny's cell, first thing. I opened his tray slot, pulled up a chair, and greeted Lenny. I was determined to win him over with kindness—to make every effort to be his friend rather than his enemy. That was the best way to ensure my safety. Lenny was not happy to see me and began his incessant talking and cursing. I determined I would not become offended; instead, I would actively listen to his problems the best I could. I said, "Lenny, I came back to pray with you." Lenny replied, "I reject your prayer!" Lenny continued his incessant chatter for forty-five minutes, and I listened. After a while, his intensity and tone let up, and amazingly he began to speak with civility and respect. An hour later, Lenny said, "Pray for me." I prayed.

Then Lenny prayed. He said, "God forgive me for the way I treated this chaplain." Then Lenny told me that he loved me! For the rest of the twenty-three months that I worked at that prison, Lenny always treated me with respect though he continued to curse other staff. First Corinthians 13:8 says, *"Love never fails...."* If you have God on the inside of you, and you choose to love, then you never fail. "God is love" (1 Jn. 4:8); God never fails, so love never fails! For any Christian to accurately represent God to a lost world, he needs to consistently walk in love. For any husband or wife to accurately represent God to his or her spouse, he or she needs to consistently walk in love. Love is the key to success in marriage, in parenting, and in all interpersonal relationships. Determine today to put on love and keep it on; it is the bond of perfection (Col. 3:14). Hallelujah!

Chapter 2

Lord, Help Me Tame My Tongue!

All of us have spoken words that we later came to regret. Perhaps we spoke words that were overly critical or offensive, that caused strife, or caused a fellow believer to stumble. Perhaps we slandered or gossiped about someone for whom Christ died. Perhaps we lied, or told unclean joke, or used profanity. Perhaps we spoke the truth, but not in love, and our tone was ungracious. Perhaps we complained instead of giving thanks.

The words you speak are very important because they indicate to a large degree what is in your heart: Jesus said, "For out of the abundance of the heart the mouth speaks" (Mt. 12:34b). The good news is that Jesus Christ died for your sins and rose from the dead, and if you have faith in Him (that is, faith produced by the Holy Spirit, not merely mental assent), you have divine forgiveness of all your sins, including the sins of ungodly speech. And only by renewing your mind by the Word of God and being empowered by the indwelling Holy Spirit can you have victory in all areas of life, including in the Biblical command to tame your tongue.

My favorite Bible verse pertaining to taming the tongue is Ephesians 4:29. Let us to take an in-depth look at it.

Ephesians 4:29 Let no corrupt word proceed out of your mouth, but what is good for necessary edification, that it may impart grace to the hearers.

God does not want you to only reduce the amount of corrupt words you speak, but He wants you to eliminate them. This is because God said, "Be holy, for I am holy," and because Jesus said, "...be perfect, just as your Father in heaven is perfect" (1 Pet. 1:16; Mt. 5:48). Jesus also said you will have to give an account for every idle word you speak (Mt. 12:36). An idle word is a useless, wasteful word; a word that does not glorify God, nor edify man. So the will of God is that you speak no idle words and no corrupt words, but instead "speak as the oracles of God" (1 Pet. 4:11). That is a tall order. Actually, with man, it is impossible. But with God, all things are possible! In John 15:5, Jesus said, "I am the vine, you are the branches. He who abides in Me, and I in him, bears much fruit," including the fruit of self-control (Gal. 5:22-23). Through Christ, the believer should control, or tame, his tongue. I want to share a few scriptural strategies that can help you reduce or eliminate corrupt and idle words from your speech, and increase the percentage of godly, edifying, and gracious words you speak.

Strategy one is **be humble**. James 4:6 says, "God resists the proud, but gives grace to the humble." My definition of humility is my acknowledgement that God is infinitely bigger than me, that I will give an account unto Him for all things I have said and done; therefore I fully submit to Him. The opposite of humility is pride. Proverbs 16:18 says, "Pride goes before destruction...." So if a marriage dissolves, pride occupied the heart of at least one of the spouses. Proverbs 13:10 says, "By pride comes nothing but strife...." So if marital strife occurs, at that moment both spouses are being prideful. If one is prideful but the other remains humble and tames his or her tongue, strife can be avoided. In the past, I have found myself quite motivated to tame my tongue *after* I have offended my wife with my words. But an aspect of humility is being proactive—taming your tongue at all times so as to *prevent* offending your spouse and others with your words. I have committed to being proactive in this way, and it has brought greater joy and peace in my marriage and in my heart.

Strategy two is **be slow to speak** (Jas. 1:19). This does not mean one must talk s-l-o-w, taking several minutes to say a few sentences.

Rather being slow to speak means not being hasty in one's speech. Proverbs 29:20 says, "Do you see a man hasty in his words? There is more hope for a fool than for him." Conversely, Proverbs 15:28 says, "The heart of the righteous studies how to answer...." The righteous person (one who trusts in Christ, our Righteousness), before speaking, may consider, "How can my response be truthful, edifying, gracious, and glorifying of God?" The impetus behind your words should be God's will rather than selfish desires. Proverbs 10:19 says, "In the multitude of words sin is not lacking...." Again, Ecclesiastes 5:3 says, "a fool's voice is known for his many words." Again, Proverbs 17:27 says, "he who has knowledge spares his words." So gregarious people, extroverts, and people with strong personalities should be especially careful to avoid hastiness in speech, and to not speak too much. The Miranda Rights, which are read to people who are being arrested, are quite Biblical: "You have the right to remain silent. Anything you say can and will be used against you in a court of law...." Similarly, Jesus said, "For by your words you will be justified, and by your words you will be condemned" (Mt. 12:37).

Strategy three is to make the Word of God the basis for your **continual confession and meditation.** God required this of Joshua, the new commander–in–chief of Israel: "This Book of the Law shall not depart from your mouth, but you shall meditate in it day and night, that you may observe to do according to all that is written in it. For then you will make your way prosperous, and then you will have good success" (Josh. 1:8). Proverbs 4:20-22 says: "My son, give attention to my words; incline your ear to my sayings. Do not let them depart from your eyes; keep them in the midst of your heart." So Joshua 1:8 says: "This Book of the Law shall **not depart** from your mouth...", and Proverbs 4:21 says, "Do **not** let them (God's Words) **depart** from your eyes." So an important aspect of taming your tongue, and pleasing God in general, is to continually confess and read God's Word. God requires a stare, not a glance. Glancing at God's Word (meaning confessing it and reading it occasionally) is inconsistent with Christ's command to abide in Him (Jn. 15:1-8) and to walk in Him (1 Jn. 2:6; Col. 2:6). Stare at God's Word—"Do not let them depart from your eyes." Psalm 1 contains an instruction and promise similar to Joshua 1:8: "But his delight is in the law of the LORD, and in His law he meditates day and night....And whatever he does shall prosper" (Ps. 1:2-3). Anything you delight in more than God's Word is an idol to you, and idolaters will not inherit the kingdom of God. But hiding God's Word in your heart will enable you to avoid sinning against God and others.

Necessary Edification and Grace

Ephesians 4:29 says the words you speak should be "good for necessary edification...." Webster's Dictionary defines edify as "to instruct or benefit...uplift."[16] All of the words you speak should instruct, benefit, or uplift the hearers, including your spouse. Unedifying words are idle words or harmful words; you are to avoid them.

God also requires that your words impart **grace**. This is because you are the beneficiaries of God's amazing grace. Grace is unearned favor; it is receiving blessings you do not deserve. Consider God's grace on the natural level. What do you have that you did not receive? Did you make your heart to beat, your lungs to breathe, your eyes to see, your ears to hear, or your feet to walk? Did you cause the sun to rise and set, or the rain to refresh the earth? No; these and much more are gifts to you from God. Also, consider God's grace on the spiritual level. Ephesians 2:4-9 says:

> But God, who is rich in mercy, because of His great love with which He loved us, (5) even when we were dead in trespasses, made us alive together with Christ (by **grace** you have been saved), (6) and raised us up together, and made us sit together in the heavenly places in Christ Jesus, (7) that in the ages to come He might show the exceeding riches of His **grace** in His kindness toward us in Christ Jesus. (8) For by **grace** you have been saved through faith, and that not of yourselves; it is the gift of God, (9) not of works, lest anyone should boast.

In this passage, grace is mentioned three times. God also mentions three things He has graciously done for each believer—all past tense. He "made us alive together with Christ," He "raised us up together" (with Christ), and He "made us sit together in the heavenly places in Christ Jesus." So each believer is now, spiritually speaking, sitting in Christ

---

[16] Webster's American Dictionary, Second College Edition, (Random House, Inc. 2000), 255.

in heaven at the right hand of the Father. This is a position of reigning and ruling, so that in Christ you have authority over all demonic hosts. Therefore, believing husband and wife can submit to God, resist the devil, and the devil will leave the marriage.

Because we are the recipients of God's amazing grace, we should maintain hearts of gratitude toward God, and we should be gracious toward all others. Some people look primarily to natural, temporal things, such as food, alcohol, drugs, or secular entertainment to find contentment. But Hebrews 13:9 says, "For it is good that the heart be established by **grace**, not with foods which have not profited those who have been occupied with them." Colossians 4:6 says, "Let your speech **always** be with **grace**." So the motives and inclination of your heart and speech should always be grace. You should impart grace in all your interactions with others, including through every word you speak.

Now we will look at various verses pertaining to taming the tongue. Be proactive and regularly reflect on these verses so that you speak only words of grace and necessary edification to your spouse.

Psalm 17:3 I have purposed that my mouth shall not transgress.

It is not natural to speak what is right because the natural human heart is "deceitful above all things and desperately wicked" (Jer. 17:9), and "out of the abundance of the heart the mouth speaks" (Mt. 12:34). Therefore, you have to be intentional—you have to purpose—that you will not sin with your words. This requires abiding in God's Word (especially verses pertaining to taming the tongue) so that you will be mindful of God's will, and empowered to exercise verbal restraint.

Psalm 34:12-13 Who is the man who desires life, and loves many days, that he may see good? Keep your tongue from evil, and your lips from speaking deceit. Depart from evil and do good; seek peace and pursue it.

In order to have life (including abundant and eternal life through Jesus Christ), to love many days (longevity and a long marriage), and to see good (blessing and prosperity as well as a good marriage), you should obey the first instruction mentioned here—"keep your tongue from evil, and your lips from speaking deceit." Refraining from evil and deceit in your speech will help you refrain from evil and deceit in general, because evil speech can set in motion evil actions. This is an important aspect of "the fear of the LORD" (verse 11).

Psalm 39:1 I will guard my ways, lest I sin with my tongue; I will restrain my mouth with a muzzle, while the wicked are before me. I was mute with silence. I held my peace even from good....

The psalmist and king of Israel, David, was troubled at that moment, due to the presence of wicked people. David realized the potential for his mouth getting out of control, saying unrighteous things. As a man after God's own heart, David was determined to rein it in, saying, "I will guard...I will restrain...." David spoke figuratively here, using the example of wearing a muzzle intended for an animal, to emphasize his willingness to go to great lengths to not speak sinful words.

Psalm 101:5 Whoever secretly slanders his neighbor, Him I will destroy.

Slander means "a malicious, false...statement or report."[17] A synonym is to defame: "to attack the good name or reputation of...libel."[18] Obviously, slanderous talk is diametrically opposed to love, edification, and grace. Slander is condemned in several places in Scripture. One of the requirements for being a deacon is that his wife must not slander (1 Tim. 3:11). Second Timothy 3 warns us to turn away from people who slander. Titus 2:3 warns older women to not slander. In Numbers 12, Miriam and Aaron spoke against Moses because he had married an Ethiopian woman. They were being bigots. But God came down and rebuked them, saying Moses was the most humble man on earth, one with whom God uniquely spoke face to face; therefore they should have been afraid to speak against Moses. As God ascended from them, Miriam was immediately struck with leprosy. But Moses, demonstrating

---

[17] *Webster's American Dictionary*, Second College Edition, (Random House, Inc. 2000), 736.
[18] Ibid., 210.

forgiveness, prayed for her to be healed. Psalm 101:5 warns that God will send the unrepentant slanderer to hell. Stay away from such people lest you become tempted to participate in their evil conversation.

Psalm 139:4 For there is not a word on my tongue, but behold, O LORD, You know it altogether.

Our omniscient heavenly Father knows every word you speak. You will have to give an account to Him for every idle and ungracious word you speak (Mt. 12:36; 2 Cor. 5:10), and you will be rewarded by Him for every godly word you speak that emanates from a heart of faith and love.

Psalm 141:3 Set a guard, O LORD, over my mouth; keep watch over the door of my lips.

Pertaining to restraining the tongue, Psalm 39:1 says "I will guard." Here the psalmist asks the Lord's help with guarding his tongue. So guarding the tongue is collaboration between the believer and the Lord. You should ask the Lord to guard your tongue, and you also need to do your part by reflecting on Scriptures pertaining to taming the tongue.

Second Samuel 6 describes an occasion for great rejoicing in Israel as the ark of God was brought into Jerusalem for the first time. King David worshipped the LORD without restraint, leaping and whirling before the ark in public view. David's wife, Michal, Saul's daughter, looked through the window and saw David leaping and whirling, and thus she despised him in her heart. She came out to meet David, and said, "How glorious was the king of Israel today, uncovering himself today in the eyes of the maids of his servants, as one of the base fellows shamelessly uncovers himself!" (verse 20). David basically responded that God had been very gracious to him, so he would become even more undignified in his fervent worship of God. Verse 23 says, "Therefore Michal the daughter of Saul had no children to the day of her death."

So in Numbers 12 a sister of a man of God was struck with leprosy for speaking evil against the man of God, and in 2 Samuel 6 a wife of a man of God was struck with barrenness of womb for speaking evil against the man of God. Both suffered major physical impairments due to their slanderous speech. Close family members are among those who should heed God's warning, "Touch not My anointed ones, and do My prophets no harm" (Ps. 105:15).

Matthew 5:22 ...whoever says, 'You fool!' shall be in danger of hell fire.

Likewise, it is unacceptable to say things such as "He's an idiot" or "She's an airhead." (Actually these slanderous comments may be worse because the one about whom they are said is not present to defend himself. Remember Psalm 101:5. In godly humility, you should demonstrate love toward your neighbor instead of acting as judge over him. James 5:9 says, "Do not grumble against one another, brethren, lest you be condemned. Behold, the Judge is standing at the door!" God is the impartial Judge who is to be feared as well as loved. God will send the unrepentant slanderer and liar to hell. If you have slandered your neighbor or lied, repent and receive God's forgiveness (1 Jn. 1:9). Also seek reconciliation with the person(s) you wronged.

Ephesians 5:4-5 neither filthiness, nor foolish talking, nor coarse jesting, which are not fitting, but rather giving of thanks. (5) For this you know, that no fornicator, unclean person, nor covetous man, who is an idolater, has any inheritance in the kingdom of Christ and God.

We see here that certain types of ungodly speech—filthiness, foolish talking, and coarse jesting—are among sins closely associated with idolatry, which is the exaltation of anything above God. Unless an idolator repents, he has forfeited his inheritance in God's kingdom. In place of filthy conversation, we should have clean and pure conversation; in place of foolish talk, we should speak words of wisdom; in place of coarse jesting, we may have light-hearted comments that are not spoken for the purpose of seeking attention at the expense of another person or are contrary to the will of God. Also note that Paul encourages us to replace sinful talk with "giving of thanks." We should regularly meditate on all that God has done for us—that He who has given Jesus to atone for our sins is also willing to give us all things (Rom. 8:32). We should also be diligent to remember the many divine promises found throughout the Bible that we as believers can claim by faith.

Such mindfulness of God's abundant generosity, benevolence, and grace toward all of humanity, and especially toward His redeemed children, should certainly cause us to maintain an attitude of thanksgiving toward our heavenly Father.

Philippians 2:14-15 Do all things without complaining and disputing...that you may become blameless and harmless, children of God.

Instead of complaining, God's Word exhorts us to "bless the LORD at all times" (Ps. 34:1), "rejoice always" (1 Th. 5:16), and to give "thanks always for all things" (Eph. 5:20). To complain is to doubt that our gracious and Almighty God "shall supply all your need according to His riches in glory by Christ Jesus" (Phil. 4:19), and "shall give you the desires of your heart" as you delight in Him (Ps. 37:4). In Exodus, God delivered the Israelites from Egypt where they had been slaves. But Numbers shows us that the Israelites maintained the sinful, self-centered attitudes they had in Egypt even after they had witnessed the amazing signs and wonders of God demonstrated on their behalf as He physically set them free. Most of the Israelites did not walk by faith, evidenced by their frequent complaining when their circumstances were not what they wanted. At one point, they called God's manna worthless. On several occasions, they talked of returning to Egypt, implying that the conditions of slavery were preferable to being God's children. God is sovereign over every circumstance, and He tests us through our circumstances. Therefore, James 1:2 says to "count it all joy when you fall into various trials" because God is testing your faith in order to produce patience and perfection in you. God is willing to provide all your needs and give you the desires of your heart, but these promises can only be rightfully claimed if you delight yourself in His Word and trust His Son, Jesus (Ps. 23:1; Ps. 37:4; Mt. 6:33). When Paul and Silas underwent persecution in a Philippian jail—being unjustly beaten, incarcerated, and shackled (Acts 16)—they responded with faith, praying to God and singing hymns. God rewarded their trust in Him by ordaining a unique set of circumstances which included an earthquake, the salvation of the jailer's family, and then Paul and Silas being set free.

<u>Colossians 3:17</u> And whatever you do in word or deed, do all in the name of the Lord Jesus, giving thanks to God the Father through Him.

"Whatever" and "all" indicate that each word you speak and each deed you do should be spoken and done "in the name of the Lord Jesus." In other words, you represent Jesus—you are an ambassador for Christ—whenever you speak and act. Never speak nor act in a manner inconsistent with the Word of God. Instead, "teach and admonish one another in psalms, and hymns, and spiritual songs, singing with grace in your hearts to the Lord" (Col. 3:16). Additionally, "follow His steps" (1 Pet. 2:21).

Also, "giving thanks"—maintaining a heart of gratitude toward our generous heavenly Father "who gives us richly all things to enjoy" (1 Tim. 6:17), should be an integral part of your attitude, regularly expressed in your prayers and speech. After all, what do you have that has not been given you, even down to the atoms of your body, the hairs of your head, the oxygen that you breathe, and all of the various aspects of life within and around you? If you contemplate how you are "fearfully and wonderfully made" (Ps. 139:14), how you are graciously redeemed (1 Pet. 1:18-19) and at such a high cost (the blood of the Son of God), that God provides all your needs and desires if you know Him as your Shepherd and delight in Him (Ps. 23:1; Ps. 37:3), and if you contemplate the incomprehensible "things which God has prepared for" you if you love Him (1 Cor. 2:9), then how can you not be filled with gratitude?

<u>2 Timothy 2:24</u> And a servant of the Lord must not quarrel, but be gentle to all....

My wife and I recently agreed that whenever one of us becomes offended by the other, and if the offense needs to be addressed (many offenses should not be addressed), the offended spouse should consider writing a letter to the offending spouse. The letter will address the issue, but the letter must be written *in a spirit of love.* First Corinthians 16:14 says, "Let all that you do be done with love." Also, Galatians 6:1 says, "Brethren, if a man (or spouse) is overtaken in any trespass, you who are spiritual restore such a one in a *spirit of gentleness....*" Writing a letter may not be as convenient as simply speaking your mind. But if you are offended, speaking your mind may include speaking with a harsh tone, and overstating things, thus offending your spouse who initially committed the offense. Such an approach would likely cause strife. Writing a letter will hopefully keep your spouse calm, as opposed to your spouse becoming defensive if you were to verbally confront her/him. At a later time, you should reread and edit the letter. Writing a letter will likely allow for a more thoughtful and gracious reply to the problem, preventing hasty and harmful words from being spoken. Over the years, I have written many letters to my wife in response to offenses or sensitive issues, and I can testify that the letters have overall prevented strife, reinforced love, and addressed the issues with clarity.

Hebrews 13:15 Therefore, by Him let us continually offer the sacrifice of praise to God, that is, the fruit of our lips, giving thanks to His name.

This is the New Testament version of Psalm 34:1: "I will bless the LORD at all times; His praise shall continually be in my mouth." Both of these verses exhort the believer to praise God unceasingly. Such continual praise and worship of God by believers is an aspect of God's will being done on earth as it is in heaven, for in heaven the four living creatures "do not rest day or night, saying: 'Holy, holy, holy, Lord God Almighty, who was and is and is to come!'" (Rev. 4:8). Not only should you continually praise, thank, and bless God because He is worthy, but also because doing so will help you keep your mind stayed upon Him, which is conducive to life and perfect peace (Isa. 26:3; Rom. 8:5-6; Col. 3:2). "Sacrifice of praise" means you are to praise God even if you do not feel like doing so, just as you are to obey God even if you do not feel like doing so, just as you are to love your neighbor (especially your spouse) as yourself even if you do not feel like doing so. The following verses also advocate continual praise of God: Psalm 70:4: "Let all those who love Your salvation say continually, 'Let God be magnified!'"; Psalm 71:6: "My praise shall be continually of You"; Psalm 71:14-15, 23: "But I will hope continually, and will praise You yet more and more. My mouth shall tell of Your righteousness and Your salvation all the day....My lips shall greatly rejoice when I sing to You...." What an antidote to the complaining, negativity, self-centeredness, and strife which plagues many marriages!

James 1:26 If anyone among you thinks he is religious, and does not bridle his tongue but deceives his own heart, this one's religion is useless.

This verse indicates the necessity of bridling, or taming, your tongue if you want to please God. An unbridled, unrestrained tongue proceeds from a prideful, deceived heart. Self-control is a fruit of the Spirit, and you should bear the fruit of self-control so that you do not hastily utter words based on any and every thought that pops into your head and every fleeting feeling. Instead, you should give consideration as to whether or not your prospective comments would glorify God and impart grace to your spouse and neighbor. Walking with the Lord, acknowledging Him in all your ways, giving Him continual thanks and praise (Praise God for who He is, for the death and resurrection of Christ on your behalf, and also for His ongoing provisions for your life), and regularly meditating on verses pertaining to taming the tongue, are the best ways to bridle your tongue. James 1:26 reminds me of 1 Corinthians 13, which says if I do good works but do not have love, I profit nothing.

James 3:3-5 Indeed, we put bits in horses' mouths that they may obey us, and we turn their whole body. Look also at ships: although they are so large and are driven by fierce winds, they are turned by a very small rudder wherever the pilot desires. Even so the tongue is a little member and boasts great things.

Bits and rudders, which are very small, turn (or change the direction of) horses and ships, which are very large. Similarly, the little tongue turns the whole body. Your tongue can turn your body in one of two directions—toward the Lord (repentance) or away from the Lord (sin). What you say, and the tone with which you say it, affects your spirit, soul (including your attitude), and your body, and it certainly affects your spouse and others. Taming your tongue is imperative for having a happy marriage, for effective parenting, and being a godly witness.

James 4:11-12 Do not speak evil of one another, brethren. He who speaks evil of a brother and judges his brother, speaks evil of the law and judges the law. But if you judge the law, you are not a doer of the law but a judge. (12) There is one Lawgiver, who is able to save and to destroy. Who are you to judge another?

James 5:9 Do not grumble against one another, brethren, lest you be condemned. Behold, the Judge is standing at the door!

I will share three applications of the above two passages which instruct us to not speak evil of, or grumble against, any person. First, do not grumble to one person about another. Such would be gossip and slander, which God condemns. Second, do not grumble against a person about his or her own shortcomings. To do so would be making you judge of that person. Furthermore, it would be rude. [However, if someone has violated a Scriptural command, it is appropriate to point out his or her sin. But do so with humility and "a spirit of gentleness" (Gal. 6:1) rather than by grumbling.] Third (and this is likely the most challenging), **do not grumble within yourself** about another person. Otherwise, you would be acting as that person's judge. God is Judge and Lawgiver; you are not. Leviticus 19:17-18 affirms this, saying, "You shall not hate your brother in your heart....You shall not take vengeance, nor bear any grudge against the children of your people, but you shall love your neighbor as yourself: I am the LORD." The thoughts that a believer entertains in his or her heart about a fellow believer are vitally important to God. Do not grumble against, nor speak evil of, nor hate, nor bear a grudge against your neighbor in your heart.

1 Peter 2:21-23 ...Christ also suffered for us, leaving us an example, that you should follow His steps: "Who committed no sin, nor was deceit found in His mouth"; who, when

Tom Caldwell

He was reviled, did not revile in return; when He suffered, He did not threaten, but committed Himself to Him who judges righteously.

The Lord Jesus is our example and standard for godly and victorious living, including in taming the tongue. Three references to Christ's speech appear here: His words were 1) not deceptive, 2) nor reviling, 3) nor threatening, despite the deception, reviling, and threats which were unjustly leveled against Him. Jesus did not defend Himself when Pilate, Herod, religious leaders, and others falsely accused and abused Him. Jesus would let God the Father render judgment to each person according to what he had done. Likewise, if your spouse or neighbor speaks disrespectfully to you or mistreats you, certainly you should not retaliate, nor must you defend yourself, or even reply at all if doing so would include speaking ungracious words. [However, if your spouse or neighbor is in sin, then you *should* confront that person in love, restoring him or her gently (Gal. 6:1).] Instead, commit yourself to the Lord who is the righteous Judge. God will render to you what you deserve, and God will render to your spouse what he or she deserves.

Isaiah 53 (from which comes 1 Peter 2:24) prophesies of the atonement of the future Messiah, who is Jesus; verse seven references the Messiah's mouth while He would be falsely accused: "As a sheep before the shearers is silent, so He opened not His mouth." Matthew 27:12-14 says, "And while He (Jesus) was being accused by the chief priests and elders, He answered nothing. Then Pilate said to Him, 'Do You not hear how many things they testify against You? But He answered him not one word, so that the governor marveled greatly." The Jews and the Roman soldiers murdered Jesus, though He was their Creator and Redeemer. But they were not alone in murdering the Messiah, for my sins and your sins also caused Jesus to be crucified. Jesus willingly embraced His cross because of His love for all of humanity, ultimately demonstrated in His redemption of us through His blood. Regarding those murdering and reviling Jesus, from the cross He said, "Father, forgive them, for they do not know what they do" (Lk. 23:34). Your spouse has never treated you as hatefully and as shamefully as those who crucified Jesus treated Him. Since Jesus, the Divine Judge, freely loved and forgave each of us, do not think of yourself as greater than Him by justifying yourself to harbor hatred and unforgiveness toward your spouse and fellow man. Instead, follow God's command—"You shall love your neighbor as yourself" (Mt. 22:39), and Jesus' example, "who, when He was reviled, did not revile in return."

Chapter 3

Oneness, Authority, and Roles of Male and Female

"Let Us make man in Our image" (Genesis 1:26).

[I would like to credit James Grant for assisting me with some of the thoughts I share in this chapter.[19] I would also like to acknowledge Wayne Grudem, author of *Systematic Theology, An Introduction to Biblical Doctrine*[20], whose writing aided me in the consideration of certain verses and confirmed some of the ideas I had regarding this chapter.]

To be the best spouse possible, it is important to understand the roles of man and woman as explained by the Bible, God's infallible Word. Let us return to the creation account.

In Genesis 1:26-27, on the sixth day of creation, God the Father spoke to God the Son and God the Holy Spirit saying, "Let Us make

---

[19] James Grant, in conversation with me.

[20] Wayne Grudem. *Systematic Theology, An Introduction to Biblical Doctrine*, (Zondervan. Grand Rapids, Michigan. 1994).

man in Our image, according to Our likeness…So God created man in His own image; in the image of God He created him; male and female He created them." First Corinthians 11:7 reiterates this: "man is the image and glory of God."

One aspect of God's having made man in His image is that because there is plurality in the Godhead—God the Father, God the Son, and God the Holy Spirit, there is also plurality in mankind—man and woman. The Godhead consists of three distinct beings, but there is also unity in the Godhead. There is one divine nature, or essence, which all three persons of the Godhead possess (holiness, love, justice, omnipotence, omniscience, etc.). Also, fellowship exists within the Godhead, and mutual love (1 Jn. 4:8 says, "God is love"). So when Deuteronomy 6:4 says, "Hear, O Israel: The LORD our God, the LORD is *one*," the word "one" in Hebrew is *echad*. That is the same word used in Genesis 2:24: "Therefore a man shall leave his father and mother and be joined to his wife, and they shall become *one* flesh." Again, there is plurality in the Godhead—three distinct persons, and there is unity in the Godhead. Likewise, in marriage, there is plurality—man and woman are individuals. And there is also unity—man and woman are *one* (*echad*) flesh. And man and woman are to emulate God, who is *one* (*echad*), by walking in love towards one another and having fellowship.

Though all three persons of the Godhead have the same divine nature, they have *different roles*. For example, in creation, God the Father spoke into existence all that is; God the Son is the One through whom God the Father created (Jn. 1:3; Col. 1:16; Heb. 1:2), and certainly God the Holy Spirit was also involved in creation (Gen. 1:2). In redemption, God the Father sends God the Son to earth to die for the sins of the world. Then God the Son, after His resurrection and ascension, takes from God the Father the promised Holy Spirit and pours forth God the Holy Spirit upon the church. God the Son walked among men; God the Holy Spirit dwells within and rests upon men.

Different levels of authority seem to exist within the Godhead. Take, for instance, Genesis 1:26. God the Father takes the initiative in speaking to God the Son and God the Holy Spirit about creating man in God's image (for certainly He was not speaking to other heavenly beings since other heavenly beings do not create). We also see a submission of the Son to the Father in 1 Corinthians 15:28—"Now when all things are made subject to Him, then the Son Himself will also be subject to Him who put all things under Him, that God may be all in all." Again, 1 Corinthians 11:3 says: "the head of Christ is God." Also, John 16:13 says, "when He, the Spirit of truth, has come, He will guide you into all truth; for *He will not speak on His own authority*, but whatever He hears He will speak; and He will tell you things to come." Again, John 15:26 says that the Spirit of truth "proceeds from the Father." So within the Godhead, God the Father has the greatest authority.

Similarly, though husband and wife are one flesh and are comparable to each other (Gen. 2:18), still husband and wife (and more generally, man and woman) have distinctions in authority. First Corinthians 11:3 says, "the head of every man is Christ, the *head of woman is man*, and the head of Christ is God." And again in reference to Genesis 1:26, 1 Corinthians 11:7 says, "he (man) is the image and glory of God; but the woman is the glory of man." Again, Ephesians 5:23 says, "the husband is the head of the wife...." In biblical times, we see that the firstborn in any family was typically given greater authority. Likewise, the fact that Adam was created before Eve seems to be part of the reason why man is given greater authority than the woman. Paul references this in 1 Timothy 2:13—"For Adam was formed first, then Eve"—which is part of the explanation as to why Scripture says women should not teach or have authority over men (see verses 11-15). Also, Adam, who is given the authority to name the animals, is allowed to name the helper God brought to him—He calls her "woman" (Hebrew: *Ishshah*, Gen. 2:23). In Genesis 3, in response to the woman's sin, God said, "Your desire shall be for your husband, and he shall rule over you." The issue of husbands having authority over wives is pervasive in the New Testament: wives are to *be subject to* their husbands in everything (Eph. 5:24), wives are *to submit to* their husbands (Eph. 5:22; Col. 3:18; 1 Pet. 3:1, 5), and wives are to *be obedient to* their husbands (Tit. 2:5; 1 Pet. 3:6) as the wife is called "the weaker vessel" (1 Pet. 3:7). In contrast, the husband is to *rule* his own house well (1 Tim. 3:4, 12). In 1 Timothy 3, men alone are specified to be the bishops and deacons of the church (verses 1-2, 12). In Titus 1:6, men alone are specified to be the elders of the church.

Certainly, as with any authoritative position, the authority that God has given husbands over wives can be abused. So men must embrace the following command of God: "Husbands, *love your wives*, just as Christ also loved the church and gave Himself for her..." (Eph. 5:25). As Christ died for His bride, so the husband is to lay down his life for his wife. It is an aspect of the glory of manhood for a man to lay down his life for the woman. To do so is a chivalrous act, modeled by the medieval knights, but also widely accepted historically. When a disaster occurs, the women and children are to be saved first, such as when the Titanic sank. To lay down one's life for his wife means, in part, that the husband is to esteem his wife as better than himself (Phil. 2:3), he is to seek her well-being above his own (1 Cor. 10:24), and he is to serve (Mt. 10:27), nourish, and cherish her (Eph. 5:29).

Though man has the greater authority, I submit that men and women are of equal importance in God's eyes. Again, this follows the pattern that the three persons of the Godhead are of equal importance and value. God created both male and female to be in God's image (Gen. 1:26-27), and male and female are equal in their sharing of God's image. Furthermore, Galatians 3:28 says, "There is neither Jew nor Greek, there is neither slave nor free, there is neither male nor female; for you are all one in Christ Jesus." A woman is equal to a man in terms of access to God the Father through faith in Christ—both can "come boldly to the throne of grace" (Heb. 4:16). Some other examples of the equality of man and woman are that a woman can abide in Christ just as much as a man (Jn. 15:1-8), a woman can move mountains by faith just as much as a man (Mark 11:22-24), and a woman can store up treasure in heaven just as much as a man (Mt. 5:19-20).

Let's consider the following questions: In heaven, will there be the continued difference of gender? Also, in heaven, will men continue to have greater authority than women? The answer to these questions is probably yes. Because there will be a resurrection of the earthly body, there will be gender in heaven. One's identity of male or female will not be annihilated. Even in our intermediate state (that is, while our earthly bodies are in the ground but we are immediately with the Lord with a temporary or intermediate body—"a building from God" [2 Cor. 5:1]), our intermediate bodies will still be recognizable to one another, and gender will likely be an aspect of that. Authority of the man in heaven will not likely operate the same as in this present time on earth. There will not be sin or evil desire in heaven, so authority in terms of providing a check upon human evil will not be needed. However, there will still likely be a certain amount of leadership in heaven ascribed specifically to men rather than women simply as part of the carryover from the way things are in the here-and-now to the heavenly state.

Let us summarize man's role within mankind. Man is the spiritual leader—he is to take the lead in representing Christ to his family, to the church, and to the world. First Timothy 3:5 says, "if a man does not know how to rule his own house, how will he take care of the church of God?" Man should never forget that his ruling and leading includes the need for him to lay down his life in order to love and serve his wife, his family, and his neighbor. Matthew 20:26-27 says, "whoever desires to become great among you, let him be your servant. And whoever desires to be first among you, let him be your slave...." A husband ought to take the lead in providing for his family, as 1 Timothy 5:8 says, "But if anyone does not provide for his own, and especially for those of his household, he has denied the faith and is worse than an unbeliever."

The woman's role has three main parts. First, women are not to lead, but rather to help the man become all he should be as a leader in society. First Corinthians 11, verses 3, 7-9 say: "the head of every man is Christ, *the head of woman is man*...(7) woman is the glory of man. (8) For man is not from woman, but woman from man. (9) Nor was man created for the woman, *but woman for the man*." This passage makes clear that woman was made for man's sake, to be his *helpmate*, as in Genesis 2:18—God said, "I will make him a *helper*...." Second, women are to nurture and prepare the next generation. The mother typically spends more time with children than the father. First Timothy 2:15 says, "Nevertheless she will be saved in *childbearing* if they continue in faith, love, and holiness, with self-control." In Titus 2, the older women are to admonish the younger women "to love their husbands, to love their children" and to be "homemakers" (verses 4-5). Third, women are to perform acts of charity for the poor and needy. Proverbs 31:20 says, "She extends her hand to the poor, yes she reaches out her hands to the needy." Concerning widows worthy of honor, 1 Timothy 5:10 says, "if she has brought up children, if she has lodged strangers, if she has washed the saints' feet, if she has relieved the afflicted, if she has diligently followed every good work."

An aspect of mankind (this includes man and woman) being made in the image of God is that humans have moral ability, which means humans can choose to do right or wrong in a way much superior to the animals. Such ability brings with it responsibility and accountability.

Concerning the role of men and women, Genesis 1:26-27 indicates that humans have been given dominion over the earth and all its creatures. Humans are called to subdue the earth—to rule over all the other creatures of the earth and to utilize the various aspects of creation for the glory of God. First Corinthians 10:31b says, "whatever you do, do all to the glory of God." Such dominion means that humans are also stewards of this earth; we are to take care of this wonderful planet which God has given to us. Psalm 8:5-6 also speaks of the creation of man and the dominion God has given him: "For You (God) have made him (man) a little lower than the angels, and You have crowned him with glory and honor. You have made him to have dominion over the works of Your hands; You have put all things under his feet…." What a privilege to be made in the image of the Almighty God, to be able to know Him intimately, to love Him, to serve Him, to occupy such a special place within all His creation, and to represent Him to a world which is in such desperate need of hope and salvation. Truly, our God is worthy of all glory, honor, and praise!

Chapter 4

An Exposition of Song of Solomon

"I am my beloved's, and my beloved is mine" (Song 6:3).

The Song of Solomon, or Song, is a song or poem that celebrates expressions of love—intimate, passionate, and even erotic at times—between King Solomon and his new bride, the Shulamite, and it is exemplary of the love that can be expressed within the context of Christian marriage. Song is also a representation of the love-relationship between Christ (the Bridegroom) and the church (His bride). For that matter, any biblical passage dealing with marriage should also be seen as representative of the Christ-church relationship because human marriage is always a type of, or picture of, that ultimate union.

Song has been called an obscure book. Because of its flowery language, Song can be difficult to fully grasp, especially at the first reading of it. Commentaries can provide help. I should remind you that the headings that indicate which character is speaking are insertions by Bible commentators and are not part of the Scripture, so sometimes there are differences of opinion as to who is speaking. Nevertheless, I find these headings helpful.

Whether Solomon is a figurative character or whether he is the historical King Solomon (the focus of 2 Chronicles 1-9 and author of Proverbs, Ecclesiastes, and Song of Solomon) is debatable, but it seems the majority of writers take him to be the historical King Solomon. (I lean that way myself.) The name "Solomon" and the title "king" appear together at times in Song (3:9; 3:11). A reason to hesitate in attributing Song to the historical King Solomon is that King Solomon went on to have "seven hundred wives, princesses, and three hundred concubines" (1 Kings 11:3). Was the Shulamite his first wife? We do not know. How did this marriage turn out? We do not know. In any case, our sovereign God has graciously given us this important book, Song, and we should believe it, as we should all of the sixty-six books of the Bible, to be the inerrant Word of God and embrace God's message.

Let me share a few more introductory points, including certain aspects of Song which stand out to me and that I will address in this chapter. Other characters in Song who have lesser roles include "the daughters of Jerusalem" (1:4; 1:11; 5:9; 6:1), the Shulamite's brothers (2:15; 8:8-9), and a relative (8:5). I do not believe Song is quoted anywhere in the New Testament. Aspects of Song that I particularly like are the frequent and various terms of endearment that Solomon and his bride speak to and about each other. I have used these terms of endearment in addressing my wife. I also appreciate the pithy, power-packed one-liners about love such as "his banner over me was love" (2:4), "love is as strong as death" (8:6), and "many waters cannot quench love..." (8:7). Song has also enhanced my appreciation of the love-relationship Christ is desirous to have with me as well as with the church as a whole. Finally, I appreciate being able to take the terms of endearment and compliments spoken by each spouse toward the other and apply them in my declaration and adoration of my Savior Jesus. Indeed, Jesus, Your name is wonderful, "better than wine" (1:2-3). You are the "chief among ten thousand" (5:10). "O you whom I love" (1:7), You are "My perfect One" (5:2). Thank You for coming to me enthusiastically and powerfully, "leaping upon the mountains" and "skipping upon the hills" like a "gazelle or a young stag" (2:8-9) in order to radically save me. You draw me to You (1:4) because You are merciful! When I found You, I held onto You and I will not let You go (3:4). Indeed, You are "the one I love" (3:1, 2, 3, 4)! Amen!

Song is typically seen as having three parts. Part 1 is 1:1-3:5, Part 2 is 3:6–5:1, and Part 3 is 5:2–8:14. I encourage you to read Song verse by verse as you read this chapter. I will expound on only some of the highlights. Like the other commentators, my own interpretation is simply that—mine. Part of my purpose in writing about Song is to whet your appetite for your own further study of this wonderful book.

Part 1

In 1:1-1:8, the Shulamite expresses her longing for her beloved husband, King Solomon. They appear to be married in this chapter due to the intimacy that is expressed (1:4, 1:13, and 1:16), even though their wedding seems to take place in 3:6-5:1. (In this case, Song would not be in chronological order.) In 1:2 she says, "your love is better than wine"—wine being a metaphor for pleasure and exhilaration.[21] Do pleasure and exhilaration characterize your relationship with your spouse? Do they characterize your relationship with Jesus? We should pursue this as a goal for both relationships. In accordance with Ecclesiastes 7:1, "A good name is better than precious ointment," the bride praises the name (which represents the character) of her husband, saying his name is "ointment poured forth." Solomon's character and reputation likely attracted his bride to him, and even the other virgins of the land can identify with what she sees in him (verse 3). In verse 4, she says, "Draw me away." In other words, "Get me off by yourself." She wants exclusive time with her beloved. On a spiritual level, whenever we draw near to our Bridegroom, Christ, He promises to also draw near to us (James 4:8). That's a loving Bridegroom, and a good example to us husbands! We find Solomon affirmatively responding to her request in 2:10 and 2:13: "Rise up...and come away." Husband and wife ought to try to carve out quality and quantity time together. Finding such time can become more challenging when children arrive, but a good marital relationship requires relating with each other, and having the time and energy to do so. In 1:5-6, the bride reveals some of her background— that she was a vineyard keeper, probably a commoner in the land rather than royalty. Her humble origin does not hinder the king's choosing her to be his bride. What an exaltation for her—to go from commoner

---

[21] *The MacArthur Study Bible*, NKJV, (Thomas Nelson Publishers. Nashville. 1997), 942.

to queen! Likewise, what an exaltation for us who are Christians—to go from sinner to saint, from wretched to redeemed. Christ chose us despite our background of ordinariness and sin. Through our union with Him, we ourselves become royalty, namely "kings" (Rev. 1:6) and "a royal priesthood" (1 Pet. 2:9). Hallelujah!

Terms of Endearment

I find the terms of endearment expressed between the husband, Solomon, and his bride to be very loving and meaningful, and you can use these terms and similar terms in the way you address your spouse. I am now going to list for you most, if not all, of the terms of endearment in Song so you can have them handy to speak them to your spouse and also so you can use them in your time of worship and prayer to our divine Beloved, Christ.

"My love," "O love," and "My beloved" are the terms of endearment that appear the most. Solomon calls his bride "my love" and "O love" about eight times. The bride calls Solomon "my beloved" about nineteen times. She calls him "the one I love" four times.

I will first list the terms of endearment Solomon spoke to his bride and then comment on them: "O fairest among women" (1:8), "my filly" (1:9), "Behold, you are fair, my love! Behold, you are fair! You have dove's eyes" (1:15), "You are all fair, my love, and there is no spot in you" (4:7), "How fair is your love, my sister, my spouse" (4:10), "My sister, my spouse" (5:1), "O my love" (6:4), "My dove, my perfect one, is the only one" (6:9).

In 1:8, the husband calls his bride, "O fairest among women." Here, Solomon reveals that to him, she is the absolute best; she tops all women in his eyes. He may have had his bride in mind when he wrote the virtuous wife passage of Proverbs 31. Instead of primarily seeing your spouse as one who falls short and magnifying those shortcomings in your mind or with your words, you should try to see your spouse in a higher way. This is in emulation of Christ who sees us in a higher way, namely, through His own righteousness: We are "the righteousness of God in Him" (2 Cor. 5:21b).

In 1:9, Solomon refers to her with an endearing nickname, "my filly" (a female horse). Solomon seems to be a horse lover as he imported horses (1 Kings 10:28). He might have liked Kentucky! In Solomon's eyes, the stately grace and beauty of a horse are indicative of his bride. In 1:15, Solomon compliments his wife—"you are fair." This builds her confidence in his love for her and thus gives her a sense of marital security. He says, "You have dove's eyes." Webster's says the dove is "a symbol of innocence, gentleness, and peace."[22] These are qualities that he commends in his wife. She returns this compliment in 5:12.

In 2:2, using figurative language, Solomon indicates that his bride stands out among the daughters (please read along in the Scripture). In 2:3, his bride indicates that Solomon also stands out among the sons and that she delights in him. It is significant that they see each other as outstanding, as a cut above the rest. Solomon drives this point home when he calls her "my perfect one...the only one" (6:9). We need to see our spouse (or a potential future spouse) as outstanding. I would not have married my wife, Kim, unless I felt she was outstanding. Any interests I may have had in other women melted away when I met Kim. When it comes to marriage, why settle for anything less than the best? You should want God's best for yourself in all aspects of your life and you should be willing to wait for God's best. If, however, you married a non-Christian, you should still wholeheartedly love God, wholeheartedly love your spouse, claim Romans 8:28, and pray to be a godly witness to your spouse.

Twice Solomon calls his spouse his "sister" (4:10, 5:1). This reminds us of the larger spiritual picture. Though you may be married, you should remember that you are part of a much larger family—the family of faith in Christ, with God as our Father, and each person who does the will of God as your brother and sister and mother (Mt. 12:50). So your wife is your sister in Christ. Marriage is not an end-all-be-all institution. All you possess in life, including your spouse, is ultimately for the purpose of glorifying God (1 Cor. 10:31). In 4:7, Solomon says, "there is no spot in you." Though all people have sinned and are flawed, this again reminds us that Christ sees us in a higher way (2 Cor. 5:21). Solomon sees his wife this way. It is important that you maintain a healthy, positive view of your spouse.

Here is the list of the bride's terms of endearment to or about Solomon, her husband: "O you whom I love" (1:7), "A bundle of myrrh is my beloved to me" (1:13), "My beloved is to me a cluster of henna

---

[22] *Webster's American Dictionary*, Second College Edition, (Random House, Inc. 2000), 241.

blooms" (1:14), "My love, my fair one" (2:10), "The one I love" (3:1, 2, 3, 4), and "This is my beloved, and this is my friend" (5:16).

In 1:7, the bride calls Solomon, "O you whom I love." When you call for your spouse's attention, perhaps for some task, it is good if you add the reminder that you love your spouse. For example, "Kim, whom I love, did you brush the kid's teeth yet?" You should not let your busy schedules or household tasks drown out love. Song 8:7a says of love, "nor can the floods drown it out." Instead, be intentional to keep love flowing like a stream in the midst of a desert of duties.

The bride speaks at times about her husband to the daughters of Jerusalem (e.g. 1:2-4; 1:12-14; 2:4-7). In 1:13 she says, "A bundle of myrrh is my beloved to me." Myrrh is a gum resin used in making incense and perfumes.[23] So, figuratively speaking, her husband is a positive fragrance to her, a sweet-smelling aroma, and pleasant to be around. This also reminds us that the Christian is "the fragrance of Christ" to other Christians, encouraging one another as "the aroma of life leading to life" (2 Cor. 2:14-15). In 1:14, she says "My beloved is to me a cluster of henna blooms." A henna is an Asian shrub or small tree with fragrant flowers; dye is made from its leaves."[24] So as the most beautiful part of a plant is the bloom, her husband, as well as their marital relationship, is beautiful to her. As dye is made from the henna plant, what her husband brings to the marriage is good. And in keeping with the bride's positive comments about her husband to the daughters of Jerusalem, you should not speak disparagingly about your spouse to others.

In 5:16, the bride calls her husband her "friend." God called Abraham his "friend" (James 2:23). Jesus calls each of us who obeys Him "friend" (Jn. 15:13-15). What a concept—I am a friend of God! A husband and wife should see themselves as much more than a couple who makes love together and runs a house together; they should be best friends. They show interest in the details of each other's lives. They share the news of each other's independent daily activities. They confide in each other. They share their hopes, dreams, and concerns with each other. They have fun together. And above all, they read the Bible together, pray together, and seek God's perfect will together. Make your spouse your best human friend.

---

[23] Ibid., 528.

[24] Ibid., 377.

As I reflect on the numerous, various, and beautiful terms of endearment in Song, my reaction is one of amazement. What a marriage-enhancing practice it could be for husband and wife to speak such terms of endearment to each other regularly. Jesus said, "Out of the abundance of the heart the mouth speaks" (Mt. 12:34b). You need to make sure that you maintain a right heart toward your spouse so that you do not say such terms of endearment as empty words. Romans 12:9 says, "Let love be without hypocrisy." But as you seek to love your spouse, you can speak to your spouse utilizing these wonderful terms, believing that doing so will help rightly fashion your heart and bless your marriage.

Compliments upon Physical Features and Appearance

In 1:10, Solomon comments on his bride's physical beauty. He does much of this in Song: 2:14b, 4:1-5, 4:11-15, 6:4-9, 7:1-9. Solomon compliments his wife's teeth, lips, mouth, temples, thighs, navel, waist, neck, eyes, nose, head, hair, stature, breasts, and breath, and even the roof of her mouth. His bride does this also, in 5:10-16, describing to the daughters of Jerusalem Solomon's superiority to all others with a focus on his physical qualities. She compliments his head, locks, eyes, cheeks, lips, hands, body, legs, countenance, and mouth. In 1:16, she says, "You are handsome." In 5:16 she says, "He is altogether lovely." These frequent compliments about each other's physical features point to the reality that physical attraction is typically a big deal in marriage. Often the husband sees physical looks as more of a big deal than the wife. Even if your spouse might not win a contest on the basis of objective beauty, she (or he) can still appear beautiful in the eyes of you, the beholder. Though "beauty is passing" (Pr. 31:30), still it is wise for husband and wife to be sensitive to what is beautiful in the eyes of each other. You should seek to remain beautiful to your spouse and your spouse should seek to remain beautiful to you. I encourage you to ask your spouse how you can become more attractive to him or her; this may include your attitude and actions as well as your physical shape and appearance. Then you should lay down any hindering habits, attitudes, ways, and even your own life, in order to meet your spouse's needs! Initially, this may not be comfortable, but this is love. First John 3:16 says, "By this we know love, because He laid down His life for us. And we also ought to lay down our lives for the brethren."

As Jesus died for His Bride, I ought to lay down my life for my wife, and my wife ought to lay down her life for me.

Spiritual Bonding

Since we have just discussed the focus on physical appearance in marriage, I want to put that in proper perspective. James Grant rightly says, "It is important not to have one's attraction to one's spouse or potential future spouse be built merely on physical attraction, because physical beauty is passing."[5] Here I want to submit what I believe may be the most important truth of this book. *The ultimate bonding of husband and wife to each other should be Christ!* Christ is the One who holds all things together, including your marriage (Col. 1:17)! Spiritual bonding means more than the husband and wife staying individually connected to Christ throughout the day as they raise kids and do chores together. Oh it certainly includes that. But the spiritual bonding of husband and wife that I advocate means that husband and wife *relate together spiritually.* Husband and wife are to be in the Word (the Bible) together—they study the Word together, speak the Word to each other, and perhaps memorize the Word together. They talk about the Word as they sit in their homes, walk by the way, rise up, and lie down (Dt. 6:7). They speak "to one another with psalms, hymns, and spiritual songs"; they sing and make melody together in their hearts to the Lord (Eph. 5:19). One of the best marital enhancing practices that Kim and I have discovered is for us to worship the Lord together in our home. We may use the hymnal, the CD player, or sing a cappella certain scriptural songs. Psalm 22:3 says of God: "O thou that inhabitest the praises of Israel" (KJV). Kim and I find joy, liberty, victory, and strength as God inhabits us in a special way due to our extended times of praising Him. Married couples should also pray together, knowing Christ's promise: "that if two of you agree on earth concerning anything that they ask, it will be done for them by My Father in heaven. For where two or three are gathered together in My name, I am there in the midst of them" (Mt. 18:19-20). This is one of the greatest benefits of marriage—the spiritual synergy created by coming together to seek God. Let the Word of God be the glue for your marriage, holding you together.

Brad McGill married Margaret (friends of mine from church) in 1971, when Brad was twenty-seven years old and Margaret was almost twenty-two. On the morning of his wedding, Brad went for a walk. He had peace about marrying Margaret. He said to himself, "Aside from getting saved, this is the best thing I've ever done." When I recently asked Brad, who has been married to Margaret now for forty-one years, about the difficulties of marriage, he replied, "It's not been difficult. With God in the center, it's been fabulous!...It's been worthwhile, and the companionship has been fulfilling."

Furthermore, James Grant points out that as husband and wife spend time together seeking God, they will be more unified in terms of their callings and ministry; they will reduce the likelihood of one's holding the other back in terms of what God is calling the other to do.

Other Pithy, Power-packed Phrases

In 2:4, the bride says, "He brought me to his banqueting house, and his banner over me was love." A banner identifies the troops under it and also rallies the troops. Solomon's banner of love, figuratively placed over his bride, identified her as his wife to all onlookers and also served as a reminder and source of inspiration to his wife of his love for her of the security of their relationship. Husband, is your wife convinced of, and secure in, your love for her? If not, then begin demonstrating consistent acts of love toward her so that she can be secure in your banner of love over her.

In 2:5 and 5:8, the bride says, "I am lovesick." This is an expression of her intense longing to be with her husband. She is beside herself with love for him. How many marriages do you know of where the husband and wife have been married for many years and yet love-starvation rather than lovesickness is characteristic of their relationship? I see no reason why the intense longing for each other that characterized the early days of marriage cannot continue.

In 2:7, 3:5, and 8:4 (in part) the bride says, "I charge you, O daughters of Jerusalem, by the gazelles or by the does of the field, do not stir up nor awaken love until it pleases." There is a proper context for romantic and sexual love—within the marriage relationship, one man to one woman. I believe that even kissing should be postponed until marriage. One who is single ought not to try to manufacture or force a romantic relationship, but instead one ought to seek first the kingdom of God and His righteousness so that God can bring a marital relationship to pass at the right time and with the right person. This certainly requires faith and patience, and through possessing these qualities one will inherit the promises (Heb. 6:12). This verse could also stand as a warning against one's passions' being artificially stimulated through entertainment, media, billboards, etc. that promote lust and sensuality.[25]

In 2:16 and 6:3, the bride exclaims, "My beloved is mine, and I am his." This is a declaration of the commitment of husband and wife to each other as well as the exclusive nature of that relationship—no outside suitors are welcome! While in prayer for my marriage, I will sometimes declare, "Kim is mine, and I am hers; nothing shall come between us." This also reminds me of the Christian's vertical relationship—"[nothing] shall be able to separate us from the love of God which is in Christ Jesus our Lord" (Rom. 8:39). I am Christ's, and Christ is mine! Hallelujah!

In 3:1-4, the bride repeats four times the phrase "the one I love" in reference to Solomon. She does not describe him as "the one I am married to." Instead, what is foundational and most defining of their marriage relationship is their love for each other. She sought him and when she found him she "would not let him go" (verse 4). Again, her clinging to Solomon conveys the intended permanence of their relationship—until death do them part. This reminds me of being born again—wholeheartedly seeking and finding Jesus Christ, and then never letting Christ go.

Part 2—The Wedding and Consummation of their Union

The wedding festival is the focus of 3:6-5:1; this is considered Part 2 of the Song. Solomon comes to Jerusalem with his sixty-man bodyguard, and the daughters of Jerusalem go out to greet him. His bride is carried on a palanquin (3:9), which is a wedding carriage or portable chair that Solomon had made for her in order to honor and exalt her above all other women on her special day; it is Solomon's royal version of rolling out the red carpet. Similarly, lifting up one's wife through prayer, kind words, and acts of thoughtfulness should be continual and not just relegated to the first day of marriage. The first appearance of the word "spouse" is in 4:8, and it appears six times from 4:8 through 5:1. This gives us reason to believe that 3:6-

---

[25] James Grant, in conversation with me.

5:1 is the account of their wedding. In 4:8 they have likely just been pronounced "husband and wife." In addition to Solomon's frequent compliments of his wife's physical features through Song, in 4:10 Solomon compliments the greatest quality about his wife—her love! Inspired by his wife's love, perhaps Solomon begins kissing her in 4:11 as he speaks of her lips and mouth. In 4:12, perhaps Solomon is warming up for the consummation—their first sexual union! He describes his bride as "a garden enclosed…a spring shut up, a fountain sealed." He has not yet had access to her sexually, but he excitedly anticipates their first encounter. In 4:13-15, Solomon gushes forth compliments about her plants, pleasant fruits, spices, and incense, which are likely figurative speech representing specific features of her body. In 4:16, the bride removes any guardedness and invites her new husband to access her garden, her body. The consummation of their marriage seems to occur between 4:16 and 5:1. Solomon encourages his wedding guests to eat and drink because it is truly a time of celebration.

Part 3

Chapter 5, verse 2 begins the third and final part of Song. Some commentators say that the first section of the third part, 5:2-5:8, is a dream, while others say it is the couple's first argument. Indeed, there is a brief separation of the two, but the cause of the separation is not obvious. In either case, the bride seeks Solomon. If an argument was the cause, she rightly pursued reconciliation with her husband. This leads to a lengthy description by the bride to the daughters of Jerusalem as to how special her husband is. Any point of disagreement between the two was put in proper perspective as she reflects on the larger picture—his surpassing excellence as a husband, "chief among ten thousand" (5:10). Motivated by this realization, she declares the unity, commitment, and exclusivity of her relationship with Solomon: "I am my beloved's, and my beloved is mine" (6:3). In 6:4, Solomon returns to his bride and speaks many complements to her including calling her his "perfect one" and his "only one" (6:9), even though many eligible queens, concubines, and virgins are out there. He says she is "as awesome as an army with banners" (6:10). That should smooth things over, if there had been an argument. In 6:11-13 (which some say is the most difficult part of Song to interpret), we see that the bride goes on an excursion, and Solomon longs for her to return to him. It is interesting that he calls her "Shulamite" instead of a term of endearment here. It is also interesting that he says "we" as opposed to "I" in "that we may look upon you" (6:13). Perhaps Solomon is with his friends when he speaks here. In 6:13, she asks what he sees in her, and in 7:1-9 Solomon answers her question by again giving her a multitude of compliments.

In 7:10, the bride makes a statement about their relationship that is profoundly important for all marriages: "I am my beloved's, and his desire is toward me." In any marital relationship, though commitment must be established, desire for one another is also important to maintain. Commitment can be likened to an anchor of a ship, holding the ship in place when it would otherwise drift because of contrary tide and winds. Commitment is necessary. But desire can be likened to when the tide and the wind work with the ship, taking the ship in the direction the ship's captain wants it to go. Likewise, in marriage commitment is necessary so that if desire fades, expectations go unmet, or temptations come, husband and wife will not drift toward infidelity, but instead will remain faithful to each other. But when husband and wife maintain strong desire for each other, this makes commitment a light yoke and an easier thing to maintain. Then joy remains in the marriage. When desire is present, marriage is a delight, not drudgery. So in this passage, the bride indicates that Solomon's desire for her has not faded. He is not burned out. His passions for her have not cooled down. He has not moved his affections away from her and put them elsewhere. His being with her has not degenerated from exhilaration and desire to obligation only. She does not feel taken for granted. She is still a high priority to him. Romance, passion, and attraction are alive and strong between the two. This gets down to the heart of the matter, which is the matter of the heart. Husband and wife must maintain purity of heart toward God and toward each other (Mt. 5:8). Husband and wife must continue to invest in each other because "where your treasure is, there your heart will be also" (Mt. 6:21). Do you desire your spouse? To restore or strengthen desire for one another in your marriage, I recommend you turn to the end of Chapter 1 and read the section "Nevertheless I have this against you, that you have left your first love" (Rev. 2:4). Also, another section in Chapter 1 which is relevant is "Let each of us please his neighbor for his good, leading to edification" (Romans 15:2).

In 7:11-13, it seems the bride is asking for a getaway with her husband, maybe a second honeymoon. She lets him know that if he will oblige her in this it will greatly motivate her to "give you my love… which I have laid up for you, my beloved" (7:12-13).

Some commentators see Chapter 8 as occurring at a country home. Perhaps the bride has brought Solomon to her mother's home for a visit. Verse 5 may refer to the family's first view of the newlyweds, seeing them coming down the road toward their house. In verses 8-9, commentators say the bride's brothers speak. It seems they are speaking in times past, when the bride was still a young teen, not yet physically developed. As good brothers should, they vowed to guard her from mischievous young men. In verse 10, the bride declares that she is grown up now, and she has achieved peace in her marriage to Solomon. In verses 11-12, she says that as Solomon had a vineyard, she also has a vineyard here at her old home. Perhaps she is saying, "Solomon, you are welcome to any fruit of my vineyard." In other words, "You are welcome in my home." In verse 13, it is thought that Solomon is asking his bride to sing a song. Perhaps verse 14 contains the words to her song, words that she has sung to him before, in 2:17. It has been proposed that "Bether" of "the mountains of Bether" (2:17) means "separation." But in 8:14, "mountains of spices" indicates that there is no more separation, but only blessing.[26]

In conclusion, let me comment on two more pithy, power-packed phrases from Chapter 8.

"*love* is as strong as death" (8:6)

I will point out two applications here. One, love requires death to self, as 1 John 3:16 makes clear. Christ demonstrated His love for the world by dying for the world. Likewise, you demonstrate love for Christ, your spouse, and your neighbor when you die to self (e.g., to selfish attitudes, behaviors, and agendas) for the edification of the other. Second, as James Grant points out, "Love overcomes death." This is along the lines of the statement "love never fails" (1 Cor. 13:8). The love of God, as manifested through the sacrifice of Christ, produces life

---

[26] *The Pulpit Commentary*, Vol 9. "Proverbs, Ecclesiastes, Song of Solomon," exposition by W.J. Deane and S.T. Taylor-Taswell, (Hendrickson Publishers. Peabody, MA.), 185.

beyond the grave—eternal life. It also produces a quality of life in this age—abundant life. This is life that overcomes the world; it overcomes the ordinary gravitational pull downward toward sin and death.[27]

"If a man would give for *love* all the wealth of his house, it would be utterly despised" (8:7).

To "give for love" is to try to replace love. But nothing can replace love. A husband cannot maintain solid, loving relationships with his wife and children by replacing quality and quantity time with them through buying them an abundance of nice things. For instance, at Christmas, a husband does not need to feel that he must spend a fortune on gifts in order to show love, but he can spend a reasonable amount on gifts. And a memorable display of love would be to spend time with his family. In doing so, he can take the opportunity to have his family join him in reflection upon the ultimate Lover of one's soul, the Bridegroom Jesus Christ, who demonstrated love by laying down His precious life for us all. "We love Him because He first loved us" (1 Jn. 4:19), and we are called to follow Christ's example (Eph. 5:1-2). Love requires sacrifice of self in order to obey Christ and edify others. Love never fails because Christ, who is love, never fails. Consecrate your marriage unto Christ, and let Him hold you together forever. Amen.

---

[27] James Grant, in conversation with me.

Chapter 5

Five Interviews

In late 2017 and early 2018, I interviewed three married ministers and two lay couples about marriage. After typing out the recorded interviews, I asked the participants to read the material, affording them the opportunity to make any desired changes. The five couples in these interviews collectively represent about 164 years of marriage; may we benefit from their wisdom.

The Dr. Hershael York Interview

In 2017, I interviewed a friend of mine, Dr. Hershael York, senior pastor of Buck Run Baptist Church, Frankfort, Kentucky. He is also the Victor and Louise Lester Professor of Christian preaching at the Southern Baptist Theological Seminary in Louisville. Hershael has been married to Tanya for almost thirty-seven years. They have two children and five grandchildren.

Tom: What are some of the benefits you enjoy most about marriage?

Hershael: I love the companionship and friendship of my wife, with whom I can enjoy, for example, a beautiful sunset. Such companionship is a need of the human heart. To have that satisfied and fulfilled is a real joy. Certainly, sexual intimacy is a wonderful gift, and it is used of the Lord to keep my heart fixed on her. Marital intimacy has had a sanctifying role in my life; it has protected me.

The ministry we share is also a wonderful benefit of our marriage. Ministry has bonded us, and we go through ministry together. Tanya is the most incredible pastor's wife I have ever seen. She has insight into people. She instinctively knows how people's hearts are leaning. She is great in individual interactions and relationships. She also has great insight into the ministry. She has never betrayed a confidence, has never spoken out of turn. Even if others were unkind to me, she has never responded in a hurtful way. She is the greatest Christian I know. She walks in the Spirit. To go through life with her is an wonderful delight. After all these years, my wife is a joy. I don't take that for granted.

That's not to say we don't have our moments. But they are just that—a few moments. The older we become, the less we argue. We still have arguments because we are both passionate people. But when we do, we later say, "What a waste of time."

I was on staff at Ashland Avenue Baptist Church in Lexington for seven years, beginning in 1980 as minister of music and youth; then I became the pastor. It was the church where Tanya grew up, and that is where we met. Tanya and I went out the night of my first day on the job. Thirteen days later I bought the rings. The senior pastor had concerns, and understandably so. I told him, "I am going to marry her, but I am willing to wait for you, until God shows you its right and you give me the OK." Three months later, he said to me, "You need to marry her." God brought Tanya and me together. If I had a million lifetimes, I would not marry someone else for even one of them. I would marry her every time.

Our lives are so centered and focused on me. Tanya is very compliant. For example, when we watch television, we watch what I want to watch. I don't insist on that. Some years ago, she made the unilateral decision that she would always watch whatever I would want to watch, in order to avoid ever having an argument about it. She teaches wives at the seminary, which she does because of me. (It's a little different now that we have grandchildren.) For years, Tanya and I have taken mini-vacations at a hotel in Cincinnati. I don't want to go to the mall. But she does; so we are going to do that. It's an occasion for me to say to Tanya, "Let's do what you want to do."

Tom: When your children were little, was it difficult to have quality time with Tanya? Was there ever a strain from that?

Hershael: Tanya and I didn't have the strain because we always carved out time. We had grandparents close to us for all but a three-year span. Even during seminary, we quickly found friends who would babysit our boys. All of our marriage, we have had at least one date night per week. The boys would typically spend Friday nights with Tanya's mom and dad. When I preached my mother-in-law's funeral, I said one reason why we have such a great marriage is because every week she wanted our boys to come stay with her.

A decision I made several years back was to go to bed when Tanya does. I used to let her go to bed, and I would stay up. But now I go to bed with her, early, and that's our together time. We might read or watch TV. Whatever we do, it's punctuated with conversation. We interrupt anything and everything to talk. We may go to bed at 8:30 or 9:00 p.m. and talk for a couple hours, and go to sleep by 11:00 p.m. I have togetherness with her every night.

Tom: Do you have any advice about the role of television in the family?

We would deny our boys TV in the summer. They would watch limited TV during the school year. Anything we allow to go to excess becomes a real problem, whether TV, Little League, etc. And as priest of my home, I needed to keep an eye on that.

Twenty years ago, when my wife would teach the seminary wives, she would commonly receive the question, "My husband always wants to have sex. How do I slow him down?" Now, seventy-five percent of the questions seminary wives ask Tanya is, "My husband never wants to have sex. What can I do to make him interested?" What is the difference? Pornography. People with smart phones that have no internet filters can be quickly tempted with pornography. It's an invitation for someone to come into their lives.

Tom: I am bound to love my wife whether she submits to me or not. Kim is bound to submit to me whether I love her or not. But when we both are fulfilling our God-ordained roles in this way, it is like flowing *with* the current instead of against it.

Hershael: Exactly. Some get caught in a vicious cycle—the husband doesn't give the wife love, so the wife doesn't give the husband respect; or she doesn't give him respect, so he doesn't give her love. It's what Dr. Emerson Eggerichs calls the crazy cycle. But it's great when husband and wife mutually love and respect one another.

First John says, "Everyone who loves has been born of God." So lost people do not know what true love is. One has to be born again to have the capacity to know God. A married couple, above everyone else, should demonstrate the love of Christ in their marriage. The love of Christ should be noticeable, and that is our goal. Your marriage is about so much more than just your happiness. The married couple should demonstrate Christ's love for His church. It is my goal to love my wife in such a way that submission is not even an issue for her. Why wouldn't she submit to me when I am always doing what is best for her? I am always putting her needs and desires before my own.

Tom: Do you have advice about resolving marital conflict?

Hershael: Repent. Be willing to own what you do—your attitude, tone, etc. One spouse does something that ticks the other off, then the other feels justified in saying something disrespectful. Repent. Regardless of what my wife does, I never have the right to speak disrespectfully to her. I am to love her as Christ loved the church. We need to eliminate the things that cause conflict. For me it is my tone of voice. I really have to work on that, because I can sound tense and aggravated. If I feel aggravated, it is a momentary feeling, but Tanya can become wounded and hold on to it for a while. So we should try to eliminate the behaviors that cause the tension. But when offense does happen, we ask for and grant forgiveness quickly. This many years in, we know that we are going to stay together. So the question becomes how much time are we going to waste before we get to the resolution of the matter.

The Tim and Sara Caldwell Interview

On January 1, 2018, I interviewed my brother and sister-in-law, Tim and Sara, who have been married for seventeen years. They are in their mid-forties and live in Crestwood, Kentucky. Sara brought two children to the marriage, Phoenix and Tai (both young adults now), and Tim and Sara gave birth to Sam (in 2002) and Sophie (in 2005). They have one grandchild, Ava, who was born to Phoenix and Jarrod in 2017. Tim's vocational life has been in education; he currently serves as Assistant Principal at South Oldham High School. Sara does landscaping work and cares for Ava three days per week. Tim's family and Jarrod's family attend New Life Church in Louisville.

Tom: What are some of the benefits you enjoy most about marriage?

Sara: You have a chosen partner with whom you can share your life. It's having your best friend with you daily. It's the security of knowing I can tell Tim anything and he will love me unconditionally. It's the comfort of daily waking up with someone I completely trust and with whom I enjoy spending time. It's having someone with whom I can share my hopes and dreams. It's raising our kids together. Tim and I came into marriage with very similar ideas about how we wanted to raise our children.

Tim: It's good to have a relationship where your spouse needs you and you need your spouse—the mutual dependence on each other, so you are not as self-centered. You must take into consideration how your daily decisions will impact your spouse and kids.

Sara: Of the things I mentioned before, I am not great at all of them. Some mornings I may wake up and know I do not have 100% trust in a decision Tim has made, but my goal is to get there. So marriage requires continual work; it is a work in progress.

Tim: Marriages go wrong when one or both spouses start making unilateral decisions, showing little or no concern for the input of the other. Marriage involves giving up one's independence to a large degree, and instead making decisions with the spouse and kids in mind.

Tom: Is spending quality time important to you, and what are some good ideas for quality time?

Sara: We are not the best at carving out time for just the two of us. Even though I hate spending the money, just the two of us having dinner out is good. It takes us out of our element; we are not focusing on cooking but we are face to face, focusing on each other, asking each other questions.

I like to be outdoors. So I enjoy when Tim and I ride bikes or take a walk in the park. It seems that being physically active stimulates our minds, which helps us have good conversation. And the kids need to see that Mom and Dad want to spend time together.

Tim: Sara gets up early in the mornings and so we have about fifteen minutes of time together. We read and have coffee together before I go to work.

Tom: Colossians 4:6 says "Let your speech always be with grace." If my words are not going to pass the grace test, then I should not speak. Can you comment on the importance of word choice and tone in conversation?

Sara: I think tone is really important; it communicates your unconscious feelings. An aggressive tone may communicate more than the actual words you are speaking. I am probably more sensitive to tone that Tim is, but still I am not always good at having a polite tone.

Tim: Neither one of us tend to vent our feelings. Sara can bottle things up if she is frustrated, and so can I. At times, each of us has harbored frustration against the other, and that can lead to a build-up of negative emotions. Thankfully, we do not have a lot of arguments, but negative emotions can come out in other ways. I may notice Sara is being distant and I may try to pry the issue out of her. She doesn't like it if I do that because she doesn't want to have the conflict. Sometimes Sara is trying to have a serious conversation, but I am being sarcastic or silly which can offend her. These are some of the struggles we have in conversation. It would be good to have a regular check-in with each other to see how we are doing. Are we connecting? How am I doing as a husband?

Tom: Being an educator, what impact do you see good marriages, struggling marriages, separation, and divorce have on students?

Tim: This became very clear to me when I was principal at Portland Christian. The seventh and eighth grade combined class consisted of only twelve kids. There were significant discipline issues to the point we had to dismiss some of the kids. Six of the twelve kids came from two-parent, loving households, who were regular church attenders. Basically those kids were respectful, polite, compliant, had concern for their grades, and faithful in their homework. The other six kids were from broken families. They did not care about their grades or homework; they had inappropriate relationships with peers, and they had anger issues. Our policy was that when kids were failing classes we would contact the parents. And in a lot of those situations the contact information revealed mom and dad lived in separate homes. There are exceptions to this, but generally speaking, and I think statistics will bear out that when kids come from homes where the parents are together and love each other, those kids do better socially, emotionally, and educationally.

Tom: Is the role of television and social media beneficial, harmful, neutral, or non-applicable in marriage and family?

Sara: Detrimental. One can come home in the evening and connect with the television and not connect with one's family. We don't really struggle with this issue. I have never been a big television watcher.

Tim: One of the biggest recommendations I would have for newlyweds is do not have a television in your house and do not introduce your kids to television. That way, it will not become that easy default entertainment source for them. They will develop interest in other things. Television is easy and requires nothing of the viewer.

Sara: Television is artificial living. If we could do it over again, I would never let video games in the house. Video games are pointless; one of the biggest wastes of time. They are a complete lack of productivity of any kind. So I agree with Tim that it would be good for newlyweds to not own a television. When I was a young parent, I went a long time without having a television. And I wish we had never introduced our kids to television. Joanna and Chip Gaines star in their own home improvement television series, "Fixer Upper." They are a sweet, Christian couple with four children (and Joanna is pregnant with their fifth). When they were in premarital counseling, the counselor told them one of the best things they could do would be to not own a television. For all the years of their marriage, they have not had a television in their home. Ironically, they are television celebrities. Part of the reason for their success is because they have had such productive lives through their church and work. How much more productive everyone could be if they did not have a television in the house.

Tim: Often a kid is in his room, isolated, playing video games, which can cause the kid to be antisocial as well as unproductive. From a parenting perspective, when a kid has such sensory stimulating experiences repeatedly, it makes a book or a teacher's lecture seem comparatively very boring. Too much media stimulation contributes to shorter attention spans. There are societal pressures on kids to have smart phones, but I think parents would be wise to resist this pressure as long as possible.

Tom: Instead of focusing on a spouse's imperfections, it is important to see one's spouse in a higher way. For this is how God sees us—in a higher way, as the righteousness of God in Christ. If your spouse has areas of imperfection, how do you deal with that?

Sara: You should try to remember that your spouse is an individual who will not think like you on every matter. Each spouse has different callings, gifts, skills, and interests. To put your own unreasonably high expectations on your spouse, especially if he or she does not know what your expectations are, that becomes a set-up for conflict.

Tim: There are certain extreme cases of this, such as if the husband, due to laziness, fails to get a job; or if either spouse neglects the children; or if a spouse does not fulfill his or her God-given responsibilities; or if a spouse is involved in something immoral or illegal, then the concern is certainly justified and a confrontation of that sin would need to occur. The confrontation should include "I love you and I am willing to help you through this, but I cannot allow you to continue in this destructive behavior." But many times conflict can come when the perceived shortcoming is relatively minor, but the spouse is not willing to overlook it and makes too much of it. For example, the dishes were not put away or the house was not cleaned when the spouse came home from work. In such cases, grace should be extended. One reason expectations are not met is because, as Sara said, one person does not communicate the expectations, or does not ask for help, or assumes the other person should intuitively know to do something. One might get the attitude, "I should not have to ask you for help. You saw me doing this; it would have been nice if you would have helped." So it can become unfair if one is not willing to communicate one's desire.

Tom: One should not try to micromanage one's spouse, and one should not try to be the Holy Spirit to one's spouse. As Sara said, spouses need to respect each other as separate, unique individuals. But bigger issues that negatively impinge upon the whole family unit—those need to be addressed.

Tom: Do you have any advice concerning how newlyweds should resolve marital conflict? And speak of the importance of forgiveness.

Tim: There is never a good reason to win an argument for winning an argument's sake. If there is conflict, I want to try to fix it and apologize as soon as I can so that the conflict does not linger. If that means I have to yield my point and if I have to lose the argument, I am willing to do that. I should say, "I am sorry, and I don't want us to have this conflict." I should have a submissive attitude in that way, as long as this is not one of those egregious problems we discussed earlier. By doing this, we can eliminate the vast majority of marital conflict. Recognizing if there is distance or coldness in my spouse, and then humbling myself and immediately trying to seek resolution and apologizing, that is the key. For the most part, Sara and I have been able to avoid significant strife.

Sara: One reason we do not have much strife is because both of us are willing to apologize, willing to come to the other one and say, "This doesn't feel good; I don't like having unresolved issues between us." And it takes both the husband and the wife to have this attitude of quickly apologizing and seeking reconciliation. And it must be genuine. Tim and I do not have confrontational personalities and we are both people-pleasing, and these qualities help us in this area.

Tim: Scripture says, "Do not let the sun go down on your anger," which affirms that we need to reconcile as quickly as possible. The longer one goes without reconciling, the more one magnifies the problem in one's mind, and allows bitterness to creep in. I don't see how married couples go three or four days without talking to one another. If a spouse maintains the attitude "I am going to win this argument," that person is going to lose in the long run.

The Rev. John Hallock Interview

In 2017, I interviewed a friend of mine, Rev. John Hallock of Kentucky, age forty-one, who is an ordained Lutheran minister, and has been married for almost eighteen years to Carrie. They have four children whom they homeschool.

Tom: What are some of the benefits you enjoy most about marriage?

John: For those not called to celibacy, marriage benefits the whole person: spirit, soul, and body. Also, marriage prevents loneliness. The married person has a partner with whom to share goals and purpose.

Tom: What are some of the challenges of marriage?

John: Obviously, you are marrying someone with a background different than yours, who has different ideas, and you are coming together to be one. Conflicts and disagreements are inevitable. God calls the married person to place his spouse above himself, to serve his spouse, and to lay down his life for the benefit of his spouse. That is not easy. God uses marriage as a means of sanctification—to conform each of us into the image of Christ, and the sanctification process includes times of testing and trial. If a man enters marriage thinking, "This is about me, and my wife is supposed to bring me happiness," then when his wife does not please him or feed into his self-centeredness, he gets highly upset. When this happens repeatedly, he wants a divorce. Instead, in times of trial the husband should realize, "I am to lay down my life for my wife." Its like what President Kennedy said at his inauguration, "Ask not what your country can do for you, but what you can do for your country." It is not what my spouse can do for me, but what I can do for my spouse. Any good marriage is going to encourage growth in Christ and growth in the relationship.

Marriage is a picture of Christ and the church. So as a husband, I must remember I have a higher calling—to lay down my life, to be crucified, to die to my flesh and my selfish desires for the sake of esteeming my wife higher than myself. I am to be my wife's protector and supporter. This does not mean that she does not bring anything to the equation. Paul is clear that marriage is a partnership. My wife is to be my helpmeet; she is to respect, encourage, and support me also.

Tom: What if your spouse does not live up to your expectations?

John: No mortal human is going to live up to one's expectations, whether that person is a pastor, leader, or spouse. When a man goes into marriage thinking his spouse is going to meet his expectations, he has already set both her and himself up for failure. A quality to embrace is humility, which is contemplating one's own sinfulness in light of God's holiness. When I do that, then I am saying, "Who am I to hold expectations over the head of anyone?" On the other hand, you cannot ignore sin or lukewarmness in your spouse, but you must confront it in love.

There is only One who is perfect and who can meet the longing of all our hearts—Jesus Christ. If I transfer my focus from Christ to my spouse—trying to find ultimate satisfaction and fulfillment in a mere mortal human, then I will be disappointed. So I must go into marriage realizing my wife is not going to meet my expectations. I am marrying an imperfect human who is being transformed into the image of Christ, but who is not Christ. We are all a work in progress. My wife is prone to fail my expectations, and I am prone to fail hers. The only expectations we should have are grace and forgiveness—the same expectations we want for ourselves. My wife does not meet every expectation of me, and I certainly do not meet every expectation of Jesus Christ. I fail every day. The good news is that Christ has done for us what we could not do for ourselves, so that through our faith in Christ, we are forgiven. So we must be merciful and humble toward one another.

Tom: Is spending quality time important to you and your wife?

John: Yes. Every couple is different, and every person is wired different. Every couple has to find what works for them. My wife became pregnant about one month into our marriage; therefore our entire marriage has revolved around our kids. We have never had date nights as other couples do. Our quality time has usually included the kids. But now that our older kids are high school age, my wife and I take lots of walks together.

Tom: What does your wife like?

John: Acts of service, such as when I mow the grass, wash the car, clean, etc. Then she will be all over me. Financial security is also important to her.

Tom: What do you like?

John: I like having a wife that stays at home, homeschools our kids, and takes care of the home front, the practical things. Both parents working can contribute to the high divorce rate. It is important for me to come home and know my wife has a meal cooked, and that she is a role model for my kids. We get along very well. She can rearrange the house, and that doesn't bother me. I am laid back when I am home. She is hand's on, so it works.

Tom: Do you have advice about resolving marital conflict?

John: Die. Jesus said, "Deny yourself, take up your cross, and follow Me." I have counseled many couples about their marital struggles, and I find that many are unwilling to humble themselves and die to selfish desires and the need to be right. God's intent for marriage is to have peace and joy. Someone who is unwilling to die daily, to decrease himself that Jesus may increase, is someone who will not know peace.

The Ron and Linda Adkins Interview

In 2017, I interviewed two Christian friends of mine, Ron and Linda Adkins of Frankfort, Kentucky, who have been married for fifty-two years. Ron's trade has been building houses (in 2017, he built a beautiful addition to my house), and Linda worked many years in a law office.

Tom: What are some of the benefits you enjoy most about marriage?

Linda: I enjoy the fact that my husband has been so sweet, affectionate, and good to me. Knowing that my best friend is my husband is very important to me.

Tom: Do you have advice about how to resolve marital conflict?

Linda: Keep the communication lines open. Stand by each other when times get hard. Go through problems together and be supportive of your spouse no matter what the situation might be. In the end, you grow through those problems.

Tom: Is spending quality time with your spouse important to you? What are some activities you enjoy doing together?

Ron: Sometimes we are busy, but it is important to wind down and do something together. We try to refresh the feelings we had when we were first married. We are still sweethearts.

Linda: We still hold hands, which is special.

Ron: The activity we have enjoyed the most is fulfilling our call to the music ministry. (Ron and Linda have led singing in churches, with Ron playing the keyboard. They have been doing this together since they were teenagers, before they were married.) That has been something we have done together that has kept us excited. Some things we do not have in common: Linda likes the mall and I like hunting. But the one thing we do have in common is our love for music and for the church.

Linda: Our traveling and singing have bound us together.

Tom: Do you have any advice about the role of television in marriage?

Ron: I don't think television adds anything to a marriage. Television can get in the way if you spend too much time watching it.

Linda: We have two TVs in two different rooms, so he can watch what he wants and I can watch what I want. Some shows we watch together.

Tom: Do you have any advice for newlyweds?

Ron: Christ should be central to the marriage. Newlyweds should start the marriage right and join a good church.

Linda: Newlyweds need to keep the romance and affection going, such as holding hands, cuddling, and being sweet to one another.

Ron: I remember the way it was when we were dating, and I have tried to mimic that through the years. There is no reason why the initial romance cannot continue. I don't think I have ever taken Linda for granted.

The Rev. Manuel Cordero Interview

In 2017, I interviewed a friend of mine, "Manny" Cordero, who serves as the Senior Director of Chaplaincy Ministries for the Assemblies of God. He is also a retired federal prison chaplain. Manny has been married to Christine Joy for forty years, and they have two children and six grandchildren.

Tom: What are some of the benefits you enjoy most about marriage?

Manny: Having companionship and a loving relationship. Having a partner who will pray with me. A helpmeet who will walk with me and help me.

Tom: Is spending quality time important to you and your wife?

Manny: Yes. In counseling married couples, I have seen how many of them have grown apart from each other. Christine and I combat this in our marriage by taking trips together; we go on vacation. We also enjoy going out to dinner, just the two of us. My daughter and her kids live with us, so at a restaurant Christine and I can concentrate on just the two of us. We need time to replenish, to reconnect. And doing so doesn't take that long. Some couples do not make time for each other. As a result, their marriages and their ministries suffer.

Tom: Do you have advice about resolving marital conflict?

Manny: It's a matter of communication. Sometimes we need to take a breather, because the communication resulting from conflict needs to become devoid of emotions. If I speak with an angry tone, no progress will be made. Each spouse needs to try to see the other person's side of the argument, and have compromise.

Tom: Do you have advice about maintaining boundaries with the opposite sex?

Manny: Familiarity with a person of the opposite sex does breed the prospect of temptation. I will not travel with a female staff member by myself in a car. I will have a third person present, so as to avoid even the appearance of impropriety.

Tom: Colossians 4:6 says "Let your speech always be with grace." If my words are not going to be gracious, I probably should not speak. Also, hasty words can bring immediate strife.

Manny: You are absolutely right. You can spark an argument just by the way you have spoken. It is a difficult thing, and I still struggle with my tone even after forty years of marriage. Sarcastic words or a sharp tongue can set the spouse off. Words have tremendous power and can create conflict. On the other hand, words have tremendous power to solve conflict and to soothe. Loving, beautiful words can change the tone of a conversation. Tone, body language, and posture are all aspects of communication, and one needs to guard one's tongue so as not to offend. James tells us to tame our tongue, and that would include our tone and posture.

Tom: Instead of focusing on my spouse's imperfections, it is important that I see my spouse in a higher way.

Manny: I agree. If you value your spouse, you will see her in a higher way and treat her that way. Instead of looking for negative things and putting her down, you can look for the best in her. It really bothers me if I am with another couple, and one spouse demeans the other. There is an African story of a wealthy man who went to get a wife. All the women wanted him because of his wealth. Even though many of the women in his village were beautiful, he was not interested in any of them. But he fell in love with a woman who was not the most attractive physically and she did not come from a prominent family. He asked the town's people what was the most anyone had ever paid for a dowry for a wife. They pointed out a very talented and beautiful wife and said her husband gave such and such amount for her—a very high dowry. So the wealthy man gave a dowry double in value for the woman he loved. He demonstrated to his wife that she was by far the most valuable woman to him. We see from this story that, in addition to saying "I love you," demonstrating love and speaking words of affirmation will cause the wife to have self-confidence, and she will blossom. My wife used to feel she was not pretty. But I affirmed her beauty so much that she now believes she is beautiful to me.

In marriage it is imperative that we forgive. A small disagreement can grow into something much worse if we do not forgive. Ironically, we tend to inflict the most hurt on the one we love the most. Hopefully our offenses are not intentional, but without apologies and forgiveness, the hurt from the offenses may fester. If forgiveness is not extended, then one spouse may go to work the next day and not be able to concentrate. Seeking forgiveness and giving forgiveness are tremendously important.

My wife is a gift from God. If I do not treasure her, then I am disrespecting God and what He has given me. Any deep relationship such as marriage takes time and work. Marriage is a struggle because we all have edges that need to be smoothed. Other friendships can be superficial compared to the marriage relationship. Marriage is the most beautiful relationship, but it takes work.

I am glad you are writing this book, Tom, because I am concerned about pastoral marriages. I lead marriage seminars in Cuba and Africa, because I have seen many of those couples in the ministry not do well in taking care of their marriages. My doctoral degree is in marriage and family therapy. Part of my degree project was to lead a marriage retreat which I tailored specifically for pastors. We must see marriage and family as our first ministry. The ministry of the church or chaplaincy is secondary. We need to get our priorities straight.

Chapter 6

An Exposition of Ephesians 5:22-33

Wives, submit to your own husbands, as to the Lord. (23) For the husband is head of the wife, as also Christ is head of the church; and He is the Savior of the body. (24) Therefore, just as the church is subject to Christ, so let the wives be to their own husbands in everything. (25) Husbands, love your wives, just as Christ also loved the church and gave Himself for her, (26) that He might sanctify and cleanse her with the washing of water by the word, (27) that He might present her to Himself a glorious church, not having spot or wrinkle or any such thing, but that she should be holy and without blemish. (28) So husbands ought to love their own wives as their own bodies; he who loves his wife loves himself. (29) For no one ever hated his own flesh, but nourishes and cherishes it, just as the Lord does the church. (30) For we are members of His body, of His flesh and of His bones. (31) "For this reason a man shall leave his father and mother and be joined to his wife, and the two shall become one flesh." (32) This is a great mystery, but I speak concerning Christ and the church. (33) Nevertheless let each one of you in particular so love his own wife as himself, and let the wife see that she respects her husband.

Ephesians 5:22-33 is probably the most in-depth passage in the New Testament on the husband-wife relationship and deserves exceptional attention. (First Corinthians 7 also deals with marriage, but much of its focus is on singles and whether or not they should marry. It is discussed in Chapter 14.) In Ephesians 5:22-33, some form of the word "love" appears six times—five times in reference to husbands toward their wives and one time in reference to Christ toward the church. Note that no command is given in this passage for wives to love their husbands. Titus 2:5 does say for wives "to love their husbands, to love their children...." But in this central text on marriage, when it comes to love, the overwhelming emphasis is on the husband to love his wife. Why do you think this is?   The husband is the one whom God ordained to be the head of the house, and thus the one most responsible to lead the home by godly example. Verse 25 says, "Husbands, love your wives, just as Christ also loved the church and gave Himself for her." Love is exemplified from the top down: Christ, the Head of the body, loves the body. Likewise, the husband, the head of the home, is to love his wife. Also, Christ loved the church before the church loved Christ (Rom. 5:8); likewise, the husband is to lead in love and persevere in love toward his wife even if his wife does not respond with love as quickly or as fully as he would like.

The husband is to love his wife to the degree that Christ loved the church. Christ demonstrated His love for the church in the ultimate way—Christ laid down His life for the church. In John 15:13, Jesus said, "Greater love has no one than this, than to lay down one's life for his friends." So one's laying down his or her life for the benefit of another is the greatest love that can possibly be shown. Jesus calls all of us who would be saved from our sins to love Him in this way—by laying down our lives for Him. We see this, for instance, in 2 Corinthians 5:14b-15: "if One died for all, then all died; and He died for all, that those who live should live no longer for themselves, but for Him who died for them and rose again." Again, in Matthew 10:39b, Jesus said, "he who loses his life for My sake will find it." We must love Jesus more than we love ourselves and we must put obedience to His holy Word above yielding to our fleshly desires and human wisdom. And we love Him because He first loved us. In marriage (which is a picture of the relationship between Christ and the church, verse 32), the husband should demonstrate love to the fullest degree by laying down his life, including his daily selfish agenda, for the benefit of his wife and for the glory of God. And the wife is called by God to love her husband in the same self-sacrificing way. Acting selfishly is contrary to walking in love. Dying to self for the benefit of the other is necessary for love. First Corinthians 16:14 says, "Let all that you do be done in love." Therefore, one must always resist temptations to live selfishly. In what area of your marriage could you improve in laying down your life for the benefit of your spouse?

Before Christ paid the ultimate price, death, for the benefit of the church, Christ daily was a servant to the church. Again, being a servant also requires death to self in terms of death to your personal agenda when that agenda differs from God's agenda for you. Jesus said, "The Son of Man did not come to be served, but *to serve*, and *to give* His life as a ransom for many" (Mt. 20:28). Jesus daily gave of Himself and served others, such as when He washed the feet of the disciples or when He forsook a meal or forsook His rest in order to spontaneously minister to others in need. Likewise, a loving spouse will display regular acts of service and generosity toward his or her spouse. Love is much more than having positive feelings toward your spouse; love includes maintaining a heart of generosity and service. If you will generously and consistently serve and give to your spouse, the feelings of love you want to have for your spouse will likely develop in you. Also, you will increase the likelihood that your spouse will respond to you in kind.

Submission of the Wife

In Ephesians 5:22–33, as there is an emphasis on husbands to love their wives (mentioning this five times), there is also an emphasis on wives to submit to their husbands. (It is hypocritical for a husband to be unwilling to walk in love toward his wife, yet expect that his wife submit to him. And certainly the husband should not oppress or abuse his wife in any away, thinking he has the right to do so because of biblical submission.) Verse 22 says, "Wives, submit to your own husbands, as to the Lord." Verse 23 says, "the husband is the head of the wife...." Verse 24 says, "let wives be (subject) to their own husbands in everything." Verse 33 says, "let the wife see that she respects her husband." In summary, the wife is to submit to, be subject to, and respect her husband who is her head. Webster's defines "submit" as "to give over or yield to the power and authority of another...to defer to another's judgment, opinion, decision, etc."[28] As Colossians 3:23 says, "And whatever you do, do it heartily, as to the Lord and not to men," the wife is to submit to, be subject to, and respect her husband from her heart. If a wife displays a level of submission outwardly toward her husband, but in her heart she is not submissive, but rather resistant, perhaps even resentful, to his leadership, then she is in disobedience to the biblical command to submit to her husband. The Baptist Faith and Message states the role and attitude of the wife concerning submission to the husband with these words: "A wife is to submit herself graciously to the servant leadership of her husband even as the church willingly submits to the headship of Christ."[29] As Ephesians 5:21 says: "submitting to one another in the fear of God," there is a general sense is which all Christians are to submit to one another in terms of putting the other person first as a demonstration of love. Though Christ serves the church, He certainly does not submit to the church in terms of subordinating His authority to the church's authority. And nowhere does the Bible say "Husbands, submit to your wives," yet Scripture repeatedly emphasizes that wives are to submit to their husbands. Let's explore what this means and what it does not mean.

Galatians 3:28 says, "There is neither Jew nor Greek, there is neither slave nor free, there is *neither male nor female*; for you are all one in Christ Jesus." A woman can come just as boldly to the throne of grace in prayer as a man can (Heb. 4:16). A woman can move mountains, heal the sick, and do miracles by faith in Christ just as much as a man (Mk. 11:23, Gal. 3:5). A woman can store up treasure in heaven just a much as a man (Mt. 6:20). So in terms of access to the Father through Jesus Christ, men and women are the same. Also, in terms of value and importance to God, men and women are equal, as they are equally made in the image of God (Gen. 1:26-27). Nevertheless, God has established certain roles that are gender distinct within the functioning of this earthly society— roles that He intends to be fully conformed to by His people despite pressures of political correctness and other secular views.

Generally, the man is to exercise headship, which includes being the spiritual leader—leading his family, the church, and the world in knowing and fulfilling the will of God as revealed by the Bible and

---

[28] *Webster's American Dictionary*, Second College Edition, (Random House, Inc. 2000), 784.

[29] *The Baptist Faith and Message*, 2000.

the Holy Spirit. And as leader, this includes man's being a servant—his willingness to lay down his life for the benefit of his wife, his family, and his neighbor. Matthew 20:26-28 says: "whoever desires to become great among you, let him be your servant. And whoever desires to be first among you, let him be your slave—just as the Son of Man did not come to be served, but to serve, and to give His life a ransom for many."

Let's take a look at other passages where submission of the wife to the husband is emphasized.

1 Corinthians 11:3, 7-9 But I want you to know that the head of every man is Christ, *the head of woman is man*, and the head of Christ is God. (7) For a man...is the image and glory of God; but *woman is the glory of man.* (8) For man is not from woman, but woman from man. (9) Nor was man created for the woman, but *woman for the man.*

We note here that the order of headship from the top down is God, then Christ, then man, then woman. We also note in verse nine that woman was made for man, which lines up with the concept of woman as man's helper in Genesis 2:18—"And the LORD God said, 'It is not good that man should be alone; I will make him a *helper* comparable to him." Therefore, wives are to be the husband's helpers, or assistants, in whatever God has called the man to do. When a wife is not willing to be her husband's helper and submit to her husband, then the husband will likely be held back by her to some degree in fulfilling his God-given calling and mission. By contrast, the virtuous wife—the one who submits to her husband and who fulfills her role according to Proverbs 31:10-31—will allow her husband to "have no lack of gain." Indeed, she will do him "good and not evil all the days of her life" (Pr. 31:11-12).

1 Corinthians 14:34-35 Let your women keep silent in the churches, for they are not permitted to speak; but they are to be *submissive*, as the law also says. (35) And if they want to learn something, let them ask their own husbands at home; for it is shameful for women to speak in church.

Though there are a variety of ways people interpret this passage, it is still to be noted that the woman is to be submissive to the man. Furthermore, as man is the head of the house (1 Tim. 3:4, 5, 12), we see here that man is to be the human leader in the house of God (under Christ of course).

<u>Colossians 3:18-19</u> *Wives, submit to your own husbands*, as is fitting in the Lord. (19) Husbands, love your wives and do not be bitter toward them.

These verses reiterate the roles laid out in the Ephesians 5:22-33 passage, which are for the wife to submit to the husband and the husband to love the wife.

<u>1 Timothy 2:11-15</u> Let a woman learn in silence with all *submission*. (12) And I do not permit a woman to teach or to have authority over a man, but to be in silence. (13) For Adam was formed first, then Eve. (14) And Adam was not deceived, but the woman being deceived, fell into transgression. (15) Nevertheless she will be saved in childbearing if they continue in faith, love, and holiness, with self-control.

It is often said that this passage was intended only for a particular point in time—the time it was written—and it should be viewed is irrelevant today. However, verses 13-14 negate that argument by going all the way back to the first couple, Adam and Eve, as the reason for the command for women to submit to men and not to teach or have authority over men. This passage also emphasizes that a primary role for the woman is child-bearing—nurturing and preparing the next generation. Such a role is vitally important, one to be taken seriously and with gratitude toward God.

<u>1 Timothy 3:1-13</u> This is a faithful saying: If a man desires the position of a bishop, he desires a good work. (2) A bishop then must be blameless, the husband of one wife, temperate, sober-minded, of good behavior, hospitable, able to teach; (3) not given to wine, not violent, not greedy for money, but gentle, not quarrelsome, not covetous; (4) one who rules his own house well, having his children in submission with all reverence (5) (for if a man does not know how to rule his own house, how will he take care of the church of God?); (6) not a novice, lest being puffed up with pride he fall into the same condemnation as the devil. (7) Moreover he must have a good testimony among those who are outside, lest he fall into reproach and the snare of the devil. (8) Likewise deacons must be reverent, not double-tongued, not given to much wine, not greedy for money, (9) holding the mystery of the faith with a pure conscience. (10) But let these also first be tested; then let them serve as deacons, being found blameless. (11) Likewise, their wives must be reverent, not slanderers, temperate, faithful in all things. (12) Let deacons be the husbands of one wife, ruling their children and their own houses well. (13) For those who have served well as deacons obtain for themselves a good standing and great boldness in the faith which is in Christ Jesus.

This passage clearly teaches that bishops and deacons are to be men. Furthermore, requirements for both positions include ruling one's house well. Webster's defines "rule" as "to exercise dominating power, authority, or influence over; govern…to exercise authority, dominion, or sovereignty."[30] If men do not rule their own houses well, then they are not fit to take care of God's house. It is also noteworthy for bishops to be "gentle, not quarrelsome," which is congruent with husbands loving their wives.

<u>Titus 2:3-5</u> the older women…(4) admonish the *young women* to love their husbands, to love their children, (5) to be discreet, chaste, homemakers, good, *obedient to their own husbands*, that the word of God may not be blasphemed.

Again we see the submission theme of wives to men again, this time with the use of the word "obedient." Teaching young wives to love and obey their husbands is necessary because loving and obeying one's husband is not the direction toward which women naturally gravitate in this secular society.

James Grant says discreet means "refraining from doing certain things that one's flesh would like to do; the ability to say 'no' to certain temptations."[31] Chaste in this passage refers to remaining sexually pure within marriage.

<u>1 Peter 3:1, 5-7</u> Wives, likewise, be *submissive* to your own husbands…(5)…in former times, the holy women who trusted in God also adorned themselves, being *submissive* to their own husbands, (6) as Sarah *obeyed* Abraham, calling him lord, whose daughters you are if you do good and are not afraid with any terror. (7) Husbands, likewise, dwell with them with understanding, giving honor to the wife, as to the weaker vessel, and as being heirs together of the grace of life, that your prayers may not be hindered.

Wives are to submit to their husbands as well as follow the example of Old Testament holy women, including Sarah, who obeyed her husband and called him "lord." As in many of these passages, an exhortation also goes to the husband. He is to maintain a heart of understanding as he dwells with his wife whom he is to honor. Webster's says the

---

[30] *Webster's American Dictionary*, Second College Edition, 688.

[31] James Grant, in conversation with me.

word "understanding" means in part: "cooperation...empathy."[32] The husband is to empathize with his wife, remembering that, as "the weaker vessel," she may not be quite as strong or as disciplined in some areas as he is. Webster's defines "honor" as "to hold in high respect... to show courteous regard for."[33] The husband is to honor his wife, meaning he must greatly respect her and be courteous towards her. If husbands and wives do not obey the exhortations of the Word of God, then such disobedience will result in their prayers being hindered (verse 7; Ps. 66:18). If a wife does not submit to her husband whom she can see, then she also does not submit to God whom she cannot see. If a husband does not love his wife whom he can see, then he does not love God whom he cannot see. Again, the husband-wife relationship is a type of the Christ-church relationship. Husbands, write down some ways in which you could improve in demonstrating honor and courtesy toward your wife. Husbands, also write down some ways in which you could improve in being the godly leader within your home. Wives, write down some ways you could improve in the area of submitting to your husband.

What If My Wife Does Not Submit?

After I know that my wife has been exposed to and understands the Biblical passages that detail her responsibilities as a wife and mother, I am not responsible for my wife's willingness to submit to me or respect me. She will have to give an account to God for her responsibilities and behavior as a wife and mother, as I also will have to give an account to God for my responsibilities and behavior as a husband and father. God wills for me to love, honor, be gracious to and patient with my wife no matter what she says or does. Colossians 3:19 says: "Husbands, love your wives and do not be bitter toward them." It is never appropriate for me to cease loving my wife or allow bitterness towards her to come into my heart. First Peter 3:7 says: "Husbands, likewise, dwell with them (your wives) with understanding, giving honor to the wife as to the weaker vessel...." It is never appropriate for me to cease honoring or having an understanding attitude toward my wife. If my wife does not submit to me or respect me, my response should be to love her, be

---

[32] *Webster's American Dictionary*, Second College Edition, 857.
[33] Ibid., 388.

patient with her, and not pressure her into doing what I want. Let me reiterate: if my wife disrespects me, I am to respond by loving her. I should pray to the Lord to do a work in her to become more like Christ, as I also should pray to the Lord to do a work in me to become more like Christ. I must allow the Holy Spirit to do the work in my spouse that only the Holy Spirit can do. For me to try to usurp the Holy Spirit's role in this matter would be sin. Philippians 2:13 says: "For it is God (not the spouse) who works in you both to will and to do for His good pleasure." So pray, don't pressure. Love, don't lash out. Be patient, not pushy. Be humble, not haughty. I am not to judge my wife. Again, I am to pray for her, be patient with her, overlook any shortcomings she may have (realizing I also have shortcomings), and continuously love her as Christ loved the church.

Respect

Ephesians 5:33 says, "Nevertheless let each one of you in particular so love his own wife as himself, and let the wife see that she *respects* her husband." As this passage points out the special call for the husband to love his wife, it also points out that the wife is uniquely obligated to respect her husband. Webster's defines "respect" as "to hold in esteem or honor; admiration."[34] A wife who respects her husband should not belittle her husband, nor should she despise the leadership he shows on behalf of the household. Even if his family background includes men being more passive and not being strong leaders, she still should respect even his small efforts and the small beginnings he makes in leading his family. And this respect she demonstrates should not be in pretense, but it should emanate from a heart of respect for him. She should encourage her husband all along the way, and this will likely help him grow in his role as the family leader. Wife, how could you improve in showing respect to your husband?

Love Your Wife As Your Own Body

Verses 28-29 say, "So husbands ought to love their own wives as their own bodies; he who loves his wife loves himself. For no one ever hated his own flesh, but nourishes and cherishes it, just as the Lord

---

[34] *Webster's American Dictionary*, Second College Edition, 388.

does the church." Because your physical body is part of who you are (1 Thessalonians 5:26 says one is comprised of spirit, soul, and body. Also, body and self are linked in verse 28), then there is a certain love and care you should have for your body, which is the temple of God. Second Corinthians 3:17 says, "If anyone defiles the temple of God, God will destroy him. For the temple of God is holy, which temple you are." You should take care of your physical body through proper nutrition, regular exercise, and rest. Also, you care for your spouse when you care for your body for a number of reasons: you can increase your longevity on this earth, you can feel better and thus be more pleasant to be around, and you can be more physically attractive for your spouse. Verses 28-29 indicate that not only should a husband care for his body in order to love his wife, but he should love his wife *as* his own body. As the husband nourishes and cherishes his own body, he should nourish and cherish his wife. Therefore, I recommend that he not spend more time in the gym working out than he spends in quality time with his wife. As the husband nourishes his body, he should also nourish his wife by feeding her love, spiritual edification, emotional bonding, financial provision, and support around the house. A husband can cherish his wife by holding her in high esteem and treating her as valuable and precious. Husbands, what specific actions could you take to better nourish and cherish your wife?

Jesus Christ as the Bridegroom

Larry Blackford (a good friend of mine with whom I have done weekly prison ministry) has been married to Nancy for twenty-six years. Larry and Nancy included in their wedding invitations, "Today, I marry my best friend." Larry says, "This still holds true. She is my lover and my best friend." Larry appreciates how Nancy gives him the freedom to spend a lot of his time doing ministry. (Larry ministers in a variety of venues—prison, jail, churches, and schools.) Larry says, "Nancy is very supportive in my ministry. If I feel that God is leading me to do something, I have her support to do it without question." Nancy reveals the key to their marital success with these words: "We love the Lord." Larry says, "Our marriage is a good love story that always points to the greatest love story ever told—that God sent His Son Jesus Christ to be our loving Bridegroom."

In Ephesians 5:22-33, another marriage spoken of in addition to the marriage of husband and wife is the marriage of Christ to the church. The purpose of human marriage and the roles within marriage can be better understood as we remember that human marriage is a type, or picture, of the ultimate and eternal marriage, that of Christ to the church. Therefore, human marriage should not be seen as an end in itself. Human marriage, as everything else in life, is to be viewed as a means to an end—to glorify God in all that one does! That is a major purpose of marriage—to glorify God. Husband and wife, do you glorify God in the ways you relate to each other day by day? There are several references to the theme of Christ as Bridegroom and the church as His bride in the Bible, such as Revelation 19:7—"Let us be glad and rejoice and give Him glory, for the marriage of the Lamb has come, and His wife has made herself ready." In Matthew 25:1-13, the parable of the ten virgins, verses.6-7 say, "And at midnight a cry was heard: 'Behold, the bridegroom is coming; go out to meet him!' Then all those virgins arose and trimmed their lamps." (We also see this theme in Hosea and Song of Solomon.) So we who are Christians, whether male or female, are the bride of Christ. (So I, Tom, am a bride as well as a husband!) We see in this Ephesians 5 passage that Christ as the head of the church is the One who served and loved the church in the ultimate way—He died on the cross for the benefit of the church, His bride. Part of this benefit was for the sanctification and cleansing of the church, which is the process of departing from all evil and becoming more like Christ.

Once my mother-in-law washed a pair of my jeans. But she did not check the pockets before she put them in the wash, and I had a New Testament Bible in one of the pockets. The wash obliterated the pages of the Bible, and when the jeans came out of the wash, letters and words could be seen covering every inch of my jeans. As my jeans had been washed in the Word of God, so the church also needs to be cleansed "with the washing of water by the word" (Eph. 5:26). This is the means of sanctification and preparation of the bride for her wedding day—exposure to the Holy Scripture, upon which all believers should meditate throughout the day and night (Ps. 1:2; Ps. 119:97). Christ, the Bridegroom, is returning for a church, His bride, which is "glorious… not having spot or wrinkle or any such thing, but that she should be holy and without blemish" (Eph. 5:27). We as Christians and as married couples are called to holiness. Holiness means to be set apart from that which is evil. We must purge evil from our individual lives and from our homes. Without holiness, "no one will see God" (Heb. 12:14)! Let's now focus more intensely on the importance of the Word of God in a marriage.

The Concept of *Shema* within Marriage

Its one thing to know God's standard when it comes to love, holiness, honor, respect, etc.; it's another thing to live up to that standard. How can I possibly love my wife to the degree that the Bible commands? I will now share a key concept which I have gleaned from two passages of Scripture, so I urge you to now open your Bible to Ephesians and read 5:22 through 6:9 and also to Colossians and read 3:18 through 4:1. Each of these two passages deals with particular roles within the family as well as within the bondservant–master relationship (commonplace in biblical times). Also, each of these two passages lists the relationship roles in the exact same order which are as follows: wives, husbands, children, fathers, bondservants, and masters. (When the Bible repeats something, it is typically for emphasis.) Furthermore, preceding both of these passages are two verses with similar wording—Ephesians 5:19 and Colossians 3:16. Ephesians 5:19 says, "*speaking to one another in psalms and hymns and spiritual songs, singing and making melody in your heart to the Lord….*" Colossians 3:16 says, "*teaching and admonishing one another in psalms and hymns and spiritual songs, singing with grace in your hearts to the Lord.*" I believe these similarly worded verses give emphasis and clear instruction as to how people, especially within the important relationships listed just below them, are to communicate with each other as well as jointly glorify God in word and song. *They are to speak the Word of God to each other as well as sing songs together that are based on the Word of God.* In other words, Scripture is to be the basis for conversation and interaction within these vital relationships. Also, with much of the focus on singing, and singing being linked with the Word of God, a significant amount of time that the husband and wife spend together should be used for praise and worship. After all, Jesus said, "For where two or three are gathered together in My name, I am there in the midst of them" (Mt. 18:20). Jesus also said, "if two of you agree on earth concerning anything that they ask, it will be done for them by My Father in heaven" (Mt. 18:19). So the husband and wife (and we might include the children as well, which could be represented by "or three" in Matthew 18:20) should cultivate a powerful family prayer life as well as a routine of genuine family worship. Deuteronomy 32:30 talks about one person putting a thousand, but two putting ten thousand to flight. So there can be real spiritual synergy when the husband and wife come together to share the Word of God in conversation, song, and prayer. Kim and I call our times of speaking and singing the Word of God to each other, and /or with our kids, "Shema Time." This is based on Deuteronomy 6:4-9, the passage from which Jesus quoted when He declared the two greatest commandments of the entire Bible, Matthew 22:36-40. (Take a moment and read these passages.) "Shema" is the Hebrew word for "hear," which is the first word of Deuteronomy 6:4. The Deuteronomy and Matthew passages declare that you are to love God with all of your being and you are to love your neighbor (including your spouse) as yourself. It also tells you *how* to cultivate and demonstrate love toward God and each other—you are to hide the holy Word of God in your hearts and speak the Word of God to each other throughout the day. After all, God said in Deuteronomy 32:47 that the Word of God "is your life." So speaking the Word of God to one another promotes the life and love that you so desperately need, especially in marriage. There really is no substitute.

I cannot attribute any success in my marriage to the natural abilities (e.g. personalities) that Kim or I possess. Any success we have experienced is due to the practice of Kim and me abiding in the Word of God, speaking the Word of God to each other, making decisions based on the Word of God, taming our tongues, and being mindful to treat each other according to the Word of God. (I certainly do not mean to insinuate that Kim and I have mastered being a Shema couple, but we are working on it.) Sometimes Kim and I use the hymnal and sing hymns together in a variety of situations, such as while cooking dinner or riding in the car. Our daughters have enjoyed the unified family celebration and they have often initiated our family hymn-singing themselves. Also, I sometimes read or recite a verse pertaining to love to Kim and then I reword the verse into a declaration I make to Kim about my love for her. For instance, I will read to Kim Philippians 2:4b—"let each esteem others better than himself." Then I will say, "Kim, I esteem you better than me," or "Kim, you are more important than me." I will recite to Kim 1 Corinthians 10:24—"Let no one seek his own, but each one the other's well-being." Then I will declare, "Kim, I seek your well-being over my own." I will read Romans 12:10b—"in honor giving preference to one another...." Then I will say, "Kim, I honor you and I prefer you above me." I will read Romans 13:10a—"Love does no harm to a neighbor...." Then, I will say something like, "Kim I determine to never harm you, Emma, or Anna with my words, thoughts, or deeds, because you are precious to me." Often, I will give Kim a back rub (Kim loves backrubs and I can practice being a servant) while I read the verses to her and follow each verse with a declaration of love and commitment to her. Such practices make Kim feel loved and respected by me, and it draws us closer together. Furthermore, our minds become renewed with the Scriptural standards by which God commands us to live, and the Word of God inspires and empowers us to deeply love and serve each other. Without such renewing of your mind by the Word of God, your heart naturally gravitates toward selfishness. If this goes unchecked, then you find yourself irritable and easily offended by your spouse. However, speaking the Word of God to each other truly enhances the quality of your marriage as well as inclines your heart toward your loving heavenly Father. You cannot please God, walk with God, nor love God if you do not hide God's Word in your heart (Ps. 119:11). Similarly, you cannot please your spouse, walk in unity with your spouse, nor display agape love toward your spouse without hiding the Word of God (especially Scriptures pertaining to loving and serving your spouse and your fellow man) in your heart. This is the ultimate key to a successful, God-glorifying marriage. The Word of God is the ultimate healer and sealer of relationships; nothing else can compare!

Testifying to the importance of husband and wife receiving love and encouragement through their local church, Reverend Alvin Worthley (retired Director for Chaplaincy, U. S. Assemblies of God) shared with me the following concerning his marriage to Adeline. (They have been married for over fifty years.)

> We were blessed by accepting the responsibility of pastoring a wonderful rural church in Northern Minnesota right after our honeymoon. The love of that congregation pouring into our lives was invaluable. The stability of their lives and the depth of their commitment made pastoring a delight. It turned out to be one of the richest learning experiences for our marriage.

We were the youngest couple in a congregation that taught and nurtured many young people that became pastors, district leaders, missionaries, and active laypersons. Today, we still look back and give thanks for a good foundation. We believe that the time of bonding with the ability to focus on each other that took place in that idyllic setting set the course for a great marriage.

Indeed, a husband and wife can benefit greatly from surrounding themselves with other believers who are spiritually mature and who model continuously upholding the Word of God in faith and practice.

The practices mentioned above are *positive* investments that *build* marital relationships. Another important aspect of marriage is to *avoid* making negative investments through one's thoughts, words and actions that would *tear the relationship down*. Do the positive and avoid the negative. Amos 5:15a says, "Hate evil, love good." I include "thoughts" in how one invests because a negative word or action we might demonstrate likely originated from a negative thought or attitude. First Corinthians 13:5b says, "(love) thinks no evil." Again, Proverbs 12:5a says, "The thoughts of the righteous are right...." Again, Matthew 12:34b says, "For out of the abundance of the heart the mouth speaks." A friend of mine, Kevin Black (who has enjoyed over twenty years of being married to Holly) said of his marriage, "Having Christian values gives us the temperament to not say things in the heat of the moment, or even think things, that would be regrettable." So it is imperative to honor one's spouse even with one's thoughts, desires, and attitudes so as to avoid the hypocrisy that the psalmist describes—"the words of his mouth were smoother than butter, but war is in his heart" (Ps. 55:21).

Remember Your Vows

Clarence and Mayme Vail, from Hugo Minnesota, were married for 83 years and 117 days before Clarence passed away on June 14, 2008 at 101 years old. Mayme explained the reason for their enduring marriage in the following way: "You take your vows, for better or for worse, for richer or for poorer. I guess you just stick to it, come what may." She also said her husband was the strong, silent type and never spoke out of turn.[35]

The following are the vows I wrote and used in my wedding, December 15, 2001. I mistakenly left out "forsaking all others" then, so I have vowed it to Kim since then.

> I, Tom, receive you, Kim, to be my wedded wife. I accept you as a precious gift from God. I love you with a love only Christ Himself could place within my heart. I give myself to you as Christ gave Himself to the church. I wish to have and to hold you from this day forward, for better or for worse, for richer or for poorer, in sickness and in health, to love and to cherish, forsaking all others, as long as we both shall live, according to God's holy ordinance.

Reading over your wedding vows should remind you of the great commitment you made to your spouse. If your vows were similar to mine, then you vowed to love and cherish your spouse, to give yourself to your spouse, to have and to hold your spouse, *even when matters are worse.* And you would keep that commitment for the rest of your natural life. Think about how Jesus, our divine example, was and is committed to the church. When Jesus was carrying His cross toward Golgotha, having already been viciously tortured, He was aware of the great pain and death He was about to endure. But Jesus did not bail out. Jesus did not say, "I have loved and served the church faithfully for thirty-three years, and I have endured long enough. People do not appreciate nor understand My sacrifice. Even My own disciples abandoned Me last night." No, Jesus was committed to obeying His Father and loving His bride until He died! That is the commitment you are to model within your marriage! So be a person of your word. When difficulties arise, do not look for a way out of your marriage, but look to God for a way to navigate through the difficulties. God will provide.

Should One Divorce? Can One Remarry?

Let's consider a scenario: Bill and Jill are married. Jill has an affair. What should Bill do? James Grant says:

---

[35] Mike Celizic. *Couple, married 83 years, share their secret,* www.today.msnbc.com

Bill should seek to stay married. It is difficult to lay down absolute law here. Bill has a right to divorce in the eyes of the church in that the church doesn't have to take disciplinary action. But if Bill divorces, he may have an underlying sinful attitude of resentment and unforgiveness in his heart. In the sum total of Scripture, God does forgive. And it would be good to follow God's example and forgive, thus preserving the marriage after infidelity. If Bill did divorce, could he marry again in the future? Yes. If one is within his or her biblical rights to divorce, then he or she is within his or her rights to remarry. If Bill did everything he could to preserve a marriage, but divorce was inevitable, then Bill could remarry in the future.[36]

Let's consider another scenario: A woman and man divorced by mutual consent. Afterwards, the woman becomes a Christian. Can she ever marry again and it not be considered adultery? James Grant says:

If there's the prospect that the earlier marriage could be reconciled, that would be ideal. But if the man has already remarried or is not willing to reconcile, then 1 Corinthians 7:15 would apply. This verse says, "If the unbeliever departs, let him depart; a brother or a sister is not under bondage in such cases...." I interpret "not under bondage" to mean free to remarry. Again, if there is no prospect of reconciliation, then she could likely remarry. But her heart must be right. She should do more than just a token or surface level attempt at reconciliation (in that first marriage). She should do all in her power to be faithful to that first marriage commitment.[37]

Marriage requires persistence and forgiveness. Never give up. Do not look for an easy way out, but rather for the way through. Rely upon knowledge from the Bible and empowerment by the Holy Spirit; do not primarily rely upon feelings.

In 2004, boys at a certain high school raised money for a secret cause. They used the money to buy over nine hundred roses, one for each of the girls in the school. They also attached to each rose a Bible verse about the love of Jesus. On Valentine's Day, those boys pleasantly

---

[36] James Grant, in conversation with me.
[37] Ibid.

surprised the girls of that school by giving each of them a rose. What a beautiful display of thoughtfulness and what a morale boost to that school those boys must have caused. Likewise, men need to lead their families by initiating love and by setting the example of love. As Christ loved the church before the church loved Christ, and as Christ laid down His life for the church, husbands need to lay down their lives by way of humble service, kindness, honor, and godliness reflected in their thoughts, words, and actions day in and day out for the sake of loving their wives. Likewise, wives need to love, honor, and submit to their husbands just as the church needs to love, honor, and submit to Christ, it's Head. When husbands and wives both embrace the familial roles divinely given them, then the American society will find itself greatly improving, one family at a time.

Chapter 7

Sexual Immorality

"Flee sexual immorality" (1 Cor. 6:18).

A story is told of a preacher who struggled to tell a good joke. So he went to a Joke-impaired Preachers Conference. He wrote down a joke he heard at the conference: "The best years of my life were spent in the arms of another woman, not my wife...my mother." His first Sunday back in the pulpit, for the first time in a long time, he tried to tell a joke—"The best years of my life were spent in the arms of another woman not my wife." Then he paused. He couldn't remember the punch line! Who was the other woman?! So he finally finished the joke by saying—"And I can't remember who the other woman was." That final admission made it even worse! What a pathetic attempt at telling a joke. Hopefully, he had a solid marriage, and his wife did not doubt his fidelity. But sexual infidelity is no joking matter. Neither is fornication, pornography, homosexuality, or any other category of sexual sin.

Many Americans are in bondage to sexual immorality. The National Coalition for the Protection of Children and Families states—"Approximately forty million people in the United States are sexually involved with the Internet. Sex is the number one topic searched on the internet."[38] One statistic said that twelve percent of all total websites are pornographic.[39] Remember the bride's words to the daughters of Jerusalem: "Do not stir up nor awaken love until it pleases" (Song. 2:7). Forty million Americans are inappropriately stirring up sexual passion—a passion they ought to reserve for their spouses. An Associated Press report said, "Twenty-two percent of men and fourteen percent of women admitted to having sexual relations outside their marriage sometime in their past."[40] This statistic is similar to the results of a national study performed by the University of California, San Francisco: "About twenty-four percent of men and fourteen percent of women have had sex outside their marriages."[41] And such sexual promiscuity often finds its beginnings during teen years. The National Campaign to Prevent Teen Pregnancy states, "Nationally, one-quarter of fifteen year old females and less than thirty percent of fifteen year old males have had sex, compared with sixty-six percent of eighteen year old females, and sixty-eight percent of eighteen year old males who have had sexual intercourse."[42] I could go on and on with statistics from various sources, but the point is substantiated that many Americans engage in sexual immorality. In this chapter, we will look at Scriptural passages that warn us of sexual sin—what it is, what consequences come with it, and how the Christian can guard himself or herself from falling into sexual sin.

The Immoral Woman of Proverbs

The immoral woman of Proverbs obviously stands in sharp contrast to the virtuous wife of Proverbs 31. Proverbs gives us at least four passages focusing on the immoral woman.

---

[38] www.nationalcoalition.org

[39] Womansavers.com (Research & Rate B4U Date!), citing the Associated Press.

[40] Womansavers.com (Research & Rate B4U Date!), citing the Associated Press.

[41] According to a Dec. 21, 1998 report written by Karen Peterson, *USA Today*, where she cited a national study of 5,000 men and women who have been married (by the Center for AIDS Prevention at the University of California, San Francisco).

[42] *A Statistical Portrait of Adolescent Sex, Contraception, and Childbearing*, National Campaign to Prevent Teen Pregnancy, (Washington, DC, 1998).

Proverbs 5:3-6, 8, 20 For the lips of an *immoral* woman drip honey, and her mouth is smoother than oil; (4) but in the end she is bitter as wormwood, sharp as a two-edged sword. (5) Her feet go down to *death*, her steps lay hold of *hell*. (6) Lest you ponder her path of life—her ways are unstable; you do not know them. (8) Remove your way far from her, and do not go near the door of her house. (20) For why should you, my son, be enraptured by an immoral woman, and be embraced in the arms of a seductress?

I encourage you to read all of Proverbs 5 as the entire chapter is related to the theme of the immoral woman. Her lips, mouth, and words—though they are enticing (physically sweet like honey and smoother than oil), they are not indicative of the condition of her heart. Her heart, or core being, is "bitter," perhaps because of certain hardships of her past and/ or because she has been wronged by others. Ultimately she is resentful toward God who has not given her the circumstances of life just the way she would like to have them. She is "sharp as a two edged sword": her words will cut away one's peace and her actions may cut a man's feet out from under him. She is "unstable." This is due to her making decisions based on what is appealing to her flesh because she is either ignorant of the counsel of the Word of God or rejects it outright. She is tossed like a wave of the sea by her changing moods and desires. One day she wants this; another day she wants that. She may speak kindly one moment, but use filthy, cutting language the next. As sin leads to death, so do her feet. She walks in paths of unrighteousness, and such paths lead to the eternal damnation of hell. Do not become familiar with her ways lest you also fall and possibly end up at the same horrible destination.

Proverbs 6:23-29, 32-35 For the commandment is a lamp, and the law a light; reproofs of instruction are the way of life, (24) to keep you from the *evil woman*, from the flattering tongue of a *seductress*. (25) Do not lust after her beauty in your heart, nor let her allure you with her eyelids. (26) For by means of a *harlot* a man is reduced to a crust of bread; and an *adulteress* will prey upon his precious life. (27) Can a man take fire to his bosom, and his clothes not be burned? (28) Can one walk on hot coals, and his feet not be seared? (29) So is he who goes in to his neighbor's wife; whoever touches her shall not be innocent... (32) Whoever commits adultery with a woman lacks understanding; he who does so destroys his own soul. (33) Wounds and dishonor he will get, and his reproach will not be wiped away. (34) For jealousy is a husband's fury; therefore he will not spare in the day of vengeance. (35) He will accept no recompense, nor will he be appeased though you give many gifts.

The immoral woman is described in several ways in this passage: evil woman, seductress, harlot, and adulteress. She is also a predator—"an adulteress will *prey upon* his precious life" (verse 26). Clear warnings of grave consequences are given concerning her: If a man "goes in to" her and "commits adultery" with her, he "shall not be innocent," but will be "reduced to a crust of bread"; he "destroys his own soul" (verse 32); "wounds and dishonor he will get, and his reproach will not be wiped away" (verse 34). Furthermore, vengeance rather than forgiveness is what he will likely receive from the victimized husband. Contrary to popular belief these days, grave consequences are not only applied to those who get caught in adultery by a spouse or some other person, but every person who commits adultery will be found guilty before our holy God who sees all (Heb. 4:13). The sin of adultery is likened to "fire" and "hot coals"—all participants will be burned. This may refer figuratively to a type of judgment manifest in this earthly realm; also, anyone who fails to repent of sexual immorality and believe on Christ will suffer the eternal flames of hell. It is interesting that three of the four passages in Proverbs that deal with the immoral woman mention hell (5:5, 7:27, 9:18), and Proverbs 6 implies it—"destruction of the soul" (verse 32). Also, Revelation 21:8 says: "But the cowardly, unbelieving, abominable, murderers, *sexually immoral*, sorcerers, idolators, and all liars shall have their part in the lake which burns with fire and brimstone, which is the second death."

The immoral woman uses several features to lure her victims—her flattering tongue, her physical beauty, and her eyelids. But Proverbs 31:30 warns that "charm is deceitful." That's why you can more accurately discern the character of a woman by the fruit she bears (see Gal. 5:19-23: the works of the flesh or the fruit of the Spirit), rather than by her outward appearance. First Peter 3:3-4 says that a woman's adornment should not be "merely outward...rather let it be the hidden person of the heart...."

A major reason that so many men fall into adultery is because they "lack understanding" (verse 32). They are either ignorant of the Word of God or they simply disregard it. Verses 20-23 provide the antidote (preventative) to falling into adultery, or any other sin. The antidote is devotion to the Word of God—keeping it, not forsaking it, "binding it continually upon your heart," and "tying it around your neck."

Proverbs 7:4-27 Say to wisdom, 'You are my sister,' and call understanding your nearest kin, (5) that they may keep you from the *immoral woman*, from the *seductress* who flatters with her words. (6) For at the window of my house I looked through my lattice, (7) and saw among the simple, I perceived among the youths, a young man devoid of understanding, (8) passing along the street near her corner; and he took the path to her house (9) in the twilight, in the evening, in the black and dark night. (10) And there a woman met him, with the attire of a *harlot*, and a crafty heart. (11) She was loud and rebellious, her feet would not stay at home. (12) At times she was outside, at times in the open square, lurking at every corner. (13) So she caught him and kissed him; with an impudent face she said to him: (14) "I have peace offerings with me; today I have paid my vows. (15) So I came out to meet you, diligently to seek your face, and I have found you. (16) I have spread my bed with tapestry, colored coverings of Egyptian linen. (17) I have perfumed my bed with myrrh, aloes, and cinnamon. Come, let us take our fill of love until morning; (18) let us delight ourselves with love. (19) For my husband is not at home; he has gone on a long journey; (20) he has taken a bag of money with him, and will come home on the appointed day." (21) With her enticing speech she caused him to yield, with her flattering lips she *seduced* him. (22) Immediately he went after her, as an ox goes to the slaughter, or as a fool to the correction of the stocks, (23) till an arrow struck his liver. As a bird hastens to the snare, he did not know it would cost his life. (24) Now therefore, listen to me, my children; pay attention to the words of my mouth: (25) Do not let your heart turn aside to her ways, do not stray into her paths; (26) for she has cast down many wounded, and all who were slain by her were strong men. (27) Her house is the way to *hell*, descending to the chambers of *death*.

The Lord gives us here a lengthy passage about a young man's encounter with the immoral woman in order to emphasize the seriousness of the warning against adultery that all men ought to heed. As in previous passages, the immoral woman is also called a seductress and a harlot. She is also an adulteress as she admits to having a husband. What are her tactics and characteristics? In verse 10, we see that she dresses provocatively— "with the attire of a harlot," and seeks to use her God-given physical features to lure someone other than her husband. Typically, men are highly attracted to women's physical looks, so the Scripture commands women to dress modestly (1 Tim. 2:9). Verse 10 also points out that she has a "crafty heart," which reminds me of the serpent of Genesis 3 who was the most cunning of all beasts. In verse 11, we see that she is "loud and rebellious," which stands in contrast to "the incorruptible beauty of a gentle and quiet spirit (of the woman of God), which is very precious in the sight of God" (1 Pet. 3:4). Verses 11-12 also point out that she is not content to stay at home, nor anywhere else. She is restless, not knowing God's peace. First Timothy 6:6 says, "Godliness with contentment is great gain" (see also Phil. 4:11). She is not committed to taking care of her household, which stands in contrast to the virtuous wife who "watches over the ways of her household" (Pr. 31:27). In verse 13, she hastily kisses the young man, not even desiring to play hard to get or to be won over. She immediately lets him know he can have her. Perhaps she is in a hurry to get this affair going because the devil working through her is in a hurry to see this young man fall. Perhaps the devil is mindful of the prospect of this strong young man's future exposure to the gospel, his getting saved, and consequently wreaking havoc upon the devil's kingdom. In verses 14-21, we see the unfolding of verse 5 (she "flatters with her words"). She speaks of "peace offerings" and says that she has paid her vows. But she is a liar, for a willful adulteress does not know peace (Rom. 5:1), nor does she keep vows, since she readily breaks her wedding vows. She lets the young man know that she greatly desires him. Desiring to be desired is a temptation for many people. But we should have our desires fulfilled through God's provision and in God's timing. Then she makes a strong appeal for the simple young man to sleep with her. She indicates that he can have sex with her as she immediately references her bed and invites him to spend the night. She mistakenly calls this love, for she does not know or obey our wonderful God, who is love (1 Jn. 4:8). Again, she breaks her wedding vows which likely included something along the lines of "forsaking all others as long as we both shall live." All her luring tactics worked, as the young man yielded to her invitation "immediately" (verse 22).

Let's now take a look at her victim. He was a simple, young man—maybe a youth, or close to it, in age. The man was strong (verse 26). He may have been strong in any number of ways: perhaps physically, or in terms of his potential vocationally, or his ability to accomplish things, or in his leadership skills. Yet, the man was weak in an area of great importance—Biblical understanding. He was devoid of it, and as a result, he fell. He offered no resistance. Perhaps he had received Scriptural instruction in his past, but since then he had departed from the fear of the Lord. The fear of the Lord is a key to one's not falling into sin (Pr. 16:6).

Now read verses 21-23 where the author paints pictures of the young man's fall using several metaphors. He is likened to an ox, a fool, and a bird in order to emphasize the gravity of his unwise decision to participate in adultery. And what did this sin cost him? The bottom line is that it cost him his life. Perhaps the husband returned home, caught him in the adulterous act, and murdered him. Proverbs 6:34 says, "For jealousy is a husband's fury; therefore he will not spare in the day of vengeance." Why would the young man have believed her? If she was willing to commit adultery, then she was willing to commit other evil acts, including telling a lie. If a person will not trust God, why should you fully trust him or her? If this happens to a young man, and he does not have time to repent of his sin of adultery and get right with God before he dies, then he will likely die in his sins and go to hell forever.

What does this passage present as the main antidote, or preventative, to yielding to the immoral woman? As in the Proverbs 6 passage, the Word of God is the antidote. Read 7:1-5. We are told to keep and treasure the commands and law of God. Figuratively speaking, bind them on your fingers so that whenever you reach out your hand to do something, you are reminded to act within the parameters of God's law. Most important, "write them (the Words of God) on the tablet of your heart" (verse 3). You will prosper in every area of your life if you maintain a pure heart before God (3 Jn. 2, Pr. 4:23). The Word of God is infinitely more beneficial than the words ("enticing speech" and "flattering lips") of the immoral woman. This chapter seems to indicate that, more than anything else, her words caused him to fall (verse 21). Satan is a liar (Gen. 3:4-5; Jn. 8:44) and the immoral woman is a liar. You defeat Satan's lies with truth. The entirety of the Word of God is truth (Psalm 119:160). Hallelujah! May we daily hide the truth—God's Word—in our hearts (Ps. 119:11).

Proverbs 9:13-18 A *foolish woman* is clamorous; she is simple, and knows nothing. (14) For she sits at the door of her house, on a seat by the highest places of the city, (15) to call on those who pass by, who go straight on their way: (16) "Whoever is simple, let him turn in here"; and as for him who lacks understanding, she says to him, (17) "Stolen water is sweet, and bread eaten in secret is pleasant." (18) But he does not know that the dead are there, that her guests are in the depths of hell.

Of the four passages in Proverbs dealing with the immoral woman, three of them mention wisdom. Wisdom is typically described as a female throughout Proverbs, so Proverbs presents a clear contrast between the wisdom of God and the foolishness of the immoral woman.

This is especially seen in Proverbs 9 as you compare verses 1-6 (the invitation of wisdom) with verses 13-18 (the invitation of the foolish woman).

As the Proverbs 7 immoral woman was loud and rebellious (verse 11), so this foolish woman is clamorous: noisy and boisterous. (Contrast with 1 Pet. 3:4 and Pr. 31:26.) The foolish woman "knows nothing," which means she is completely void of the knowledge of God and how to please God (see verse 10). The foolish woman is also a crafty predator. She positions herself in a strategic place to access passersby so she can lure any man who is also void of understanding to come and be with her. She is a tool of Satan who is predatorial himself—he "walks about like a roaring lion, seeking whom he may devour" (1 Pet. 5:8). However, if you who know Christ submit to God, then you can successfully resist Satan as well as any person he may use (Jas. 4:7). She describes what she has as stolen water for drinking and bread for eating in secret. But nothing can be kept as a secret from God: "For God will bring every work into judgment, including every secret thing, whether good or evil" (Eccl. 12:14. See also Heb. 4:13). Furthermore, she calls these things "sweet" and "pleasant." But such sweetness and pleasure will be only enjoyed temporarily, because if one sows sin, one will certainly reap judgment (Gal. 6:7). And to be intimate with a woman to whom you are not married is thievery—taking what does not belong to you. Perhaps she has a husband; then intimacy with her would be adultery. If she does not have a husband, then intimacy with her would be fornication. Death and damnation are the likely future of those who heed the invitation of the foolish and immoral woman and who do not later find repentance and believe on Christ.

Sexual Sins of Galatians 5:19-21

Galatians 5:19-21 Now the works of the flesh are evident, which are: *adultery, fornication, uncleanness, lewdness,* (20) idolatry, sorcery, hatred, contentions, jealousies, outbursts of wrath, selfish ambitions, dissensions, heresies, (21) envy, murders, drunkenness, revelries, and the like; of which I tell you beforehand, just as I also told you in time past, that those who practice such things will not inherit the kingdom of God.

Galatians 5:19-21 is a list of seventeen sins or "works of the flesh." They stand in contrast to the nine fruits of the Holy Spirit listed in verses 22-23, the fruits that every Christian should seek to always bear.

Make sure you are not currently committing sins from the sin list of verses 19-21, for verse 21 says, "those who practice such things will not inherit the kingdom of God." The phrase "and the like" (verse 21) indicates that this is not an exhaustive list; there are other sins not mentioned here that are also works of the flesh. If committing such works of the flesh is normal for you, then you must repent and believe on Christ to avoid going to hell. The context of this passage tells us that if we do not walk in the Spirit, then by default we are walking in the flesh and bearing to some degree some or all of the works of the flesh.

There are three categories into which these works of the flesh fit: 1) sexual sins (four in this category), 2) sins associated with anger and division (nine is this category), 3) sins of getting high, intoxication, and associated wild parties (three in this category). That totals sixteen sins. Also, idolatry is listed. It is a general term and could fit into any of the three categories. These same three categories of sin also appear in Romans 13:13, "Let us walk properly, as in the day, not in revelry and drunkenness, not in lewdness and lust, not in strife and envy."

Adultery is having sex with someone other than your spouse. The seventh of the Ten Commandments is: "You shall not commit adultery." Jesus raised that standard when He said, "But I say to you that whoever looks at a woman to lust for her has already committed adultery with her in his heart" (Mt. 5:28). In God's eyes, you are guilty of adultery if you have sexual lust in your heart even if you never physically engage in sex outside of marriage. Shortly, we will examine a biblical example of adultery, that of David with Bathsheba.

Fornication is premarital sex. Around 2000, a USA TODAY/Gallup Poll randomly interviewed 1007 adults and found that forty-nine percent of those interviewed said living together first makes divorce less likely, thirty-one percent said living together first makes divorce more likely, thirteen percent said living together first makes no difference, and seven percent had no opinion. Half the sample was asked if an unmarried couple who have lived together for five years is as committed as a couple married five years; fifty-seven percent said yes. The report also said that in Denmark, Norway, and Sweden, roughly fifty percent of all children are born to unmarried couples. And those countries lead the way in Europe in the percentage of children born out of wedlock.[43]

---

[43] *USA TODAY*: Poll: "Cohabitation Can Be Good For Marriage," Updated 7/28/08.

These statistics confirm the great amount of ignorance and rebellion in the world today when it comes to the teachings of the Word of God, and specifically as it pertains to sexual immorality. High percentages of people dismiss the grave Biblical warning that fornicators and adulterers will not inherit the kingdom of God (Gal. 5:19-21).

Uncleanness is what may happen in your body or spirit as a result of pursuing sex outside of marriage. Sexually transmitted diseases are examples of uncleanness. Masturbation is a sin. (It's motivation is self-gratification rather than demonstration of love toward another person. Furthermore, one's thoughts typically become impure during masturbation.) Scripture warns us: "do not present your members as instruments of unrighteousness to sin..." (Rom. 6:13). Sexually impure thoughts would fall into the category of uncleanness. Proverbs 12:5a says, "The thoughts of the righteous are right." Viewing pornography is sin; it is lustful and adulterous. James Grant says that sexual immorality such as pornography is "dehumanizing. Because you're taking someone else—a human being—and making that person an object to satisfy your own depraved desire."[44]

Lewd means lustful, sensual, or vile. It conveys the idea of evil desire. An inappropriate sexual comment would constitute a lewd comment. Ephesians 5:4 says, "neither filthiness, nor foolish talking, nor coarse jesting" are appropriate, "but rather giving of thanks." Some television shows seem to rely on lewd comments for the bulk of their humor.

Hollywood has increasingly promoted sexual sin over the last two decades. In the 60's, 70's, and 80's, popular sitcoms included *The Andy Griffith Show, The Jeffersons, The Dick Van Dyke Show, I Love Lucy,* and *The Bill Cosby Show*. These shows contained virtually no sexual content. In some of these sitcoms, husband and wife did not even sleep in the same bed. But when the 90's rolled in, modesty on TV sitcoms rolled out. *Friends* (1994-2004) regularly glorified fornication and lewdness. *Ellen* (1994-1998) condoned homosexuality. *Sex and the City* (1998-2004) and *Desperate Housewives* (began in 2004) both contain sexually immoral content. Avoid all programs that condone sexual immorality and glorify sin. Even during ballgames or other relatively innocuous or wholesome programs, you still have to guard against commercials that flaunt sexuality and glorify other sinful themes. Psalm 101:3a says, "I will set nothing wicked before my eyes." You cannot obey

---

[44] James Grant, teaching on 2 Samuel 11-12, September 29, 2012.

this verse and willfully view pornography, or watch shows, or read literature that glorifies the works of the flesh. With the drastic increase in sexual immorality in our country over the last thirty years, remaining sexually pure will be an even greater challenge for young Christians. But remaining pure can be done through guarding one's mind and heart and by truly loving and abiding in the Word of God.

2 Samuel 11

Probably the most famous example of a Biblical character committing adultery is King David with Bathsheba. Though David was overall deemed a man after God's own heart, it seems David's heart drifted from God after he had been king for some years. When his daily life consisted of danger and discomfort, running from Saul, and relying upon God to protect him, David remained close to God. But after David had been established as king of Israel for some time, it seems that a lack of natural opposition as well as plush palace living allowed David to become complacent in terms of his devotion to God as well as his service to his country. Verse 1 indicates that David should have been with his troops who were out fighting battles; but instead David remained at his palace. One way to protect yourself against falling into sin is to be on the front lines of whatever activity God has called you to do. Colossians 3:23 says, "And whatever you do, do it heartily, as to the Lord and not to men." One evening, David arose from his bed. Perhaps he could not sleep well. If he had been mindful of Psalm 119:62a—"At midnight I will rise to give thanks to You," he would likely have stayed out of trouble. But his thoughts were not made captive unto the exhortations and holy standards of God's Word. From the roof of his house, he saw a beautiful woman bathing. Had David been close to God, he would have turned his eyes away from her and instead he would have renewed his mind through the Word of God. Second Corinthians 10:5b says believers should bring "every thought into captivity to the obedience of Christ." Turning from temptation and turning to God's Word is the right course of action for attaining victory. But even if David could not have shaken the arousal of his sexual passions, he could have redirected them toward his own wife. However, David chose neither of these better options. Instead, David yielded to lust and pride. David sent someone to inquire about the woman. He was told her name and that she was married. But finding out that this woman was married did not deter David; he was far from the conviction of God. Also, what a bad witness David was to his staff in that he utilized them to bring her to him! He used his prominent political position for personal gain—an abuse of power. Then David committed adultery; he had sex with this married woman, Bathsheba.

When Bathsheba sent word to David that she was pregnant, David schemed even further. David had Bathsheba's husband, Uriah, who was one of David's soldiers and out risking his life on the battlefield as David should have been doing, brought to David (another distraction from the good of the country). David planned to deceive Uriah by having Uriah sleep with his own wife, Bathsheba, so that when her pregnancy became obvious, Uriah would wrongly assume it was his baby. But Uriah did not go to his house and see his wife, though this was contrary to the king's orders, because Uriah's heart and spirit remained loyal to the Ark of God and his fellow soldiers who were at battle. So David tried a second time to get Uriah to be with his wife. This time David got Uriah drunk. Perhaps the alcohol, David reasoned, would dull Uriah of any conviction by his conscience and of a prevailing concern for his comrades. But again, Uriah stayed away from his wife. So David stooped to probably the morally lowest point in his life, as he sought to cover his sin. He had Uriah carry a sealed letter written by David to Joab, the commander of the army, instructing Joab to position Uriah in battle in such a way so that Uriah would be killed. Again, David was far from God. The scheme succeeded: Uriah was killed, Bathsheba became a widow, and David married her. Verse 27 says: "But the thing that David had done displeased the LORD."

God brought judgment upon David on account of his sin: the child that David and Bathsheba had together would die seven days after birth. Also, Israel would suffer great political turmoil as Absalom, David's own son, would temporarily rise in power and run King David out of Jerusalem. These consequences troubled all of Israel because David strayed from God and yielded to the temptation to lust, which led to adultery, deceit, and murder. In recent times, many prominent people in our nation have fallen from their powerful positions of leadership due to committing adultery or other types of sexual immorality. Think of the disgrace to their families, the agencies or other groups of people they represented, as well as the great amount of time and money spent as a result of their sexual sin and its consequences.

I used to drive a Ford Crown Victoria. In time, it developed warped rotors. If my car was traveling above fifty miles per hour, and I applied the brakes, the car would shake, or shimmy. Though I knew it was a problem, I postponed fixing it. Months later, a friend of mine, Andrew, was riding with me in my car. When I hit the brakes, the car shook so badly that it scared Andrew. He wanted to get out of my car immediately. I had become so used to the shaking that it had become normal to me. What was abnormal and a problem had become normal to me. My car had eventually become dangerous, not only to myself, but also to my passengers, as well as other cars around me. Likewise, a person can get used to, and comfortable with, committing sin. Though he may realize that a particular action is sinful, he may refuse to repent. He may justify to himself that his sin is not that big of a deal, or that it is inconsequential. But no sin is inconsequential. Colossians 3:25 says, "But he who does wrong *will be repaid* for what he has done, and there is no partiality." As time goes on, if he does not repent, his heart will likely become more and more hardened to any conviction by God and his sin can develop into a powerful idol in his heart. Like a growing cancer, the ignored sin will likely grow in frequency and size, and his sin may lead to other types of sin. Again, we see that David's lust led to adultery, which led to deceit, which led to murder. Hopefully, an outsider can point out one's sin and perhaps the Lord will grant the sinner the ability to repent. This happened with David. In 2 Samuel 12, God led Nathan to rebuke David, and David repented. But if there is no repentance, then a fall will certainly come. The fall will likely be embarrassing and painful to the sinner and damaging to others as well. (Usually one's sin negatively affects others also, as David's sins negatively impacted his entire kingdom.) The ultimate consequence is that sin separates one from God. Isaiah 59:2 says, "But your iniquities have separated you from your God; and your sins have hidden His face from you, so that He will not hear." If one is separate from God, one leans on his own understanding rather than leaning on God's wisdom and direction. One makes continuous poor choices, resulting in a serious mess.

Sexual Immorality in 1 Corinthians

Paul addresses sexual immorality frequently in his first epistle to the Corinthian church. In 1 Corinthians 5, we learn that a male church member at Corinth had his father's wife. Perhaps the man and woman had married, or perhaps they were just sexually involved. In either case, any incestuous relationship is forbidden (Lev. 18:8; Dt. 22:30). But the church allowed the offender to remain in the congregation. Therefore, Paul says that he has already pronounced judgment on the man and he instructs the church to "deliver such a one to Satan for the destruction of the flesh, that his spirit may be saved in the day of the Lord Jesus" (5:5). Satan would likely bring physical sickness upon the man, and hopefully that would bring the man to repentance so that he might be allowed to go to heaven. Paul rebukes the church for permitting the unrepentant man to remain an active member of the church. He reminds the church "not to keep company with anyone named a brother (a brother is a Christian) who is **sexually immoral**, or covetous, or an idolater, or a reviler, or a drunkard, or an extortioner—not even to eat with such a person" (1 Cor. 5:11). Christians who refuse to repent of sexual immorality are to be cut off from all church fellowship.

In 1 Corinthians 6:9-10, Paul continues to address sexual immorality:

> Do you not know that the unrighteous will not inherit the kingdom of God? Do not be deceived. Neither *fornicators*, nor idolaters, nor *adulterers*, nor *homosexuals*, nor *sodomites*, (10) nor thieves, nor covetous, nor drunkards, nor revilers, nor extortioners will inherit the kingdom of God.

Among this sin list (which is similar to the works of the flesh list in Galatians 5:19-21), Paul condemns homosexuality. Here, along with passages such as Romans 1:18-32, Genesis 19, and Leviticus 18:22, we see that homosexual desires and practices are unacceptable before God. The church should reach out in love with the good news of Jesus Christ to homosexuals. Homosexuals can come to church, hear the gospel, and seek repentance. But it is unacceptable for an unrepentant homosexual to be allowed to be an active, voting church member, and he or she should certainly *not* occupy a position of leadership within a church. Any church that ordains homosexuals to be ministers is a church that has rejected the Word of God.

But in verse 11, Paul reminds the church, "And such were some of you." Some of them, and us, used to commit sexual sins and other works of the flesh. With humble gratitude, we should remember from where God has brought us—from sin to salvation, from disgrace to grace. Paul himself admitted that he is the chief of sinners (1 Tim. 1:15). He was a conspirator to the murder of Stephen (Acts 7:58) and a lead terrorist against the Christian church. But when anyone repents and turns to Christ, as Paul did on the road to Damascus (Acts 9:6), then certainly that person is eligible to be a church member, a preacher (Acts 9:20), and eventually one who holds office within the church (1 Tim. 3:1-13).

First Corinthians 6:13b-20 says:

> Now the body is not for *sexual immorality* but for the Lord, and the Lord for the body. (14) And God both raised up the Lord and will also raise us up by His power. (15) Do you not know that your bodies are members of Christ? Shall I then take the members of Christ and make them members of a harlot? Certainly not! (16) Or do you not know that he who is joined to a harlot is one body with her? For "the two," He says, "shall become one flesh." (17) But he who is joined to the Lord is one spirit with Him. (18) Flee *sexual immorality*. Every sin that a man does is outside the body, but he who commits *sexual immorality* sins against his own body. (19) Or do you not know that your body is the temple of the Holy Spirit who is in you, whom you have from God, and you are not your own? (20) For you were bought at a price; therefore glorify God in your body and in your spirit, which are God's.

These verses repeatedly indicate that the physical body of a Christian is to be consecrated unto God. Verse 13 says, "the body is…for the Lord"; verse 15 indicates that your body is a member of Christ; and verse 19 says, "your body is a temple of the Holy Spirit." So your physical body is not your own, but rather you are God's property. "You were bought at a price" (verse 20), meaning God paid for you. And the cost was unmatchably high—the precious blood of His Son, Jesus. To commit a sexual sin is to sin against your own body, and to sin against your own body is to sin against the temple of the Holy Spirit. Therefore, "flee sexual immorality" (verse 18). Be joined to the Lord—become one spirit with Him; do not be joined to a harlot, becoming one flesh with her. The Holy Spirit wants to dwell in a holy temple.

First Corinthians 7:2 says, "Nevertheless, because of *sexual immorality*, let each man have his own wife, and let each woman have her own husband." Verse 9 says, "but if they (the unmarried and widows) cannot exercise self-control, let them marry. For it is better to marry than to burn with passion." Part of the benefit of marriage is the ability to channel one's sexual desire in the appropriate direction—toward one's spouse. It is better to marry than to lack self-control in the area of sexual desire. (I deal more with 1 Corinthians 7 in Chapter 14 of this book.)

Consequences of Sexual Immorality

The first part of 1 Corinthians 10 was written to serve as a warning to New Covenant believers of the dire consequences for sexual immorality. Concerning the Israelites in the wilderness, verse 8 says, "Nor let us commit *sexual immorality*, as some of them did, and in one day twenty-three thousand fell." Numbers 25 records how the Israelites committed harlotry with the women of Moab. They also sacrificed to the gods of Moab and worshipped them; thus they were "joined to Baal of Peor" (verse 3). Therefore, the LORD sent a deadly plague, and the LORD commanded Moses to have the offenders hanged "out in the sun, that the fierce anger of the LORD may turn away from Israel" (Num. 25:4).

In Revelation 2:18-29, the letter to the angel of the church at Thyatira, we again see God's promised judgment upon sexual immorality. Verses 20b-23 says:

> Nevertheless I have a few things against you, because you allow that woman Jezebel, who calls herself a prophetess, to teach and seduce My servants to commit *sexual immorality* and eat things sacrificed to idols. (21) And I gave her time to repent of her *sexual immorality*, and she did not repent. (22) Indeed I will cast her into a sickbed, and those who commit *adultery* with her into great tribulation, unless they repent of their deeds. (23) I will kill her children with death, and all the churches shall know that I am He who searches the minds and hearts. And I will give to each one of you according to your works.

If the church at Thyatira would have expelled Jezebel and anyone who persisted in committing adultery with her, then the Lord would have been pleased with the church's stance against sexual immorality. Instead, the Lord had a few things against the entire Thyatira church body because they tolerated sexual immorality among some of the members. We also see in this passage the Lord's patience as He gave those who committed sexual immorality time to repent. But there is a definite limit as to how long God will allow such sin to exist within His body. Sickness, tribulation, and death may await those who persist in sin. But more sobering is God's promise that the lake of fire will be the final dwelling place for those who refuse to repent of sexual immorality. Revelation 21:8 states: "But the cowardly, unbelieving, abominable, murderers, *sexually immoral*, sorcerers, idolators, and all liars shall have their part in the lake which burns with fire and brimstone, which is the second death."

More on the Consequences of Sexual Immorality

What are other possible consequences for committing sexual immorality? One consequence is unwanted pregnancy. Nationally, close to 2,800 teens become pregnant each day.[45] Typically, a teen is not mature enough to responsibly raise a child. Certainly the teen is not grounded spiritually since he or she is having sex outside of wedlock. (The exception, of course, is those few instances where an eighteen or nineteen year old marries in the Lord.) Another consequence of sexual immorality is sexually transmitted diseases. Note the number of new cases that arose nationally for each of three diseases in 2007: syphilis—40,920, chlamydia—1,108,374, and gonorrhea—355,991.[46] "By the end of 2003, in thirty-three states, an estimated 4,911,727 persons were living with HIV/AIDS."[47] Another consequence is the loss of one's virginity with someone other than one's future spouse. What a blessing it is when Christian husband and wife have kept themselves sexually pure their entire lives in anticipation of their wonderful wedding day. Another consequence of sexual immorality is sexually inappropriate thoughts embedded in one's memory that may resurface and prove difficult to eradicate. But again, the most dire consequence for sexual immorality is that those who practice such things and are unrepentant will not inherit the kingdom of God (Gal. 5:19-21). If you are struggling with a sexual addiction, a major aspect of your seeking deliverance is to intensely study the Word of God, including passages dealing with God's judgment upon sin, for "by the fear of the LORD,

---

[45] *Facts in Brief: Teen Sex and Pregnancy*, The Alan Guttmacher Institute, (New York, 1996).

[46] Centers for Disease Control and Prevention, (cdc.gov).

[47] Ibid., Surveillance Report, Vol. 18, 2006.

one departs from evil…" (Pr. 16:6b). Second, I recommend that you confide in a Christian friend of your same gender about your struggle. I recently heard a man say that he only gained victory over his addiction to pornography after he had confessed his addiction to a friend. James 5:16a says: "Confess your trespasses to one another, and pray for one another, that you may be healed." Third, you may need to fast about the matter. After Jesus had cast a demon out of a boy, he told His disciples who had failed in their efforts to cast out the demon, "this kind does not go out except by prayer and fasting" (Mt. 17:21). An extended fast can be very effective for acquiring a spiritual breakthrough. (Please fast within the parameters of good health, safety, and your own level of faith. You may want to consult your pastor and/or a reputable author for guidance on fasting.)

Proper Attire

Women (little girls and teens included) should not dress in any sexually provocative way, but rather they should dress modestly. First Timothy 2:9 says: "women adorn themselves in *modest apparel*, with propriety and *moderation*, not with braided hair or gold or pearls or costly clothing…." First Peter 3:3-4 supports this point, reiterating that apparel does not make the woman, but inner righteousness and humility make the woman: "Do not let your adornment be merely outward— arranging the hair, wearing gold, or putting on fine apparel—rather let it be the hidden person of the heart, with the incorruptible beauty of a gentle and quiet spirit, which is very precious in the sight of God." I realize that such modesty in dress is counter-cultural, but being obedient to the Word of God is certainly more important than fitting in with the secular culture and what it views as fashionable.

An Important Step in Avoiding an Affair—Boundaries

A story is told of a father and son sitting amongst the congregation witnessing a wedding ceremony. At one point in the ceremony, the bride and groom light a single candle and then blow out their individual candles. The father asks the son if he understands the significance of that act. The son replies, "No more old flames!" Whether or not that was what the father had in mind, the son was on target. Husband and wife typically state in their marriage vows that they will forsake all other romantic and sexual relationships in order to be exclusively committed to one another. Christian spouses almost never set out to get into an extra-marital affair. When an affair occurs, the usual reason is that a spouse has developed a friendship with someone of the opposite sex, perhaps a work colleague, committee member, or neighbor. But such a development begs the question, "Why befriend someone of the opposite sex when your spouse should be your best friend?" I recommend that all spouses develop *boundaries* with those outside of their marriage who are of the opposite sex. Certainly married people have acquaintances of the opposite sex and should be courteous and polite with those acquaintances. But I recommend that married people avoid having regular, in-depth, one-on-one conversations with those of the opposite sex to whom they are not married (obviously this rule does not apply to certain immediate family members). Such relating can lead to emotional bonding, and emotional bonding can lead to temptation. If you as a spouse are experiencing romantic and sexual temptation with someone of the opposite sex, then flee. Turn away from that illicit relationship, and the associated feelings will eventually die. At the same time, turn to God through His Word and prayer, and perhaps also confide in a reliable Christian friend (of your same gender) about your struggles, so that you may "cleanse (yourself)...from all filthiness of the flesh and spirit, perfecting holiness in the fear of God" (2 Cor. 7:1). Furthermore, you may want to connect with any of the following internationally renowned ministries that specialize in providing assistance in the area of pursuing sexual purity: Pure Life Ministries[48], Exodus International[49], and Focus on the Family[50].

---

[48] Purelifeministries.org

[49] Exodusinternational.org ("The largest information and referral ministry in the world addressing homosexual issues.")

[50] *Couple tie the knot while running marathon*, by Brian Gillie, Examiner.com. February 1, 2011.

"And we know that all things work together for good to those who *love* God, to those who are the called according to His purpose" (Rom. 8:28).

A story is told about a king who thought it was time to find a husband for his daughter. So he offered a challenge to the young men of his kingdom. He said, "Anyone who can swim across the moat full of alligators, touch the castle wall, and swim back across the moat has shown true bravery and is worthy to marry my daughter and be prince in the land. Is there anyone brave enough? Anyone?" A few minutes went by; there were no takers. The king said, "How sad that we have no brave souls," and he turned around to walk away. Then suddenly the king heard a splash. He turned back to see a man swimming the moat. The man fought off alligators, touched the castle wall, swam back across while still fighting off alligators, until he exited the moat near the king, huffing and puffing. The amazed king heralded the young man's success. The king exclaimed, "Congratulations, Brave Young Man! You may take my daughter in marriage, and be the prince of the land!" The man said, "Sir, I do not want your daughter, nor do I want to be prince. All I want is the name of the person who pushed me in."

You may feel like your marriage has so far been one big trial. Perhaps the alligators of selfishness and strife have battled you throughout your entire marriage, and you feel it has been a real struggle to survive. If this is the case, then you can claim Romans 8:28 for yourself, provided you love God, which includes keeping His commandments (Jn. 14:15), and provided you are called by God. As you love God, as you display patience toward your spouse, as you tame your tongue, and as you love your spouse despite any shortcomings he or she may have, then, despite whatever issues about your spouse bother you, you can be assured that God will work for good from those issues. If you steadily love God, then God works for your good! God can use those difficult marital issues to develop godly qualities such as patience, perseverance, and a willingness to die to self in both husband and wife (Rom. 5:3-5; Jas. 1:2-4). Furthermore, in the future, you and your spouse will likely be able to minister more effectively to others who are experiencing marital problems because you have experienced the faithfulness of God and the fruit of your own perseverance. In the midst of difficult marital issues, do not become sluggish, resentful, faithless, or hopeless, but rather seek

Tom Caldwell

God for faith and patience so that you may inherit all of His wonderful promises (Heb. 6:12). Among those promises are prosperity and victory in whatever you do (Ps. 1:3; 3 Jn. 2; 1 Cor. 15:57; 2 Cor. 2:14), and this includes prosperity and victory in your marriage.

Chapter 8

Raising Children

**"I have no greater joy than to hear that
my children walk in truth"
(3 John 4).**

At this point, my wife, Kim, and I have been blessed to have two children, Emma (born in 2005) and Anna (born in 2007). The personal joy these children have brought us has exceeded our expectations. Perhaps we will be blessed to have more, either naturally or by adoption. Having children has also enhanced my marriage. Emma and Anna have caused Kim and me to realize how much we need each other. I need Kim to nurture, train, and homeschool the children while I am at work. Kim needs me to earn a living for the family, and to help nurture, discipline, and homeschool our children. The responsibilities of raising children should cause husband and wife to come together as a team.

The Call to Have Children

Some married couples today opt to not have children. That's understandable if the married couple is physically unable to have children or if they are living in poverty. But should a couple opt out on having children simply because they do not desire children? In this section, I intend to show that the desire to have children by husband and wife is a godly desire, that having children is a great blessing from God and should be considered part of the marital package.

In Genesis 1:22 and 28, God says, "be fruitful and multiply...." God never retracted this command. God says these words again after the flood in Genesis 8. Also, God tells Jacob at Bethel, "Be fruitful and multiply" (Gen. 35). Jacob seemed to have taken God's command to heart as he had twelve sons and a daughter.

To have children was a godly desire by godly women in the Bible. Consider *Sarah,* Abraham's wife. When ninety-year-old Sarah, who had been barren, gave birth to Isaac, she said, "God has made me laugh" (Gen. 21:6). Her newborn gave her joy as well as amazement at this miraculous provision from God. When Isaac was married, he "pleaded with the LORD for his wife (*Rebekah*), because she was barren; and the LORD granted his plea, and Rebekah...conceived," giving birth to Jacob and Esau (Gen. 25:21). So Rebekah went from barrenness to twins! Jacob's wife, *Rachel*, was barren also, and she said to Jacob: "Give me children, or else I die!" (Gen. 30:1). What a strong desire for children Rachel had, and what a contrast to many women and men today who seem to despise the idea of raising children. After a long time, "God remembered Rachel, and God listened to her and opened her womb. And she conceived and bore a son, and said, 'God has taken away my reproach.' So she called his name Joseph" (Gen. 30:22-23). It is noteworthy that all three women were barren (that's three consecutive generations of barren women in the same family), all three were considered godly, all three desired children (it was a righteous desire), the prayers of all three were eventually answered by God as God granted all three at least one child, and all three children grew up to be used of God. Isaac, Jacob, and Joseph—Jewish patriarchs, important people in Jewish and Christian history, were born to these formerly barren women who through their faith and patience received God's blessing of children.

In Judges 13, Manoah's wife was also barren. Verse 3 says, "And the Angel of the LORD appeared to the woman and said to her, 'Indeed, now, you are barren and have borne no children, but you shall conceive and bear a son…the child shall be a Nazirite to God from the womb; and he shall begin to deliver Israel out of the hand of the Philistines.'" That child to be born was Samson, a man of great physical strength whom God used to defeat to Israel's enemies. This is another example of a barren woman giving birth to a special son as a result of God's visitation.

In Luke 1, Zechariah and Elizabeth "were both righteous before God…blameless. But they had no child, because Elizabeth was barren, and they were both well advanced in years" (verses 6-7). An angel said to Zechariah:

> your prayer is heard; and your wife Elizabeth will bear you a son, and you shall call his name John. And you will have joy and gladness, and many will rejoice at his birth. For he will be great in the sight of the Lord…He will also be filled with the Holy Spirit, even from his mother's womb (Lk. 1:13-15).

God visited this righteous couple and honored their prayers so that Elizabeth, who had been barren and was now old, gave birth to John. Thus joy came to her, Zechariah, and many others. And as their son was filled with the Holy Spirit in the womb, you can pray for the Holy Spirit to fill your child even while in the womb. And was John a special son? John the Baptist was the greatest man born of women from the time of Adam and Eve until the birth of Jesus.

We can also remember that the Shunammite woman of 2 Kings 4 was barren. Because she had blessed Elisha by providing him living quarters, he wanted to bless her in return. When Elisha was told that she had no son and her husband was old, Elisha spoke to her, "About this time next year you shall embrace a son…the woman conceived, and bore a son when the appointed time had come…" (verses 16-17).

So several of the great people in the Bible were born to previously barren women. The Lord did a special work, not only through the lives of the ones who were born, but also by opening the womb of the mothers. Therefore, God received much glory in those instances. Another practical application is as follows: If the fulfillment of your dreams and desires has so far been barren, do not give up. Instead, pray and obey God, believing that He can give birth to great things in and through you in due time. Psalm 37:4 says: "Delight yourself also in the LORD, and He shall give you the desires of your heart." When married couples desire children, that is a good desire, and God can bring that desire to fruition.

Concerning women in general, 1 Timothy 2:15 says, "Nevertheless she will be *saved in childbearing* if they continue in faith, love, and holiness, with self-control." We are saved by faith in Christ. But "faith without works is dead" (James 2:26). For the wife, having children is part of the works that demonstrate her faith. When possible, having children should be considered part of the package of having a spouse.

Some women, because they have not been able to have children naturally, have opted to adopt or be a foster parent. Other women (perhaps not married) help care for nieces, nephews, or other children (including in the church nursery). I admire women who do that. God bless you! Jesus said that "the last shall be first" (Mt. 19:30). I would not be surprised if, among those who are first in heaven, we will see women and men who have greatly invested in the lives of children of whom they are not the natural parents.

First Timothy 5:9-10 says, "Do not let a widow under sixty years old be taken into the number, and not unless she has been the wife of one man, well reported for good works: *if she has brought up children...*." Bringing up children is an eligibility requirement for a widow to receive from the church's distribution.

First Timothy 5:14 says, "I desire that the younger widows marry, *bear children*, manage the house...." Raising children and managing the house is not a second rate job. Instead, you who do so are training the next generation! America's future, to a large degree, will depend on your efforts. Again, God bless you who raise children. You have a high calling because children are highly valuable.

If you and your spouse are seeking to have children, there are two relevant Scriptural promises on which you can meditate. In Exodus 23:25b-26a, God says, "And I will take sickness away from the midst of you. No one shall suffer *miscarriage or be barren* in your land...." Also Deuteronomy 28:4 lists as part of the blessings for obedience—"Blessed shall be the fruit of your body...."

The Sanctity of Life

Did you know that our nation has committed approximately 1.37 million abortions each year since 1973?[51] That is approximately fifty-two million abortions from 1973 (Roe vs. Wade) through 2012. Also, approximately forty-two million abortions occur world-wide annually.[52] Let's consider some Scripture on this topic. The Bible says that God saw that *Leah* was unloved, so "He opened her womb" (Gen. 29:31); of *Hannah* it says God "closed her womb" (1 Sam. 1:6); of *Ruth* it says, "The LORD gave her conception" (Ruth 4:13). So God opens wombs, God closes wombs, and God grants conception. God is the author of life; life is precious in God's sight. We need to respect the sanctity of life, which begins at conception. Psalm 22:10 says, "From My mother's womb, you have been my God." Again, Jeremiah 1:5 says: "Before I formed you in the womb I knew you; before you were born I sanctified you; I ordained you a prophet to the nations." Again, Psalm 139:13-14 says, "For You formed my inward parts; You covered me in my mother's womb. I will praise You, for I am fearfully and wonderfully made." Again, life begins at conception, and God is the author of that life. God, have mercy on this country which is guilty of approximately fifty-two million abortions over the last thirty-eight years.

Psalm 127:3-5a: Behold, children are a heritage from the LORD, the fruit of the womb is a reward. Like arrows in the hand of a warrior, so are the children of one's youth. Happy is the man who has his quiver full of them....

When children are raised into being righteous young adults, then the parents can aim them as sharp arrows and send them out into the world. The parents can know that God will guide their flight all the way, that they will strike a blow against the enemies of God, and that they will participate in the advancement of God's kingdom on earth. I have heard it said that a major problem on this planet is overpopulation. I submit that a much bigger problem is an under population of holy, righteous, and God-fearing people.

In *Exodus*, manna from heaven was a blessing from God. But the Israelites called it worthless, and thus they incurred God's wrath.

---

[51] Alan Guttmacher Institute (www.agi-usa.org, 1996-2008).
[52] Ibid.

Unfortunately, some people today treat embryos, infants, and children as worthless. But embryos, infants, and children are valuable! They are a heritage, a reward, and a blessing from God. Children should not be despised, but rather embraced. Will God judge those who willfully harm children? Matthew 18:6 says, "But whoever causes one of these little ones who believe in Me to sin, it would be better for him if a millstone were hung around his neck, and he were drowned in the depth of the sea."

And not only are we to teach children, but we can learn at least three lessons from children. Matthew 18:3-4 says, "unless you are converted and become as little children, you will by no means enter the kingdom of heaven. Therefore, whoever humbles himself as this little child is the greatest in the kingdom of heaven." One, children are teachable. Likewise, we should not think we have all the answers; instead, we should be teachable—learning God's will from God's Word and the Holy Spirit, our Teacher (Mt. 11:29; Jn. 14:26). Two, children have a freshness about them. Likewise, we should not get ourselves into a rut of mundane, mediocre living; instead we should believe that God wants to do new and exciting things in and through us. Three, young children are dependent upon their parents. Likewise, we should not lean on our own understanding; rather we should acknowledge God in all our ways (Pr. 3:5-6).

Proverbs 23:22-25: Listen to your father who begot you, and do not despise your mother when she is old. (23) Buy the truth, and do not sell it, also wisdom and instruction and understanding. (24) The father of the righteous will greatly rejoice, and he who begets a wise child will delight in him. (25) Let your father and your mother be glad, and let her who bore you rejoice.

We see that obedient, righteous children can bring joy, delight, and gladness to parents. But many parents today experience regular disappointments with the behavior of their children. This is often because some children, as they have become older have become sinful, disrespectful, and rebellious. They reject the council of Proverbs 23— they do not listen to their father, and they despise their mother when she is old. They reject truth, wisdom, instruction, understanding, and righteousness. Proverbs 29:15b says, "a child left to himself brings shame to his mother." So the mother and father need to tend to the child and train the child in righteousness. Third John 4 shows the fruit of such an investment—"I have no greater joy than to hear that my children walk in truth." The willingness or unwillingness of the children to obey God and parents determines to a large degree the joy or sorrow of the parents. In the remainder of this chapter, I will address some of the key things children need in order to grow in righteousness and be a blessing to their parents. We will look at their need for quality and quantity time with their parents, discipline, the Word of God abiding in them deeply, and the importance of protection from evil influence.

Remember, Parents, "Love Does Not Seek Its Own" (1 Cor. 13:5)

At the age of twenty-three, after I had finished college, I was living at home and working temporarily for the county's Department of Social Services. My dad was making arrangements to purchase a tract of land and turn it into a golf driving range so I could manage it and develop my own business. Dad was not doing this for his own benefit, but simply to assist me, and I was appreciative of his help and excited about the prospect of managing my own small business. At the time, I had not yet become a Christian, but I was actively seeking God and reading the Bible nightly. One night, I was inspired by what I read in Matthew 7:7, "Ask, and it shall be given unto you...." I earnestly prayed, "Lord, please show me what kind of career path you want for me." I did not expect an immediate answer. Two days later, a friend in my Sunday School class gave me a brochure about the Southern Baptist Theological Seminary, in Louisville, Kentucky. I thought little of the prospect of my attending seminary, until later that same night. As I lie in bed, flipping through the pages of the seminary booklet, suddenly the Lord visited me and revealed to me that I was to attend Southern Seminary! (This was the first time I had ever been visited by God that I was aware of, and it amazed me. It made me more zealous in seeking Him.) The next morning, I called Southern Seminary to see if I would be eligible to enroll there, and if I could begin in the spring semester. They said that I could. I believe it was the next evening when I shared the news with my parents. As they were watching television, I said, "I have something important to tell you. I am going to seminary." As I stated this, I began to cry. I suppose I cried because I wanted to be a good person in God's eyes, and I wanted to please my parents. I'll never forget Dad's reaction.

I imagine Dad wanted some explanation as to how I came to such a decision since the prospect of my going to seminary had never been mentioned before, and because Dad and I had been planning for me to manage a driving range, and Dad was making investments to that end. (In hindsight, I could have worded my announcement of my calling to seminary differently, showing more sensitivity to my plans with Dad.) Nevertheless, Dad, sensing the importance of that moment in my life, almost immediately came over to me and gave me a big hug. That was an unforgettably loving reaction on his part. He and Mom supported my decision to attend seminary, and they paid for my tuition, and more. My attending seminary was the right decision. And incidentally, I received Jesus as my Lord and Savior during that first semester!

Q. T. (Quality Time and Quantity Time)

A survey of elementary children was conducted which indicated the ten most appreciated qualities in dads. Children said: 1) he takes time for me; 2) he listens to me; 3) he plays with me; 4) he invites me to go places with him; 5) he lets me help him; 6) he treats my mother well; 7) he lets me say what I think; 8) he's nice to my friends; 9) he only punishes me when I deserve it; and 10) he isn't afraid to admit when he's wrong. In the survey, the top five qualities involve time—quality and quantity time. Just as husband and wife need quality and quantity time together, children also require quality and quantity time with each parent. Relationships require relating. And love requires time. Within the family, there are three relationships to nurture: the God-family relationship, the husband-wife relationship, and the parent–child relationship. For husband and wife to fit all this relating in, they must use their time wisely. Hobbies, outside friendships, sports, and television in general need not be sacrificed altogether, but these activities must take a far back seat to these most important relationships.

We as a family go over Scripture and act out Bible stories. Often, Emma, Anna, and I put the full armor of God on together to begin our day (Eph. 6:10-18). We also sing and praise-march through the house together. We as a family play together with legos, play-dough, and coloring books. We go on wagon rides down our street, and we go to the playground together. Also, I sometimes take the girls with me to a restaurant for breakfast to have daddy-daughter time.

Disciplining Your Child

As our loving heavenly Father chastens all of His spiritual children, so we parents are to also chasten our children.

Hebrews 12:7-11 If you endure chastening, God deals with you as with sons; for what son is there whom a father does not chasten? (8) But if you are without chastening, of which all have become partakers, then you are illegitimate and not sons. (9) Furthermore, we have had human fathers who corrected us, and we paid them respect. Shall we not much more readily be in subjection to the Father of spirits and live? (10) For they indeed for a few days chastened us as seemed best to them, but He for our profit, that we may be partakers of His holiness. (11) Now no chastening seems to be joyful for the present, but painful; nevertheless, afterward it yields the peaceable fruit of righteousness to those who have been trained by it.

The correction that human fathers give their children causes the children to respect them (verse 9). Children must learn to respect authority. This does not come naturally; it must be taught. If children do not learn to respect human authority, how will they learn to respect and humbly serve the invisible God? Chastening is part of training (verse 11), and "it yields the peaceable fruit of righteousness" and "holiness" (verses 10-11). Note also Proverbs 3:11-12: "My son, do not despise the chastening of the LORD, nor detest His correction; for whom the LORD loves He corrects, just as a father the son in whom he delights." So we should be thankful rather than resistant for the Lord's chastening in our lives; His purpose is to correct us and make us more like His perfect Son.

Proverbs 13:24 He who spares his rod hates his son, but he who loves him disciplines him promptly.

I acknowledge that spanking is a controversial topic in today's society, but my purpose in this book is to give exposure to what Scripture says about marriage and family. Naturally, parents desire that their children like them; however, parents have a higher responsibility before God. A parent who loves his or her child disciplines the child and trains the child to know and obey God. The Lord is serious about the parent's eradicating rebellion from the hearts of their children.

Proverbs 19:18 Chasten your son while there is hope, and do not set your heart on his destruction.

When a child is not regularly disciplined, hope can diminish in terms of the child's willingness to turn to righteousness. (Please also read Pr. 23:13-14.) Parents must raise children "in the training and admonition of the Lord" (Eph. 6:4). When a parent disciplines a child, the motive should always be love (1 Cor. 16:14), never destruction. If a parent becomes full of anger and gets "in the flesh," then he or she should not spank at that time. Child abuse is rightly a felony, and no parent or guardian should ever cross that line.

Proverbs 22:15 Foolishness is bound up in the heart of a child; the rod of correction will drive it far from him.

Foolishness is repeatedly condemned in Proverbs, and a child at his or her core, or heart, is naturally foolish. The rod of correction drives the foolish tendencies far away. The opposite of foolishness in Proverbs is wisdom. Proverbs 4:7 says, "Wisdom is the principle thing; therefore get wisdom." Proverbs 29:15a says, "The rod and rebuke give wisdom." Disciplining one's child is conducive to developing wisdom in the child.

Proverbs 29:15, 17 The rod and rebuke give wisdom, but a child left to himself brings shame to his mother...(17) Correct your son, and he will give you rest; yes, he will give delight to your soul.

Children cannot successfully raise themselves, but children require the consistent love, attention, and investment of the parents. Such investment reinforces to the child the parent's love for the child, and it also gives opportunity for the parent to model godly behavior for the child. Children should not have large blocks of unsupervised time.

Children Need the Word of God

Perhaps the most central passage in all the Old Testament is Deuteronomy 6:4-9; it is called the Shema (pronounced shê-mah´). Shema is the Hebrew word for "hear" in verse 4. The Shema is the passage which Jesus quotes in Matthew 22:36-40, Mark 12:29-31, and Luke 10:27—saying it is the first and greatest commandment in the Bible. Deuteronomy 6:4-9 says:

Hear, O Israel: The LORD our God, the LORD is one! (5) You shall love the LORD your God with all your heart, with all your soul, and with all your strength. (6) And these words which I command you today shall be in your heart. (7) You shall teach them diligently to your children, and shall talk of them when you sit in your house, when you walk by the way, when you lie down, and when you rise up. (8) You shall bind them as a sign on your hand, and they shall be as frontlets between your eyes. (9) You shall write them on the doorposts of your house and on your gates.

This passage contains great instruction for parenting. Loving God with all of one's being is the greatest biblical commandment. The first way that the parent can demonstrate loving God is to hide the Word of God in his or her own heart. Hiding the Word of God in one's heart is closely linked to loving God, as Jesus said in John 14:15, "If you love Me, keep My commandments." Second, the parent is commanded to train the next generation to also love God—"teach them (the Holy Scriptures) diligently to your children." Third, Scripture is to be a regular part of a family's focus and conversation throughout the day— talk of the Scripture "when you sit in your house, when you walk by the way, when you lie down, and when you rise up." When our family is out driving, we often quote or discuss Scripture. This practice is similar to Ephesians 5:19 (which occurs just before instruction on family relationships)—"speaking to one another in psalms and hymns and spiritual songs, singing and making melody in your heart to the Lord." Ephesians 5:19 focuses on sharing the Word of God through song. So family singing, praise, and worship can regularly occur at home and in the car, as well as at church. Fourth, this passage teaches that the Word of God is to be secured to the hand (figuratively) so that whenever one reaches out to perform some task, he is reminded to do so in accordance with the Word of God (verse 8). The Word of God is to also be placed between the eyes (figuratively) so that one's outlook and perception are always filtered through the lens of Scripture (verse 9). Furthermore, the Word of God is to be written on the doorposts of the house and the gates so that whenever you are coming or going, you are reminded to conduct yourself according to the Word of God (verse 9). It is fundamental that Christians are to be people of the Word. Deuteronomy 32:47 says, "The Word of God is your life." And if the Word of God is your life, then you must diligently train your children to make the Word of God central to their lives as well. The Sunday School teacher and pastor should not be the primary source of biblical learning for your children. We certainly thank God for their contribution, but the primary responsibility for the Biblical training of your children is you, the parents. Other passages that exhort teaching the Word of God to your children are Deuteronomy 4:9-10, 11:19, and Psalm 78:5-8. Also, Deuteronomy 32:46 says, "Set you hearts on all the words which I testify among you today, which *you shall command your children to be careful to observe*—all the words of this law."

Judges 2:7, 10 So the people served the LORD all the days of Joshua, and all the days of the elders who outlived Joshua, who had seen all the great works of the LORD which He had done for Israel. (10) When all that generation had been gathered to their fathers, *another generation arose* after them who did not know the LORD nor the work which He had done for Israel.

The people of Joshua's generation had seen with their eyes many great miracles of God. In Joshua 3, the Jordan River supernaturally stood as a heap upstream so the Israelites could cross on dry ground. In Joshua 6, God caused the walls of Jericho to fall down flat. In Joshua 10, God listened to the petition of Joshua and caused the sun to stand still for about a whole day while the Israelites finished defeating the Amorites. And many other military victories occurred because of the intervention of God on behalf of the children of Israel. Joshua's generation had personally witnessed God's power. God's miracle intervention in conjunction with God's Word, on which they were commanded to constantly meditate (Josh. 1:7-8), caused them to serve God faithfully. But their children— the next generation—did not personally witness the manifest power of God, nor did they faithfully embrace His Word. As a result, "everyone did what was right in his own eyes" (Judg. 17:6)—a situation that we see manifesting more and more in our country today. The body of Christ in America needs revival! And a wholehearted return to the Word of God in our homes will pave the way for God to pour out His Holy Spirit in America. Paul said to Timothy, who was a strong leader in the early church, "when I call to remembrance the genuine faith that is in you, which dwelt first in your grandmother Lois and Your mother Eunice, and I am persuaded is in you also" (2 Tim. 1:5). Timothy's mother and grandmother both modeled faith in God and in His holy Word for

Timothy. What better legacy can a parent and grandparent leave a child? Paul went on to say to young Timothy in 2 Timothy 3:15-17:

> and that from childhood you have known the Holy Scriptures, which are able to make you wise for salvation through faith which is in Christ Jesus. (16) All Scripture is given by inspiration of God, and is profitable for doctrine, for reproof, for correction, for instruction in righteousness, (17) that the man of God may be complete, thoroughly equipped for every good work.

It is incumbent upon parents and grandparents to "train up a child in the way he should go, and when he is old he will not depart from it" (Pr. 22:6). Again, Deuteronomy 4:9 says, "Only take heed to yourself, and diligently keep yourself, lest you forget the things your eyes have seen, and lest they depart from your heart all the days of your life. And teach them to your children and your grandchildren."

Kim and I read Bible stories to our children, and they love to do role play and act out Bible stories. Also, when each of our children were very young I began teaching them Bible verses when I put them to bed each night. They did not want me to leave the room, so I had (and still have) their full attention. By age two and one half, Emma could quote the Lord's Prayer, Psalm 23, as well as a few other verses. A child's memory is sharp at that age, and they are very impressionable, so teaching the Word of God to your children as soon as possible is imperative. Then one day, when our children become young adults, as Psalm 127 indicates, we will be able to aim and shoot them as sharp arrows into the world to make a godly difference. I pray that you, reader, as well as Kim and myself, will always be able to truthfully claim the following regarding our children—"I have no greater joy than to hear that my children walk in truth" (3 Jn. 4). Indeed, nothing can make a parent happier.

The Age of Accountability

The age of accountability is when a person is old enough to know right from wrong. When this age is reached, the person needs to be saved, or born again (Jn. 3:3; Rom. 10:9-10). Otherwise, if the person dies, he or she will be eternally lost. So at what age is the age of accountability typically reached? Certainly it differs for each child. But my opinion is that perhaps as early as age two and probably by age five (under normal conditions), a child has reached the age of accountability. Children at this age will likely know right from wrong to a certain degree, and will choose wrong. That is sin. James 4:17 says, "Therefore, to him who knows to do good and does not do it, to him it is sin." So it is imperative to share Scriptures as well as the plan of salvation with your children as soon as possible. When Anna was two and a half years old, she began to repeatedly tell me that she did not know the Lord. This concerned me, so I more diligently began teaching her about the Bible and praying for her. Then one night as I was praying with Anna, I felt led by God to explain the gospel to her right then. As I was explaining to Anna that Jesus died to take away her sins, Anna began repeatedly exclaiming that the Lord was taking away her sins right then! She said she felt the Lord touch her and take away her sins! Praise the Lord! She was about thirty-four months old at the time. Since that moment, when I ask Anna if she knows the Lord, she always says, "Yes!" I believe Emma also received Jesus as her Savior when she was around the same age. Praise God for that! And now comes the continuous, life-long work of discipleship.

Children Need Protection from Evil Influences

Evil content of any sort that enters one's mind can quench the Holy Spirit within. Internet, satellite TV, cable TV, network channels, primetime shows, movies, and commercials regularly display themes of murder, violence, premarital sex, adultery, fornication, homosexuality, and witchcraft. These themes hinder the renewal of one's mind and can desensitize one to horrific matters that ought to be considered inappropriate for societal entertainment.

The Gossip Girl Series is a series of books written for teen girls that have sold more than two million copies; the first was produced in 2002 and the eleventh in 2007. Messages of the book include lesbianism sex is cool, value is found in status rather than in one's character, there are no boundaries, promiscuity is acceptable, and with enough money you can get away with anything.[53] Each of these messages oppose God's Word.

---

[53] Jill Rigby, *Raising Respectful Children in a Disrespectful World*. (Howard Books, 2006), 120.

The Harry Potter book series is the best-selling book series ever, selling over 450 million copies by June 2011,[54] and it is highly read by young, impressionable kids and teens. Peter Chattaway writes, "Harry exhibits a flagrant disregard for rules,"[55] which advocates disrespect for authority. Also, the material embraces subjective morality rather than absolute truth. The series blurs the line between good and evil.[56] Furthermore, it glorifies sorcery. Deuteronomy 18:10-12 says that those who practice sorcery and witchcraft, among other things, "are an abomination to the LORD" (verse 12). Gossip Girls, Harry Potter, and other such material are inappropriate for Christian entertainment.

It has been reported that seventy-five percent of twelve year olds watch R-rated movies at least once per month and that ninety percent of seven year olds watch PG-13 movies regularly (a PG-13 movie today would likely have received an R rating around 1994). Sixty-five percent of these kids said their parents allowed them to see such movies.[57]

Before the age of eighteen, the average child will witness over 200,000 acts of violence on television, including 16,000 murders.[58] The average time that an American kid spends watching television each day is four hours. Children spend more time watching television than any other activity except sleep.[59]

Parents need to exercise godly discernment concerning the types of television shows and movies their children watch, what kind of music they listen to, what kind of literature they read, and what websites they visit. Philippians 4:8 gives the criteria for appropriate Christian thought—"Finally, brethren, whatever things are true, whatever things are noble, whatever things are just, whatever things are pure, whatever things are lovely, whatever things are of good report, if there is any virtue and if there is anything praiseworthy—meditate on these things." Again, Psalm 101:3a says, "I will set nothing wicked before my eyes."

---

[54] *Harry Potter.* Wikipedia.

[55] Peter Chattaway, "Harry Potter and the Prisoner of Azkaban", in *Christianity Today*, April 24, 2004.

[56] Jill Rigby, *Raising Respectful Children in a Disrespectful World*, 122.

[57] Ibid., 133-134.

[58] *American Psychiatric Association Report*, 2004.

[59] A.C. Huston and J.C. Wright, "Television and socialization of young children," in T. MacBeth, ed., *Tuning in to Young Viewers* (Thousand Oaks, CA.: Sage), 37-40.

Also parents need to guard what kind of friendships they allow their children to have. Proverbs 12:26 says, "The righteous should choose his friends carefully, for the way of the wicked leads them astray." If I spend day upon day and year upon year training my children in the Word of God, teaching them to have good manners and respect for others, why would I let that positive investment begin to unravel by sending my children to a school where they will be exposed to other children many of whom were not trained in such a manner? First Corinthians 15:33 says, "Do not be deceived: 'Evil company corrupts good habits.'" Children are impressionable, and I am responsible for the impressions my children receive. Proverbs 13:20 says: "He who walks with wise men will be wise, but the companion of fools will be destroyed." If our children are around wise people, then wisdom will accrue to our children. But if our children are allowed to become regular companions of fools (and a fool is someone who "has said in his heart, 'There is no God...'", Ps. 14:1), then destruction is heading toward our children. A few weeks ago, a mother leveled accusations against my wife for our choosing to homeschool our children. One of her arguments was that homeschooled children are sheltered from the problems of society, so when they turn eighteen and are exposed to the real world, they won't be able to cope. I strongly disagree. First Peter 1:16 says: "Be holy for I am holy." Holy means, in part, to be set apart from that which is ungodly. Second Corinthians 6:14 and 17 say, "Do not be unequally yoked together with unbelievers. For what fellowship has righteousness with lawlessness? And what communion has light with darkness?...come out from among them and *be separate*...." Even though a child is properly trained by the parents, when a child is in a secular school system thirty to forty hours per week, nine months per year where they are exposed to rampant profanity, disrespect for authority, sexually mature and immoral conversation, pornography, homosexuality, alcoholism, marijuana, other drugs, violence, secular curriculum, and a worldly mindset in general, is that not going to be a substantial influence on that child? It certainly will be.

I am not saying that all parents must homeschool. There are financially-strapped families and single parent homes, and in such situations, homeschooling perhaps cannot be realized (I certainly salute those mothers who must work full-time to make ends meet.). We are blessed that Kim is a stay-at-home mother and has the time to homeschool. Who could better train one's children than the one who best knows them and most loves them?—their mother (of course with the assistance of the father). But I believe that such lengthy exposure of a child at school to ungodliness is dangerous. The parent who sends the child to a secular school must be even more diligent to train that child in righteousness to combat the corruption that will necessarily come from evil company in the school. But whether one's children are in public school, private school, or are homeschooled, we parents are responsible for the types of influence to which our children are exposed.

Parenting is a wonderful privilege, and children are a reward from God. Children can bring great joy to parents and great blessing to a marriage. Parents have the opportunity to perpetuate the legacy of their faith through their children. And the raising of a child will hopefully draw husband and wife even closer to each other. Parenting should also be seen as a stewardship from God. God has entrusted these little ones into our care, and we parents are fully responsible to God for our children's upbringing. May we who are parents fully embrace the opportunity and responsibility that parenting requires. May we invest in our children by giving them the quality and quantity time that they desire and need. May we diligently teach our children the Bible with diligence, daily. May we model for our children the righteousness that God requires of His redeemed people. May we protect our children from ungodly influence. And at the right time, when our children turn into young adults, may we send them out into the world, fully trained and fully equipped to glorify God and advance His kingdom in all they say and do.

Chapter 9

Biblical Definitions of "Love"

"God is love" (1 Jn. 4:8b).

The *Chicago Tribune* newspaper reports the following story. In 1994, during Randy and Victoria's engagement, Randy's doctor said he needed a kidney transplant. The doctor told the couple that each year only 4,000 kidneys are available for 36,000 people who need them. Therefore, the doctor said his best option is to acquire a kidney from a family member because they usually provide the best match. But when Randy's family was tested, no adequate match was found. Therefore, Victoria volunteered to be tested for a match, and the results revealed that she was an excellent match. Randy and Victoria were married in October 1994, and in November, in what is believed to be the first husband–wife organ swap in the United States, Victoria gave her husband her kidney. Their marriage literally depended upon her sacrifice for its survival.

Godly marriages thrive when each spouse is willing to subordinate his or her own personal desires and ambitions to the will of God and for the benefit of the other. Acts 20:35 says, "It is more blessed to give than to receive." You can give without loving, but you cannot love without giving. John 3:16 expresses this well: "For God so *loved* the world that He *gave* His only begotten Son, that whoever believes in Him should not perish but have everlasting life." Again, Ephesians 5:25 says: "Husbands, love your wives, just as Christ also *loved* the church and *gave* Himself for her." So love requires sacrifice—giving of oneself for the benefit of the other. We also see this in 1 John 3:16, a verse which articulates the core meaning of love: "By this we know love, because He laid down His life for us. And we also ought to lay down our lives for the brethren." Jesus, the divine Bridegroom, willingly laid down His life to save the church, His bride. This is love—Jesus died for His bride! Likewise, each husband ought to lay down his life for his wife! Anything less is not love. First Peter 2:21 says, "Christ also suffered for us, leaving us an example, that you should follow His steps." Again, each of us needs to see Jesus Christ as our example, our ultimate role-model, our Source of strength, and the standard by which we should daily live. Though such giving and sacrifice may sound miserable, difficult, or impossible, remember that you can never out-give God. Luke 6:38 says, "Give, and it will be given to you: good measure, pressed down, shaken together, and running over will be put into you bosom. For with the same measure that you use, it will be measured back to you." Sacrifice of self for obedience to the Savior will in turn allow the Savior to supply your every need.

This chapter aids our pursuit of the understanding of love by focusing on the biblical words that we translate *love*. We will first look at the Hebrew words used for love in the Old Testament, and then the Greek words used for love in the New Testament.

Love in the Old Testament

The most common Old Testament word we translate as love (with approximately 162 appearances) is *ahab* (other forms include *aheb* and *ahabah*). It means "to have affection for,... love, like, friend."[60] It appears in what is considered the greatest Old Testament commandment, found in Deuteronomy 6:5: "You shall *love* the LORD your God with all your heart, with all your soul, and with all your strength." It also appears in reference to romantic love, as in Genesis 29:20: "So Jacob served seven

---

[60] James Strong, LL.D., S.T.D., *The New Strong's Exhaustive Concordance of the Bible*, (Thomas Nelson Publishers, Nashville, 1984), 660-661, 9.

years for Rachel, and they seemed only a few days to him because of the *love* he had for her." But *ahab* can also refer to love for things; thus, it appears at the place in Genesis 27:4 where Isaac said to Esau, "And make me savory food, such as I *love*...." So the range of meaning of *ahab* is broad. Another word we transliterate as love is *rayah*; it typically means "a female associate," such as a wife, companion, or friend.[61] It appears approximately nine times, all in Song of Solomon and in reference to the Shulamite, the wife of King Solomon. Another word, *dod*,[62] appears as love three times, such as in Proverbs 7:18—"Come let us take our fill of *love* until morning...." This is a negative use of the word love, as these are the words of an immoral woman trying to entice a man into committing adultery with her. Another word that appears three times and is translated love is *chashaq*.[63] It is used of the love between God and a believer, such as in Psalm 91:14, "Because he has set his *love* upon Me, therefore I will deliver him...." (It also appears in Deuteronomy 7:7 and Isaiah 38:17.) Three other Hebrew words which are translated as love and appear only once each in the Old Testament are: *egeb*[64] (appears in Ezek. 33:31), *chabad*[65] (in Dt. 33:3), and *racham*[66] (in Ps. 18:1). So approximately seven words are used for love in the Old Testament, and their meanings can be quite diverse. Let's now look at the three New Testament Greek words which we translate as love.

Love in the New Testament

Love is a word that has a wide range of meanings in today's society, and it is often used in ways that are a far cry from the meaning of the main New Testament word for love. Marie writes to Jimmy, "Dearest Jimmy, no words could ever express the great unhappiness I've felt since I broke off our engagement. Please say you'll take me back. No one could ever take your place in my heart, so please forgive me. I love you, I love you, I love you! Yours forever, Marie...P.S. Congratulations

---

[61] James Strong, LL.D., S.T.D., *The New Strong's Exhaustive Concordance of the Bible*, (Thomas Nelson Publishers, Nashville, 1984), 660, 109.

[62] Ibid., 660, 30.

[63] Ibid., 660, 44.

[64] Ibid., 660, 85.

[65] Ibid., 661, 36.

[66] Ibid., 660, 108.

on winning the state lottery!" Marie is insincere when she says that she loves Jimmy; rather, she lusts after his money. In another example, one might say, "I love ice cream" or "I love University of Kentucky basketball." It might be better to say one likes these things, unless of course one is willing to lay down one's life for either of them. Again, during an emotionally charged movie, a young man may tell his girlfriend "I love you," but whether or not he really loves her will be revealed by the way he daily treats her. These examples illustrate the often-superficial use of the word love in today's society. But what does the New Testament say about love?

Phileo is one of the Greek New Testament verbs that we translate love. Philadelphia, the city of brotherly love, derives its name from *phileo*, which typically means "to be a friend to...fond of...have affection for."[67] This word appears in 1 Thessalonians 4:9: "But concerning brotherly *love* (*philadelphias*) you have no need that I should write to you...." It also occurs in Hebrews 13:1: "Let brotherly *love* continue...." *Philanthropia* is the related Greek New Testament noun, from which we get the English word *philanthropy*. Again, *phileo* means love, and *anthropos* means man. Webster's defines philanthropy as "Altruistic concern for human beings, especially as manifested by donations of money, property, or work to needy persons or to institutions advancing human welfare."[68] *Philanthropian* is translated as *kindness* in Acts 28:2—"And the natives showed us unusual *kindness*; for they kindled a fire and made us all welcome, because of the rain that was falling and because of the cold." Variants of *phileo* or *philanthropia* occur about nineteen times in the New Testament.

Agape is the most common word translated love in the New Testament, appearing 253 times: 137 times as a verb and 116 times as a noun, emphasizing that love should lead to action or demonstration. (For example, Galatians 5:13b says, "through love serve one another.") James Grant defines love as "*a spiritual quality that manifests itself in a decision of the will.*"[69] Another way of saying this is: *Agape love is a spiritual quality that manifests itself when a person chooses to put others ahead of himself.* Let's break the definition down into two parts.

---

[67] James Strong, LL.D., S.T.D., *The New Strong's Exhaustive Concordance of the Bible*, (Thomas Nelson Publishers, Nashville, 1984), 661, 76.

[68] *Webster's American Dictionary*, (Second College Edition. Random House, Inc. 2000), 593.

[69] James Grant, in conversation with me.

One, love is a spiritual quality. In other words, love is a fruit of the Spirit (Gal. 5:22-23). One must have the Holy Spirit—thus, one must be a Christian in order to bear *agape* love. Colossians 1:17b says, "in Him all things consist" (or "hold together"—NASB). "Him" is Christ, and Christ is love (1 Jn. 4:8). As you, day by day, consecrate your marriage unto Christ, He can hold you together! Let me illustrate. It appears that braided hair consists of two strands. But a braid cannot consist of just two strands because it would unravel. A third strand must be utilized to hold the two strands together. That third strand can represent the Word of God and the Lord Jesus Christ, both of which are absolutely necessary for the husband and wife to consistently hold together in *agape* love.

I do affirm that nonbelievers can love. For example, a nonbeliever can genuinely care for and sacrifice for the sake of his children; that is love. A nonbeliever in the military may lay down his life for his comrades; that is love. But love is not *agape* unless the person exhibiting love abides in Christ—after all, in John 15:5 Jesus said, "apart from Me you can do nothing." *Agape* love is blind to who the other person is, which can be exemplified when a Christian missionary goes overseas to minister to strangers, or when a church volunteer donates numerous hours at a soup kitchen. *Agape* love empowers a believer to love his enemies, to bless from his heart those who curse him, to do good to those who hate him, and to pray for those who despitefully use him and persecute him (Mt. 6:44). While Jesus hung on the cross, He prayed for those who were insulting and murdering Him by saying, "Father, forgive them, for they do not know what they do" (Lk. 23:34). *Agape* love includes forgiving others no matter how badly you have been mistreated by them.

The First Epistle of John has much to say about *agape* love. First John 4:7-8 says, "Beloved, let us love one another, for love is of God; and everyone who loves is born of God and knows God. He who does not love does not know God, for *God is love*." *Agape* love does not fizzle out, for its source is infinite—God. One cannot manufacture *agape* love out of one's flesh. God is the source and supplier of *agape* love; therefore, only as one abides in God can one abide in love. First John 5:3a says: "For this is the love of God, that we keep His commandments." Again, love is more than a mere sentiment or a feeling; love requires obedience to God. John 14:15 reiterates this: "If you love Me, keep My commandments." First John 3:17 shows how one must also extend love to one's needy neighbor: "But whoever has this world's goods, and sees his brother in need, and shuts up his heart from him, how does the love of God abide in him?" Two conditions are mentioned here: 1) if one has this world's goods, and 2) if one sees his brother in need. When these two conditions arise, one does not need to pray about it, seek counsel about it, or delay. One should demonstrate the love of God by helping one's brother in need. If one shuts up his heart toward helping his brother, then one does not have the love of God in his heart. First John 3:14 says: "We know that we have passed from death to life, because we love the brethren. He who does not love His brother abides in death." To refuse to help one's brother when one has the ability to do so is to hate one's brother. First John 4:20-21 says: "If someone says, 'I love God,' and hates his brother, he is a liar; for he who does not love his brother whom he has seen, how can he love God whom he has not seen? And this commandment we have from Him: that he who loves God must love his brother also." We must do everything within our power to make our horizontal relationships right (with our brother) if we expect to have our vertical relationship right (with God).

Second, love is a choice. In early March 2003, Los Angeles Lakers basketball coach Phil Jackson underwent treatment for a kidney stone. The anesthesiologist leaned over the coach and said, "We named your kidney stone 'Kobe.'" (Kobe Bryant was a great player for the Lakers.) "Why?" asked Coach Jackson. The anesthesiologist replied, "Because it's not passing." As the kidney stone was not passing, Kobe was not passing the ball, according to the anesthesiologist; but then again, Kobe was that good. In marriage, none of us are that good. We must each pass the ball, meaning we must each choose to share, serve, and give to our spouse. We must choose to include our spouse in our time, attention, efforts, and plans.

I will use my own marriage as an example. Every time I interact with my wife, Kim, I have a choice to make—whether or not my attitude and behavior will be in accordance with loving her. If circumstances do not turn out as I want, will I speak to Kim with a kind tone or not? When I come home from work, will I typically choose to spend some quality time with my family or will I instead choose self-centered activities? If Kim is falling short in some area of her life, will I demonstrate patience and encouragement toward her or will I regularly harp on her failure in that particular area? Consider how other-centered the following verses are and how our meditating on them can shape the attitude we can have toward our spouse. Philippians 2:3-4 says, "Let nothing be done through selfish ambition or conceit, but in lowliness of mind let each esteem *others* better than himself. Let each of you look out not only for his own interests, but also for the interests of *others*." First Corinthians 10:24 says, "Let no one seek his own, but each one the *other's* well-being." These other-centered verses show me that I am to esteem Kim better than myself, to look out for her interests over my own, and to seek her well-being over my own. Again, Romans 14:21 says, "nor do anything by which your brother stumbles or is offended or is made weak." I am never to cause Kim to stumble; instead, I want to help her to have sure footing in every step of her life. I am never to offend Kim; instead, I am to consistently encourage and edify her. I am never to make Kim weak; instead, I am to inspire her to look to Christ for her strength. First Corinthians 16:14 says, "Let all that you do be done with love." So there is never a time when it is acceptable for me to quit honoring Kim and preferring her above myself. At the end of my life, I want Kim, my children, and others who know me well, including the Lord, to be able to truthfully say, "More than how often or how well Tom preached, more than how much money Tom earned, or what accolades Tom may have received, what most characterized Tom (as a Christian, husband, daddy, son, brother, and minister) was that he was continuously a man of godly love." My priorities for my life are as follows: I want to be an excellent Christian, excellent husband, excellent father, and excellent minister, in that order. Excellence, first and foremost, requires love, because love is the greatest quality of all.

Love is "above all." Colossians 3:14 says, "*above all* these things put on *love,* which is the bond of perfection." First Peter 4:8 says, "*above all* things have fervent *love* for one another, for '*love* will cover a multitude of sins.'" First Corinthians 13:13 says, "And now abide faith, hope, *love*, these three; but *the greatest of these is love.*" And the two greatest commandments in the Bible, stated in Matthew 22:37-39, again emphasize that love is the top priority: "You shall *love* the LORD your God with all your heart, with all your soul, and with all your mind. This is the first and great commandment. And the second is like it: You shall *love* your neighbor as yourself." Indeed, love is the greatest Christian virtue one can possess! Are you and your spouse willing to put Christ and His Word at the center of your marriage (if that's not already the case)? What are some practical ways that you can choose to esteem your spouse ahead of yourself today? How can you improve your relationship with God so that you are empowered to love your spouse better?

Chapter 10

An Exposition of 1 Corinthians 13

Though I speak with the tongues of men and of angels, but have not love, I have become sounding brass or a clanging cymbal. (2) And though I have the gift of prophecy, and understand all mysteries and all knowledge, and though I have all faith, so that I could remove mountains, but have not love, I am nothing. (3) And though I bestow all my goods to feed the poor, and though I give my body to be burned, but have not love, it profits me nothing. (4) Love suffers long and is kind; love does not envy; love does not parade itself, is not puffed up; (5) does not behave rudely, does not seek its own, is not provoked, thinks no evil; (6) does not rejoice in iniquity, but rejoices in the truth; (7) bears all things, believes all things, hopes all things, endures all things. (8) Love never fails. But whether there are prophecies, they will fail; whether there are tongues, they will cease; whether there is knowledge, it will vanish away. (9) For we know in part and we prophesy in part. (10) But when that which is perfect has come, then that which is in part will be done away. (11) When I was a child, I spoke as a child, I understood as a child, I thought as a child; but when I became a man, I put away childish things. (12) For now we see in a mirror, dimly, but then face to face. Now I know in part, but then I shall know just as I also am known. (13) And now abide faith, hope, love, these three; but the greatest of these is love.

A man driving his car noticed a female driver tailgating him. As he approached an intersection, the light turned yellow. Instead of speeding through the intersection, he appropriately stopped for the yellow light. The woman behind him became furious—she honked, yelled obscenities, and displayed the middle finger. Immediately, a policeman's blue lights flashed behind the lady. When she pulled through the intersection and to the side of the road the policeman arrested her. He took her to the police station where she was fingerprinted, photographed, and placed in a holding cell. A few hours later, the arresting officer brought her out, returned her belongings and said, "Ma'am, you are free to go." The lady, very upset, asked, "Why did you arrest me?" He replied, "I noticed the bumper stickers on your car: 'What Would Jesus Do?,' 'Choose Life,' 'Follow Me To Sunday School,' and the ichthus fish symbol. And when I saw how terribly angry you became toward the other driver, I assumed you had stolen the car."

The woman was a hypocrite, having bumper stickers on her car that promoted following Christ, but behaving in a way contrary to the example of Christ. In John 13:35, Jesus said, "By this all will know that you are My disciples, if you have love for one another." Love, the first and greatest of the fruit of the Spirit, should always be evident in the life of a Christian, and it should be foundational to the marriage relationship.

First Corinthians 13, often referred to as "The Love Chapter," is sandwiched between two chapters dealing with the spiritual gifts, chapters 12 and 14. Chapter 12 lists the nine gifts of the Spirit: gifts such as faith, healing, prophesy, and tongues, which are of great value to the body of Christ. For instance, if one operates in the gift of healing and is used by God to deliver a fellow believer from cancer, what a great lift that would be to the person healed as well as a great witness to others of Christ's power! Chapter 14, verse 1 says, "desire spiritual gifts." Chapter 12, verse 31 says, "earnestly desire the best gifts." Even though we believers should desire to cultivate the use of these gifts of the Spirit, we should never lose sight of what 12:31 calls "a more excellent way." God has put between these two chapters on spiritual gifts a chapter on love—the excellent way—because love should be central to all we do. First Corinthians 16:14 says, "Let all that you do be done with love."

Verses 1-3 of 1 Corinthians 13 mention several spiritual gifts and noble acts. Verse 1 mentions *tongues*. Chapter 14, verse 5 says, "I wish you all spoke with tongues...." Chapter 14, verse 18 says, "I thank my God I speak with tongues more than you all." So tongues are a spiritual blessing that each believer should desire. Verse 2 speaks of *prophecy*. The office of prophet is an honorable office, ranking second in the fivefold ministry (Eph. 4:11). Chapter 14, verse 9 says, "Desire earnestly to prophesy...." Verse 2 speaks of *knowledge*. Obviously, knowledge is necessary for successful living, especially knowledge of the Bible so one knows the will and ways of God. Hosea 4:6 says, "My people are destroyed for lack of knowledge." Verse 2 also speaks of *faith*. One cannot go to heaven without faith in Jesus Christ (Rom. 10:9), nor can one walk in a way pleasing to our Lord without faith (Heb. 11:6). Furthermore, faith is the prerequisite for answered prayers and miracles—Mark 9:23 says, "All things are possible to him who believes." Verse 3 speaks of *generosity to the poor.* The World Bank estimates that 1.2 billion people in the world are trying to survive on an income of one dollar or less per day.[70] First John 3:17 says, "Whoever has this world's goods, and sees his brother in need, and shuts up his heart from him, how does the love of God abide in him?" Verse 3 also speaks of *martyrdom*. The New Testament persons Stephen, James, Antipas, and Jesus were all martyrs, and through their ultimate sacrifice—that of their lives—the gospel of Jesus Christ was greatly advanced.

Once my sister-in-law, Sara, attempted to make a coconut custard pie. When the delicious-looking pie came out of the oven and the first bite was taken, Sara quickly realized that a main ingredient had been accidentally omitted—sugar. Therefore, she called her dish "quiche" and the family ate it just the same. As sugar is a necessary ingredient for pie, love is a necessary ingredient for any ministry or marriage that is pleasing to God. Love is an imperative for the Christian, a non-negotiable. The phrase "but have not love" is repeated three times in the first three verses to emphasize this point.

James Grant once said that love is like the banks of a fast-flowing river. As long as the river remains within the banks, all is well—the river can be utilized for good purposes. But if a river gets outside of its banks, then the river temporarily becomes a liability rather than an asset, as it may flood homes, businesses, etc. All spiritual gifts, all ministries, and all that is done in the name of Jesus must emanate from a heart of love for it to be pleasing to God.

In summary, verses 1-3 say that if one speaks in tongues, prophesies, has all knowledge, has all faith, is generous, and is a martyr, but lacks

---

[70] World Bank, *World Bank Development Report 2003* (Washington, DC: International Bank for Reconstruction and Development, 2002), 3.

the necessary ingredient of God's love in one's heart, then that person is nothing, a zero in God's eyes. Furthermore, "it profits him nothing," meaning that he will receive no treasure in heaven for any of his love-void efforts at ministry and marriage. If love is absent, then the motive by which the ministry is done may be pride, self-glory, fear, or something else contrary to the heart of God. Such "ministry," if it remains void of love, will at some point be recognized as hypocritical and will become a liability to the body of Christ. Therefore, the proper priority concerning the spiritual gifts and various ministries is expressed in Galatians 5:6—what avails is *"faith working through love."* Again, when faith, like a river, flows within the boundaries of love, then great things can happen for the kingdom of God. Another way of putting it is: Bearing the nine fruit of the Spirit (Gal. 5:22-23), especially the first and most important fruit, love, is a greater priority than operating in the nine gifts of the Spirit.

Verses 4-8 contain a list of phrases that helps shape the definition of love. These phrases describe what love is and what love is not.

"Love suffers long" (verse 4)

The all-purpose lubricant/cleaner/polisher WD-40 gets its name from "Water Displacement" and the number of experiments needed to get it right. In other words, there were thirty-nine attempts that did not work. Imagine if the inventor of WD-40 had given up at thirty-nine tries; the world would then not have had WD-40. But the inventor's perseverance paid off. Likewise, a successful marriage requires perseverance—a willingness to hang in there during times of trial within the marriage. One must be willing to suffer a long time without getting into the flesh, such as by becoming anxious, stressed, or impatient. The NIV reads, "Love is patient." In certain circumstances, you will have to wait until things turn your way, and those who are patient are willing to do that. Your waiting includes humbling yourself and enduring until God gives you the victory. Psalm 27:14 says, "Wait on the LORD; be of good courage, and He shall strengthen your heart; wait, I say, on the LORD!" James 1:2-4 says: "My brethren, count it all joy when you fall into various trials, knowing that the testing of your faith produces *patience*. But let *patience* have its perfect work, that you may be perfect and complete, lacking nothing." Though counting your trials as joyful is not natural, God exhorts you to do this because you then are acknowledging that God is sovereign over your trials and circumstances, that there is divine purpose in your trials and circumstances, and that you need to participate with God in what He is doing at that moment. You should pray, "Lord, make me a willing vessel during this time of trial so You can make me more like Christ and accomplish Your purposes through me." God promises that "all things work together for good to those who love God, to those who are called according to His purpose" (Rom. 8:28). Longsuffering, or patience, includes consistently putting the other person first, whether that person is God, your fellow man, or your spouse.

"(Love) is kind"

The story is told that an elderly widow, restricted in her activities, was eager to serve Christ through acts of kindness. After praying about this, she realized that she could be a blessing to others by utilizing her skill of playing the piano. The next day she placed a small ad in the newspaper: "Pianist will play hymns by phone daily for those who are sick or dejected. The service is free." The notice included her phone number. When people called, she would ask, "What hymn would you like to hear?" Within a few months, her playing had brought encouragement to many people. Often, callers opened up to her about their problems and she was able to offer them hope from the Scriptures.

Kindness refers to the desire to do good to someone. In marriage, you can test whether or not you are kind by asking yourself the following questions: Do I consistently prefer my spouse above myself? Do I consider my spouse's desires and plans above my own (unless of course they go against God's plans)? Am I generous toward my spouse? Do I pray for my spouse? Do I do the little things to help my spouse? Do I have a good attitude toward my spouse? Ephesians 4:32 says, "And be *kind* to one another, tenderhearted, forgiving one another even as God in Christ forgave you." Here kindness is positioned close to forgiveness. Certainly you should demonstrate kindness by being quick to forgive your spouse when your spouse has failed. "Kindness" again appears in Colossians 3:12: "Therefore, as the elect of God, holy and beloved, put on tender mercies, *kindness*, humility, meekness, longsuffering...." You are to "put on" kindness because, as with the other fruit of the Spirit, kindness is a choice as well as a spiritual quality (Gal. 5:22-23). You should *choose* kindness, and you should abide in Christ to be empowered to be kind. When you are kind, you emulate Christ—"Psalm 63:3 says: "Your *lovingkindness* is better than life." What are some ways that God has demonstrated kindness to you?

The next several phrases are the "do not's" of love. These are negative, selfish, and prideful attitudes or qualities that a man or woman of God would certainly want to resist.

"Love does not envy"

To not be envious means to not be jealous, to not begrudge another person's success. Envy should not exist within the marriage relationship. If your spouse has many friends or acquires accolades, do not become jealous of your spouse because of that. (This does not mean your spouse should pursue intimate friendships with the opposite sex. You *should* have a problem with that.) Psalm 37:4 says, "Delight yourself also in the LORD and He will give you the desires of your heart." If God sees that you genuinely delight in Him rather than delighting primarily in the things and persons of this natural earthly realm, then He will see to it that your heart's desires will be met. (Matthew 6:33 emphasizes this.) Then you will experience fulfillment and contentment so that you will not need to look at how God has prospered your spouse or anyone else with an envious eye.

"Love does not parade itself"

On May 1, 1991, Major League Baseball player Ricky Henderson broke Lou Brock's record for stolen bases in a career: 939! That day, Henderson said, "Lou Brock was a great base stealer, but today I am the greatest of all time." However, Henderson's historic moment was somewhat overshadowed because on the same day, Nolan Ryan (at age forty-four) pitched his seventh career no-hitter! Proverbs 27:2 says, "Let another man praise you, and not your own mouth...." Therefore, do not say boastful things to your spouse or anyone else, nor be a showoff. If God wants you to receive recognition for your accomplishments, then He will have someone other than you acknowledge them. The Bible never gives you license to exalt yourself. God does the exalting, and He exalts those who humble themselves. Luke 18:14 says, "For everyone who exalts himself will be humbled, and he who humbles himself will be exalted."

"(Love) is not puffed up"

The NIV says "is not proud." The middle letter in "pride" is the same as the middle letter in "sin," "crime, and "anxiety"—"I." Pride is perhaps the fundamental sin—the root cause of the various sins one can commit. Pride occurs when one promotes self—"I"— above others and God. Coach Pat Riley wrote a book in 1981, *The Disease of Me Leads to the Defeat of Us*, after the Los Angeles Lakers basketball team, of which he was the coach, was defeated in the first round of the NBA playoffs. They had won the championship the year before and were expected to repeat. Perhaps they had too much pride, which allowed complacency to set in, which led to their fall. Webster's defines pride as "a high or inordinate opinion of one's own importance or superiority; conceit."[71] Pride is the exaltation of oneself, which is, in a sense, seeking to be one's own god. Adam and Eve exalted themselves when they yielded to the serpent's enticement to deny God's holy Word and attempt to be like God. That turned out to be spiritually fatal for them and for the rest of mankind. Because God is Creator and we are His creatures, it is the height of wisdom to honor Him and submit ourselves completely to His will. Husband and wife should remain humble before God and toward each other. First Corinthians 8:1 says: "Knowledge puffs up, but love builds up." Love, the bond of perfection in marriage, is not self-inflated, not full of self-importance, nor prideful. Instead, love is demonstrated through humility and service to your spouse and others.

"(Love) does not behave rudely" (verse 5)

Friday at quitting time, Jim said, "Boss, do you have any extra work I can do tonight?" The boss replied, "I sure do, but I can't pay you overtime." Jim said, "That's okay, I just don't want to go home." The

[71] *Webster's American Dictionary*, Second College Edition, (Random House, Inc. 2000), 626.

boss replied, "Why not?" Jim said, "I've been in the doghouse since last night." The boss replied, "What did you do to deserve that?" Jim said, "I was minding my own business, relaxing in front of the TV. My wife enters the room and asks, 'What's on the TV?' And all I said was, 'Dust!' She's been mad ever since!"

The wife took Jim's answer as rude. Webster's defines rude as "discourteous or impolite…rough in manners or behavior; uncouth."[72] You should not offend your spouse with bad behavior; instead you should be respectful, polite, mature, and honorable. First Peter 2:17a says: "Honor all people…." First Peter 3:8b says: "be courteous." To be courteous to your spouse and to honor your spouse are congruent with Christ's love. Christ is a Gentleman. Gentleness is a fruit of the Spirit (Gal. 5:23), and it is indicative of wisdom that descends from above (Jas. 3:17).

"(Love) does not seek its own"

The NIV says, "is not self-seeking." A story is told of a couple named Ole and Olga who had been married for a long time. Olga said to Ole, "Why don't you ever tell me that you love me?" Ole replied, "When we were married I told you that I loved you. And if I ever change my mind, I'll let you know." Ole could better demonstrate love toward his wife by giving her what she wants—telling her he loves her (assuming he does love her) simply because she wants him to. First Corinthians 10:24 says, "Let no one seek his own, but each one the other's well-being." Love is to put the well-being of the other person above the well-being of oneself. My pastor, Rev. Ernest Fridge, said: "There is a magazine called *Self*. But there should be a magazine called *Others*. God calls us to be a fountain, not a drain." Jesus, who chose to put others first when He embraced His cross, offers to everyone the Gift of the Holy Spirit which He likens to "a fountain of water springing up into everlasting life" (Jn. 4:14).

It is said that Oscar Hammerstein, a famous lyricist for American theater, while on his deathbed sent a note to an actress, Mary Martin, just as she was about to go on stage. The note said, "A bell is not a bell till you ring it. A song is not a song until you sing it. Love in your heart is not put there to stay. Love isn't love till you give it away."

---

[72] *Webster's American Dictionary*, Second College Edition, (Random House, Inc. 2000), 687.

Love requires giving. Husband and wife should regularly give of their time and attention to each other. Love ultimately requires the giving of one's life. As Jesus was crucified, and as Paul said, "I am crucified with Christ," each Christian should also die to selfishness for the sake of doing God's will and for the sake of loving one's neighbor, which includes loving one's spouse.

"(Love) is not provoked"

The NIV says, "is not easily angered." Resist becoming irritable toward your spouse. Certainly, do not entertain unjustified anger; otherwise, you could end up like the 1980s TV personality, David Banner. When he became angry, he turned into the raging and destructive Incredible Hulk. If you allow ungodly anger to simmer within you over a long period of time because you do not appropriately and quickly deal with it, anger can eventually surface to the point that you can become a monster.

On June 1, 2005, Percy (age 105) and Florence (age 100) Arrowsmith celebrated their eightieth wedding anniversary and were considered the world's longest married couple. They met in 1922 in church in Hereford, England; Percy sang in the choir and Florence taught Sunday School. They were married on June 1, 1925. The Arrowsmiths had three children, six grandchildren, and nine great-grandchildren; and they lived in the same house for seventy-eight years. When asked why their marriage has been a success, Florence said they never go to bed on a quarrel. She said, "If you've had a quarrel, you make up—never be afraid to say sorry." Florence continues, "It is all about hard work. We have had our arguments, but we work through them together. We always go to bed as friends and always make up before we go to sleep with a kiss and a cuddle." Percy said that it boils down to two words, "Yes, Dear." Percy died on June 15, 2005, and Florence died April 9, 2007. The Reverend Anthony Priddis said of the couple, "They have been churchgoers all their lives, and I am sure the family will find comfort in their Christian faith."[73]

---

[73] *World's Longest Married Couple Clock Up to 80 Years*, by Nick Britten, (Telegraph Media Group Limited 2012), Jan. 6, 2005. *World's Oldest Married Man Dies*. BBC News, published June, 15, 2005.

One reason the Arrowsmiths were able to sustain eighty-plus years of love for one another was because they practiced forgiveness toward one another. Ephesians 4:26-27 says, "Be angry, and do not sin. Do not let the sun go down on your wrath, nor give place to the devil." Deal quickly with feelings of anger toward your spouse. Make every effort to eradicate them within the same day. Replace anger with reconciliation and peace. If not appropriately dealt with, anger can turn into violence. Domestic violence and child abuse are abhorrent and stand in absolute contrast to the Christian virtue of love.

"(Love) thinks no evil"

On March 26, 2004, the *Lexington Herald Leader* reported that a sixteen-year-old Palestinian was caught by an Israeli roadblock because he was wearing a suicide bomb vest. The boy's parents were upset that he tried to be a suicide bomber and they issued a statement telling Islamic militants to quit recruiting teens. The boy said he wanted to do it because he was small for his age and had been teased by classmates. Furthermore, he said he wanted to go to Paradise. Imagine the evil that had pervaded that boy's mind—the teasing, the peer pressure, and the lies about Paradise. Hopefully he has since learned that Paradise comes only through knowing Jesus Christ.

Romans 8:5-6 indicates that the focus of your thoughts determines whether you are walking in accordance with the desires of the flesh, which leads to death, or whether you are walking in accordance with the Spirit of God, whereby you would have life and peace. Romans 12:2 says: "be transformed by the renewing of your mind…." So your entire being (including your attitude and even how you feel) can be positively affected and transformed when you make the Word of God the focus of your thoughts, motives, and confessions. Again, Proverbs 12:5a says, "The thoughts of the righteous are right." (See also Phil. 4:8 and Col. 3:1.) So you are to love others with your words, actions, and even your thoughts. Do not let negative thoughts about your spouse or your marriage pervade your mind. You should not entertain thoughts such as, "I should not have married this person." Do not entertain thoughts of intimacy or inappropriate companionship with someone who is not your spouse. Husbands and wives, keep your minds saturated with the Word of God. Study the Word of God together and speak it to one another often.

"(Love) does not rejoice in iniquity, but rejoices in the truth" (verse 6)

Pilate asked Jesus, "What is truth? (Jn. 18:38). Pilate was speaking to Truth personified. Jesus Christ is truth (Jn. 14:6). Therefore, when verse 6 says "love rejoices in the truth," this is in accordance with rejoicing in the Lord (Phil. 4:4). Also, God's Word is truth (Jn. 17:17). You are exhorted to put truth on like a belt (Eph. 6:14). As a belt holds up one's pants, truth helps hold up the robe of righteousness, which one wears by faith.

"(Love) bears all things" (verse 7)

This is similar to longsuffering (verse 4). Love does not quit because the road is difficult. Instead, one who walks in love is willing to carry whatever burden is required of her or him, including bearing the burden of another. Galatians 6:2 says, "Bear one another's burdens, and so fulfill the law of Christ." If the husband is temporarily incapacitated—unable to mow his yard or rake the leaves, perhaps the wife can demonstrate love by voluntarily bearing the burden of his yard work. Likewise, if the wife is incapacitated, the husband can cook dinner, clean the kitchen, wash and fold the clothes, and spend extra time with the children. If a spouse is struggling with an issue, then the other spouse's availability to her or him—including emotional and spiritual availability (listening and supporting in prayer), will likely help the spouse achieve the victory he or she needs.

"(Love) believes all things"

The NIV says here "always trusts." In the summer of 2005, Kim was pregnant, and we were living with her parents while we were searching for a house to buy and move into before the baby's due date (November) would arrive. One night, while I was in Denver on business, Kim called me to say she had found a house that met all of our expectations. I sensed great hope and excitement in Kim's voice. However, we would have to put a contract on it by the end of the day because Kim heard that others were planning on putting contracts on it the next day. The house was within our price range and it was a reasonable distance from my work place. Furthermore, Kim was the homemaker, the "nester," and I wanted her to be happy with the house in which she and I would raise and homeschool our children. I reasoned, "If Kim likes it, then it will probably be more than fine with me. Therefore, why not let her have it?" I asked Kim to call me back in a little while so I could pray about the matter. When Kim called back, I agreed that we could put a contract on the house. So Kim faxed me the contract; I signed it and faxed it back. A few days later, Kim picked me up from the airport and drove me to see the house for the first time that I had already committed to buy. I loved it and still do (we still live there). Kim made a great choice as I believed she would. And Kim greatly appreciated my willingness to trust her judgment.

In regard to the virtuous wife of Proverbs 31, the Scripture says, "the heart of her husband safely trusts her" (verse 11a). The virtuous spouse is trustworthy. Faithfulness to one another and consequent trust in one another are imperatives for a strong marriage. Do not be suspicious and untrusting of your spouse when there is no evidence of wrongdoing on your spouse's part. Do not assume the worst concerning your spouse (or for that matter any brother or sister in Christ). Give your spouse the benefit of the doubt. Hope and pray that your spouse is becoming more and more like Jesus—living daily in true righteousness and holiness. Conversely, however, you should not be naïve if clear signs of unrighteous behavior in your spouse appear. Nor should you endorse anything that contradicts God's Word.

"(Love) hopes all things"

Have you been praying for a loved one to get saved? Never give up! Have you felt that your marriage is shaky or crumbling? Never give up! Do you want an excellent marriage? Never give up! Jesus said, "All things are possible to him who believes" (Mark 9:23b). God parted the Red Sea; God caused the walls of Jericho (the enemy city) to fall down; God caused the sun to stand still for a day to allow Joshua to win a battle; God shut the mouths of lions to save Daniel; God protected three Hebrew youth who were cast into the midst of a fiery furnace; God took Elijah to heaven in a fiery chariot so that he did not have to experience death; and God raised Jesus from the dead. So despite barriers, God is a "God of hope," and He fills the faithful Christian "with all joy and peace in believing" (Rom. 15:13a). To the Israelites who were in exile, God said, "'For I know the thoughts that I think toward you,' says the LORD, 'thoughts of peace and not of evil, to give you a future and a *hope*'" (Jer. 29:11). Even though your present circumstances, including your marriage, may not appear hopeful, if you give top priority to obeying and having faith in God's Word, then you can have confidence that the Lord will help and prosper you as He sees fit. God promotes and exalts the one who humbles himself and clings to His Word. Romans 8:28 promises that "all things work together for good to those who love God, to those who are the called according to His purpose." Furthermore, as one lives "soberly, righteously, and godly in the present age," one can look for the "blessed *hope* and glorious appearing of our great God and Savior Jesus Christ" (Titus 2:12-13). The Christian's hope ultimately lies in the total redemption he or she will experience in and through Christ who will make all things new and will give to each one who loves Him a glorified body, and a mansion and treasure in heaven. So the hardships and afflictions of this present life are not endured by the believer in vain, but instead they are "working for us a far more exceeding and eternal weight of glory" (2 Cor. 4:17). That gives us great hope!

"(Love) endures all things"

The NIV says, "Always perseveres." In 2011 in Lexington, Kentucky, a newlywed husband and wife were driving from their wedding to their reception when they were hit by a car that had run a red light. Both husband and wife had to go to the hospital. (The wife had actually been ejected from the car, but neither had life-threatening injuries.)[74] What a rocky start to their marriage! As your life does not always go the way you planned, the same can be said concerning your marriage. When one who approaches the wedding altar has certain high expectations of his or her spouse, and then within weeks, months, or years finds some of those expectations not being fully met by the spouse, one might feel like one's feelings toward one's spouse has experienced a substantial wreck. But such circumstances present the opportunity to love. One who understands the requirements of love as expressed in God's Word and has committed to fulfilling those requirements at all cost does not quit

---

[74] www.wbko.com; posted May 22, 2011

when "the going gets tough" or when things are not playing out as one desires. After all, most marriage vows probably include something along the lines of loving one another and being committed to one another "for better or for worse...as long as we both shall live." Therefore, one spouse ought not be overly critical of the other for perceived failures or shortcomings. Instead, Galatians 6:1 says: "Brethren, if a man (or spouse) is overtaken in any trespass, you who are spiritual *restore such a one in a spirit of gentleness....*" Again, Romans 14:19 says, "Therefore let us pursue the things which make for peace and the things by which one may edify another." Husband and wife should pursue peaceful and mutually edifying solutions to problems. If progress is slow-going in an area of concern, still one needs to patiently endure. Stay the course! Make sure that marital fender-benders do not progress into core engine problems.

"Love never fails" (verse 8)

If you ever feel tempted to think that your marriage is a lost cause and that your only choice is to let your marriage fade away, most likely that is not your only choice. If you will completely surrender your heart, and your marriage, to Christ—submitting to His Lordship and His holy Word (the Bible)—then you, personally, will discover abundant new life and renewed hope. And in doing so, you will be more likely to succeed in restoring your marriage. It does "take two to tango," and your spouse's attitude is certainly a factor in the success of your marriage. But with your new demonstrations of consistent love toward your spouse through Christ, as well as your prayers, your spouse may also find new inspiration concerning your marriage. If both you and your spouse wholeheartedly turn to Christ, then you will discover a newfound love for one another, a real joy, excitement, and a Christ-centered purpose for your marriage. First Corinthians 13:8 says, "*Love never fails....*" First John 4:8 says, "God is love," and certainly God never fails! If you truly abide in God—if you truly love Him, and if you love people (which certainly includes loving your spouse), then you will generally be victorious in life, and God will tremendously bless you. Your blessings and your love will often overflow and spill onto others around you.

Conclusion

Verses 8-12 speak about how prophecy, tongues, and knowledge are not gifts that will last for eternity; they will pass away "when that which is perfect has come" (verse 10). "That which is perfect" is referring to verse 12, which foretells that unimaginably glorious moment when we will see Christ face to face! Then we will have a new and more complete knowledge of God—an eternal knowledge, based on seeing Him directly. Now, however, we only know Christ dimly, or in part. Nevertheless, the best way to prepare for that ultimate face-to-face encounter with the Lord Jesus Christ is to utilize to the fullest degree possible the time we now have on this earth to cultivate a constant attitude of *agape* love toward Christ, toward our fellow man, and toward our spouse. Love is more excellent than the nine gifts of the Spirit, and love is greater than even faith and hope.

Chapter 11

Facets of Love–Part 2

"Grace to you and peace from God our Father and the Lord Jesus Christ" (1 Cor. 1:3).

There are thirteen New Testament epistles whose authorship is attributed to the Apostle Paul. As seen in the verses below, the beginning and ending salutation in each of Paul's epistles always includes his pronouncement of grace to the hearers, regardless of what he expresses within the body of the epistles, whether rebukes or exhortations, or both. Paul also pronounces "peace" in every greeting, and three times he pronounces "mercy" in his greeting. We also see that God the Father and the Lord Jesus Christ are the Source of the grace, mercy, and peace that Paul pronounces at the beginning of each of his epistles. Therefore, one must abide in the Lord to personally experience His grace, mercy, and peace. Unique to his 2 Corinthians epistle, Paul adds "the love of God, and the communion of the Holy Spirit" in his farewell salutation (2 Cor. 13:14), acknowledging all three Persons of the Godhead as the Source of the grace and other spiritual fruit Paul pronounces to the Corinthian believers. The

Corinthian believers were probably in need of these extra words of encouragement.

Paul knew God's amazing grace first-hand. Paul (formerly named Saul) had been a terrorist; he hated Jesus Christ and anyone who followed Him, and he zealously persecuted them. But Jesus Himself appeared to Saul on the road to Damascus and revealed His will to Saul. Saul was forgiven, filled with the Holy Spirit, and called into the ministry. Paul wrote:

> For I am the least of the apostles, who am not worthy to be called an apostle, because I persecuted the church of God. But by the **grace** of God I am what I am, and His **grace** toward me was not in vain; but I labored more abundantly than they all, yet not I, but the **grace** of God *which was* with me (1 Cor. 15:9-10).

Jesus graciously guided, empowered, and protected Paul during his three missionary journeys as he preached the gospel throughout the Gentile world.

Grace is unearned favor; receiving blessings one does not deserve. Mercy is withholding or pardoning the judgments one does deserve. Peace is the absence of enmity and strife. Since God, through Jesus Christ, showers grace, mercy, and peace upon each of His children (and to a large degree upon the unredeemed also), and since each believer is to be an imitator of God (Eph. 5:1), therefore should not each believer likewise maintain a heart of grace, mercy, and peace toward each fellow believer? Yes.

In order to model the grace Paul pronounces in all of his salutations, you should approach each fellow believer with a heart of grace, and you should depart from each fellow believer with a heart of grace. Since God the Holy Spirit indwells each believer, God expects His grace, mercy, and peace to be expressed through each believer toward his fellow believer in every significant interaction they have, whether in person, in written form, via telephone, social media, etc.

Rom. 1:7 To all who are in Rome, beloved of God, called *to be* saints: Grace to you and peace from God our Father and the Lord Jesus Christ.
Rom. 16:24 The grace of our Lord Jesus Christ *be* with you all. Amen.
1 Cor. 1:3 Grace to you and peace from God our Father and the Lord Jesus Christ.

<u>1 Cor. 16:23</u> The grace of our Lord Jesus Christ *be* with you.

<u>2 Cor. 1:2</u> Grace to you and peace from God our Father and the Lord Jesus Christ.

<u>2 Cor. 13:14</u> The grace of the Lord Jesus Christ, and the love of God, and the communion of the Holy Spirit *be* with you all. Amen.

<u>Gal. 1:3</u> Grace to you and peace from God the Father and our Lord Jesus Christ....

<u>Gal. 6:18</u> Brethren, the grace of our Lord Jesus Christ *be* with your spirit. Amen.

<u>Eph. 1:2</u> Grace to you and peace from God our Father and the Lord Jesus Christ.

<u>Eph. 6:24</u> Grace *be* with all those who love our Lord Jesus Christ in sincerity. Amen.

<u>Phil. 1:2</u> Grace to you and peace from God our Father and the Lord Jesus Christ.

<u>Phil. 4:23</u> The grace of our Lord Jesus Christ be with you all. Amen.

<u>Col. 1:2</u> Grace to you and peace from God our Father and the Lord Jesus Christ.

<u>Col. 4:18</u> Grace *be* with you. Amen.

<u>1 Thess 1:1</u> Grace to you and peace from God our Father and the Lord Jesus Christ.

<u>1 Thess. 5:28</u> The grace of our Lord Jesus Christ *be* with you. Amen.

<u>2 Thess. 1:2</u> Grace to you and peace from God our Father and the Lord Jesus Christ.

<u>2 Thess. 3:18</u> The grace of our Lord Jesus Christ *be* with you all. Amen.

<u>1 Tim. 1:2</u> Grace, mercy, *and* peace from God our Father and Jesus Christ our Lord.

<u>1 Tim. 6:21</u> Grace *be* with you. Amen.

<u>2 Tim. 1:2</u> Grace, mercy, *and* peace from God the Father and Christ Jesus our Lord.

<u>2 Tim. 4:22</u> Grace be with you. Amen.

<u>Titus. 1:4</u> Grace, mercy, *and* peace from God the Father and the Lord Jesus Christ our Savior.

<u>Titus. 3:15</u> Grace *be* with you all. Amen.

<u>Philemon 1:3</u> Grace to you and peace from God our Father and the Lord Jesus Christ.

<u>Philemon 1:25</u> The grace of our Lord Jesus Christ *be* with your spirit. Amen.

Interestingly, in Ephesians 6:24, Paul attaches a condition to his pronouncement of grace: the recipients of God's grace are those who love the "Lord Jesus Christ in sincerity." This important condition negates any attempts to justify lukewarm, nominal, hypocritical Christianity. And perhaps some of the Ephesian believers were tempted with insincerity (See Rev. 2:4). Interestingly, only in Paul's greeting to Titus does Paul refer to Jesus as "Savior" in addition to His being "Lord" and "Christ." Scripture only has to say something once for it to be true; indeed Jesus is Lord, Christ, and Savior!, and His numerous benefits are available to all who believe, all who embrace His Lordship, and all who receive His grace.

<u>Ephesians 5:20</u> Giving thanks always for all things to God the Father in the name of our Lord Jesus Christ.

God wants each married person to maintain a heart of thanksgiving for his or her spouse, and to verbally express such thanks to God. In order to be thankful for your spouse, it is helpful to reflect on the many ways that your spouse is and has been a blessing to you. Intentional reflection in this way will help you not resent your spouse, have a critical spirit toward your spouse, and generally be ungrateful. I would like to share some of the many ways my wife, Kim, is a blessing to me.

- Kim believes the Bible and reads it.
- Kim attends church services with our children on Sundays and most Wednesday. [I work Sundays (I lead worship at work) and I attend church on Wednesdays].
- Kim homeschools our children. She loves and cares for them, and is conscientious regarding their well-being and safety.
- Kim cooks, cleans, washes and folds the laundry, and does other household chores.
- Kim is kind to my parents and my one sibling—Tim, and his family. They all very much love Kim and are happy that I married her. They see Kim as a good mother and wife.
- Kim loves me and is faithful to me.
- Kim is a good conversationalist. I enjoy our times of fellowship, such as our date nights. I wish we had more of them.

- Kim is intelligent. She is insightful, and also has common sense.

I should focus on the positive qualities of my wife more than on any shortcomings she may have, and she should do the same regarding me. I should work to maintain a primarily positive view of my wife. Also, I should acknowledge the sovereignty of God, that He has allowed me to have Kim as my wife. God works through Kim to help me (she is my helpmate), and also to mold me to be a patient, loving husband and father.

"It is good neither to eat meat nor drink wine nor do anything by which your brother stumbles or is offended or is made weak" (Rom. 14:21).

This verse lies within the same context as Romans 14:15, on which I commented in Chapter 1. The fact that Romans 14:21 says "anything" means that the command to not offend extends beyond food. One should not offend one's spouse in any area of life, whether that includes eating, choice of friends and social activities, use of free time, choice of television programs, habits, hobbies, or whatever.

Let's focus on some key words in this verse. We should never cause our spouse to *stumble* or fall. Instead, we ought to help our spouse find sure footing. Such sure footing is only found through faith in Christ, who is our Rock, and through obedience to His holy Word. Psalm 37:31 says, "The law of his God is in his heart; none of his *steps* shall slide."

Instead of *offending* our spouse with our words or actions, we should edify and encourage our spouse, and we should stir up love and good works (Heb. 10:24). [Sometimes, it may be necessary to *lovingly* confront our spouse (Gal. 6:1 says to "restore...in a spirit of gentleness") if he or she is disobeying God, and such confrontation may offend our spouse. To seek to bring someone closer to the Lord is an act of love, even if that person is offended.] If you wrongly offend you spouse, then quickly repent, seek your spouse's forgiveness, and make reconciliation your top priority. In Matthew 5:23-24 Jesus says, "Therefore, if you bring your gift to the altar, and there remember that your brother has something against you, leave your gift there before the altar, and go your way. First be reconciled to your brother, and then come and offer your gift." Here, Jesus indicates that we cannot rightly worship and serve God until we have done all that is within our power to reconcile with our brother or sister (and this includes our spouse) whom we have offended. We must make every effort to get all our horizontal relationships right (love our neighbor) before we can expect to have our vertical relationship right (love God).

We should never be the cause for our spouse to become *weak in faith*, or tempt our spouse to sin, and we should never be an ungodly example to our spouse. Instead, we should regularly pray for our spouse. We should seek to strengthen our spouse through encouraging words and being a godly example. We should remind our spouse that he or she can do all things through Christ which strengthens him or her (Phil. 4:13). Godly husbands and wives wholeheartedly strive to always demonstrate righteousness, love, and integrity within the home.

"Or do you not know that your body is the temple of the Holy Spirit who is in you, whom you have from God, and you are not your own? For you were bought at a price; therefore glorify God in your body and in your spirit, which are God's" (1 Cor. 6:19-20).

Though not as important as spiritual purity (1 Tim. 4:8), physical health should be a priority to any married person, and for that matter any Christian. An aspect of glorifying God with our bodies is pursuing and maintaining good physical health, which also stands as part of our witness to the world that God takes care of us and that we are stewards of all that He has given us. One aspect of having good health is knowing Jesus as our Healer (Acts 9:34; 1 Pet. 2:24; Mt. 8:1-17). Therefore, Christians with physical sickness should request of the elders to be anointed with oil and offer the prayer of faith for healing (Jas. 5:14-16). Another aspect of having good health is acquiring a sufficient knowledge of nutrition and eating nutritious meals. Exercising regularly is another aspect of pursuing good health. Walking, running, swimming, biking, and aerobics are good forms of exercise that elevate the heart rate and raise the metabolism.

Staying in shape is relevant to marriage. One reason is that it causes you to appear more physically attractive to your spouse. A story is told that a wife once said to her husband, "I want something for Christmas that will make me look good and feel good." The wife expected jewelry or clothes, but instead she got an exercise bike. To many married individuals (especially men), their spouses' physique was, is, and always will be an area of high importance. Over time, faces may not change that much, but bodies can change a lot. Maintaining a physically attractive appearance is an act of love that you can demonstrate toward your spouse. Second, as you pursue physical health, you will likely feel better. You will, therefore, likely be in a better mood, and will likely be more sociable, more productive, and generally more enjoyable to be around. This certainly is important for marriage. Third, maintaining physical health increases the likelihood for longevity. Heart disease and cancer account for approximately half of U.S. deaths.[75] However, a consistently nutritious diet, regular exercise, and abiding in the Lord's Word can greatly reduce the likelihood of debilitating diseases or premature death befalling you or your spouse.

First Thessalonians 5:23b says, "may your whole spirit, soul, *and body* be preserved blameless at the coming of our Lord Jesus Christ." This verse in part indicates that God wants us to have a blameless body. One reason is that body maintenance is temple maintenance—the Spirit of God dwells in the body of the Christian. What a privilege that we Christians have God living inside us (Col. 1:27)! Therefore, we are commanded to glorify God in our bodies, which certainly includes fleeing from any and all sexual immorality, as 1 Corinthians 6 points out. Sexual immorality includes lust, pornography, fornication, adultery, homosexuality, and lewdness. The Holy Spirit requires a holy temple.

"Let all that you do be done with *love*" (1 Corinthians 16:14).

To me, this is a monumental verse. The two greatest biblical commandments are to love God with all of your heart, mind, soul, and strength, and to love your neighbor as yourself (Mt. 22:36-40). The key verb in these two greatest commandments is "love." I define love as a spiritual quality that is manifest when you put others ahead of yourself (This is discussed in depth in Chapter 9.). According to the first part of the definition, love is a spiritual quality; therefore, you must abide

[75] www.statisticstop10.com/Causes_of_Death_in_US.html

in Christ in order to have the inner conviction to love as well as the spiritual power to love. You must abide in Christ in order to love your spouse, for Jesus said, "Without Me you can do nothing" (Jn. 15:5b). Indeed, without Jesus, I would be a sorry husband! Second, you must choose to put others ahead of yourself. To love your spouse, you must choose to look out for your spouse's best interest over your own self-interest. To do so is to give. And giving, when motivated by the love of God in your heart, is a win-win situation. Luke 6:38 indicates that we cannot out-give God: "Give, and it will be given to you: good measure, pressed down, shaken together, and running over will be put into your bosom. For with the same measure that you use, it will be measured back to you." When I give to my spouse, the Lord gives to me. Perhaps the Lord will reward me with increased victory in the here-and-now, as well as with treasure in heaven.

There is never a time when God relieves a Christian from the responsibility to walk in love. There is no break or time-out from the call to love. Every action and interaction ought to be done with the motive of, and empowerment of, the love of God. This means everything you do should be done with and through God, because "God is love" (1 Jn. 4:8b). God is the originator of love, the embodiment of love, and the source of love. That you allow God to love through you requires that you allow God's Word to abide richly in your heart, and that you diligently seek to be led by, strengthened by, and filled with His Holy Spirit throughout the day.

"Therefore, as we have the opportunity, let us do good to all, especially to those who are of the household of faith" (Gal. 6:10).

Once, my wife was sharing with the youth at church some of her experiences from the approximately twenty mission trips she had made before we were married. (The fact that she had such a heart for missions was one of the reasons I first asked her to dinner.) I had to leave church early, and when I saw my wife's car in the parking lot, I decided to write her a note of encouragement and leave it where she would find it. As I was doing this, a man I didn't know pulled up beside me in his car to ask a favor of me. He said he was in a jam. His wife was employed, but he was on disability, and they had three children. He said they just moved into a new place, but it had fleas, so he asked me for twenty dollars so he could buy flea spray. I replied with gracious words and gave him the twenty dollars without hesitation, and this seemed to amaze the man. He told me he had been a gospel singer. I asked him if he went to church. He said in the last church where he served, he was turned off because of the hypocrisy of the people. I told him that even though there are hypocrites in churches, the Lord still tells us not to forsake the assembling of ourselves together (Heb. 10:25). At the end of the conversation, I told him I'd pray for him to discern and obey God's will. He said, "Yes, I need it. God only gives us a very small view of His will." I said, "God's will includes our studying His Word." He seemed struck by this and said, "Yes. You love the Lord, don't you." I replied, "Yes." We had a delightful exchange, and hopefully as a result he would once again consider giving church a try. Also, I had the opportunity to see that in my act of demonstrating love to my wife by writing her a note, God extended to me another opportunity to minister love—to a man who needed to be reminded of God's love. Jesus said, "For to everyone who has, more will be given, and he will have abundance" (Mt. 25:29a). So consistently allow God's love to dwell richly in you, and God will give you opportunities to share His love with others.

Though we who are married have various daily responsibilities—our career, rearing children, cooking, cleaning, etc.—each of us still needs to seize the opportunity to do good to our spouse. Psalm 34:14a says, "Depart from evil and do good." Husband, perhaps you could do good to your wife by helping with household responsibilities such as vacuuming, cleaning the dishes, or spending time with the children, so that she could have some time alone. Wife, you could do good to your husband by perhaps giving him a backrub or preparing him a special dinner. If asked, could your spouse honestly say, "My husband (or wife) is good to me"?

"Speaking the truth in *love*" (Eph. 4:15a)

Many non-Christians don't believe in absolute moral truth. If they like how something feels, they may indulge themselves in it. And if a Christian challenges them on it because the Christian sees that their actions contradict the standards of the Bible, the Christian may get labeled as judgmental. But that is a wrongly applied label because

Galatians 6:1 says: "Brethren, if a man is overtaken in any trespass, you who are spiritual restore such a one in a spirit of gentleness, considering yourself lest you also be tempted." Jesus condemns being judgmental (Mt. 7:1-2) when one judges another who has not violated any Scriptural commands. They judge them for, perhaps, the way they dress, their personality, their affiliations, etc. Jesus does condemn that.

Some people do not recognize what truth is even when truth is staring them in the face. Pilate asked Jesus, "What is truth?" (Jn. 18:38). Pilate did not know that Jesus had answered that question just hours before when He told His disciples, "*I am...truth*" (Jn. 14:6). Also, Jesus prayed to the Father for His disciples, saying, "*Sanctify them by Your truth. Your word is truth*" (Jn. 17:17). The Bible, from Genesis 1:1 to Revelation 22:21, is truth. Psalm 119:160a says, "The entirety of Your word is truth...." Again, if your attitude is genuinely for another's well being, and you point out to them the error of their ways by showing them that what they are doing is clearly a violation of biblical Scripture—that is not being wrongfully judgmental; rather, that is an act of love. We are exhorted to speak the truth in love.

There is absolutely no place for deceit within the Christian marriage. Truth, honesty, and trust are nonnegotiables. How can you have meaningful conversation and share heart-to-heart with your spouse if you have doubts about what your spouse is telling you because deceit has been commonplace within the marriage? Concerning the virtuous wife of Proverbs 31, verse 11a says, "the heart of her husband safely trusts her." The opposite of truth is lies and deceit. The devil is a liar and the father of lies (Jn. 8:44). The first sin occurred when the serpent (and the devil is a serpent, Rev. 20:2) contradicted the Word of God (calling God a liar). The serpent said, "You will not surely die," in reference to God's statement that if Adam and Eve ate of the tree of the knowledge of good and evil, then "you shall surely die" (Gen. 3:4; 2:17). So knowing the Word of God is an imperative for husband and wife, as well as for all God's people, to rightly discern when the devil is at work, since it is against him and his evil army that we primarily do battle (Eph. 6:10-18). Those who side with the devil by sowing lies, if they do not repent, will one day suffer the same horrible, eternal condemnation as that of the devil. Revelation 21:8 says, "But the cowardly, unbelieving, abominable, murderers, sexually immoral, sorcerers, idolaters, and *all liars* shall have their part in the lake which burns with fire and brimstone, which is the second death." God hates lies.

The story is told of an officer who pulled over a couple in a car. The officer said to the husband, "You ran a stoplight back there." The husband replied, "Sorry officer, I didn't see it." The wife said to the husband, "Yes you did; I told you to slow down." The officer said to the husband, "I saw you put your seat belt on as I was walking to your car." The husband replied, "No, officer, I always wear my seat belt." The wife said to the husband, "No you don't, dear. I'm always trying to make you see the importance of wearing your seat belt for your own safety." The husband said to the wife, "Woman, would you can it? Can you never hold your tongue?" The officer said to the wife, "Does he always talk to you like that?" The wife replied, "Oh no, not always; only when he's been drinking."

The wife may have spoken the truth, but the motive of love seemed to be missing. As with all that we do (1 Cor. 16:14), we must speak the truth in love. If love is absent, words spoken, no matter how true, can be abrasive, can hit like a hammer, and can crush the spirit of our spouse. If my wife and I need to speak frankly about a sensitive issue between us, we ought to seek God's wisdom as to when to do so. Instead of speaking confrontational truth when either spouse is irritated, it is best to address the topic after sufficient prayer and quality time between husband and wife have occurred, where the foundation of love has been recently affirmed. First Corinthians 16:14 says, "Let all that you do be done with love." Love is mandatory. With love, we never fail. But without love, we profit nothing. In marriage, sometimes it is necessary to confront your spouse (Gal. 6:1) or to speak to your spouse about a touchy subject, but you should never set love to the side while you do so.

"bearing with one another, and forgiving one another, if anyone has a complaint against another; even as Christ forgave you, so you also must do" (Col. 3:13).

Though Jesus tells us to be perfect (Mt. 5:48), and therefore we should make every effort to do so, I don't know of any living human who has already attained a perfect attitude, walks perfectly before God, or has a perfect marriage. Instead, our personal lives and our marriages are works in progress. And because each spouse falls short—not only of

God's expectations, but also of each other's expectations, it is imperative that each spouse is always willing to forgive and patiently bear with one another in love. The exhortation to bear with one another occurs in other verses as well. Ephesians 4:2 says: "bearing with one another in love." First Corinthians 13:7a says, "(Love) bears all things." Our absolutely perfect Lord and Savior, Jesus Christ, patiently bears with us—those of us who are saved by faith in Him, though we repeatedly sin against Him. Lamentations 3:22-23 indicate that the LORD's mercies, compassions, and great faithfulness toward His people do not fail, but they are new every morning. Furthermore, Psalm 18:25 says of the LORD, "with the merciful You will show Yourself merciful." If your spouse's shortcomings tempt you to become irritated, bitter, or resentful, you must make every effort to demonstrate patience, forgiveness, and mercy towards your spouse because you certainly want God to be patient, forgiving, and merciful toward you. Remember, each of us has sinned infinitely more against our holy Creator than our spouse, or any other person, has sinned against us. As Galatians 6:2 says, "Bear one another's burdens," the Lord can empower you to come alongside your spouse and patiently walk with your spouse in joint pursuit of the perfection to which each of us is called. So be a team player and help your spouse finish life's race with excellence!

"By this we know *love*, because He laid down His life for us. And we also ought to lay down our lives for the brethren" (1 Jn. 3:16).

Love requires much more than sentimental feelings. Love requires giving and sacrifice, as we see in 1 John 3:16 (above), and in John 3:16— "For God so *loved* the world that he *gave* His only begotten Son, that whoever believes in Him should not perish but have everlasting life." In order to love God, each Christian must give of himself. He must make sacrifices concerning his time, energy, resources, and even his own life in order to follow God's Word and the Holy Spirit. When Jesus prayed "not as I will, but as You will" (Mt. 26:39)—that was sacrifice. Such giving and sacrifice is rewarded by God in several ways: He gives back a hundredfold (Mark 10:30), He gives eternal life (2 Tim. 2:11), and He gives the Holy Spirit to those who obey Him (Acts 5:32).

Likewise, in marriage, each spouse must give and must sacrifice. In order to love your spouse, you must often sacrifice your desires when your desires hinder the pleasing and edification of your spouse. Romans 15:2 says: "Let each of us *please* his neighbor for his good, leading to *edification*." In this case, your spouse is your neighbor, and you need to please your spouse (as long as in doing so you do not commit sin). For example, if your spouse wants you to stay home more, instead of focusing a lot on sports or hobbies, or spending great amounts of time with other friends, then you should do so. If your spouse wants you to watch less television and spend more quality time with him or her, then you should do so. If you love our spouse, then you will follow the example of Christ and lay down your life for your spouse.

You can never out-give God. Luke 6:38 says, "Give, and it will be given to you: good measure, pressed down, shaken together, and running over will be put into your bosom. For with the same measure that you use, it will be measured back to you." In 1 Kings 17, during the midst of a severe nationwide drought, God told Elijah to go to Zarephath for his provision of food. There Elijah met a widow and her son, and Elijah asked the widow to bring him some water and bread. She replied that she only had a handful of flour and a little oil that would last her and her son one more meal, and after they ate it they expected to die of starvation. Nevertheless, Elijah instructed her to make him a small cake first. Elijah then prophesied that the flour and oil would not be used up until God ended the drought. The widow obeyed the Word of the LORD which He spoke by Elijah, and the flour and oil were miraculously multiplied so that the three of them did not lack food for the remainder of the drought.

When, in agape love, you put God, your spouse, or anyone else ahead of yourself, then God will certainly give you a generous return on your investment. He may increase the love in your heart for your spouse and others. He may give you more efficiency in completing whatever tasks you may have put off in order to put the other person first. He may bring healing, restoration, or other blessings to your marriage. He may entrust more into your care and oversight since you have proven yourself trustworthy. And God certainly will credit your heavenly account! (Mt. 6:19-20; Phil. 4:17). This is how God's economy works. So through Christ's love, make giving of yourself for the benefit of others a way of life (as 1 Cor. 16:14 says "Let all that you do be done in love"), and know that God will greatly bless you in return.

"love your neighbor as yourself" (Mt. 22:39).

Many of the facets of love shared in this book can be applied to all relationships, and not just toward our spouse. Ephesians 5:1 says we are to imitate God. And we should never forget that God loved all the people of the world (Jn. 3:16) in that He provided His only begotten Son as an atonement for the sins of the world. This same idea is found in Romans 5:8: "But God demonstrates His own love toward us, in that while we were still sinners (rebels against God), Christ died for us." Jesus Himself, while on the cross, prayed for the very people who were persecuting and murdering Him by saying, "Father, forgive them, for they do not know what they do" (Lk. 23:34a). So Christ's example has been set before us. Therefore, in Matthew 5:44-45, Jesus says, "love your enemies, bless those who curse you, do good to those who hate you, and pray for those who spitefully use you and persecute you, that you may be sons of your Father in heaven...." A few verses earlier, Jesus tells us not to resist an evil person and gives examples of what that means, such as: "Give to him who asks you, and from him who wants to borrow from you do not turn away" (verse 42). Again, "whoever compels you to go one mile, go with him two" (verse 41). We see the same idea in Romans 12: "Repay no one evil for evil...if it is possible, as much as depends on you, live peaceably with all men...do not be overcome by evil, but overcome evil with good" (verses 17, 18, 21). So today, be mindful to love, bless, do good to, and pray for all people, no matter how they treat you. And what is the greatest love? John 15:13 says, "Greater love has no one than this, than to lay down one's life for his friends." Remember that in laying down your life for others (and certainly this is to include your spouse), you are faithfully representing our loving Lord.

"A friend *loves* at all times, and a brother is born for adversity" (Pr. 17:17).

God considered Abraham His friend (Jas. 3:23). Jesus said to His disciples, "You are my friends if you do whatever I command you."

What a privilege to be the Lord's friend! As Proverbs 17:17 indicates, if we love God at all times (and this necessitates our obeying God), then God considers us His friends.

Our spouse should be our best earthly friend. As friends, husband and wife ought to spur one another on to be friends of God, which in turn will enable husband and wife to be friends to each other. As friends, husband and wife should spend quality time together as well as enjoy the blessing of raising children together. As friends, husband and wife should pursue activities together that are mutually enjoyable. Also, true friendship in marriage means that husband and wife will love each other at all times, as Proverbs 17:17 states. If they do so, their marriage will never fail, because "love never fails" (1 Cor. 13:8a). What are some activities you and your spouse could do together that will enhance your friendship?

"For everyone to whom much is given, from him much will be required; and to whom much has been committed, of him they will ask the more" (Lk. 12:48b).

God is just (Ps. 7:11; Rom. 8:33b). In part, this means that God is fair. To say "Life is not fair" involves claiming that God is not fair, for God is sovereign over the circumstances of each person's life. God "shows no partiality" (Acts 10:34), and He commands His children to also show no partiality (James 2:4). But if God is impartial and fair, then how do we explain the estimation that "30,000 children die every day of hunger and preventable diseases"?[76] How is it fair that, according to World Bank, "1.4 billion people (one in four) in the developing world were living below US$1.25 a day in 2005"?[77] Luke 12:48b is an equalizing verse. It is one that we who have prospered (materially, educationally, spiritually, etc.) should never forget. God expects each of us to be faithful stewards of all He has entrusted to us because all that we have is His (1 Cor. 6:20; 1 Cor. 7:23; Ps. 50:12b). If you have great wealth while millions of others are dying of starvation, you need

---

[76] Oxfam America, "*Fast for a World Harvest: Fighting Hunger Takes More Than Knowing the Facts,*" (Boston: Oxfam America, 2003).

[77] Martin Ravallion and Shaohua Chen, *New Data Show 1.4 Billion Live On Less Than US$1.25 A Day, But Progress Against Poverty Remains Strong,* (World Bank Press Release No: 2009/065/DEC).

to remember that God will hold you accountable for how you have used your material resources. So I encourage you to seek God's will through His Word and prayer concerning this matter. Seek to humble your heart so that you will do whatever God wants you to do. Another important issue is your role in evangelism. If you have knowledge of Jesus Christ while so many others are ignorant of His Word, then God will keep record of what you did with your saving knowledge. Billions are born in countries where the gospel is marginalized or unknown, and the church must earnestly seek God's will concerning how to be light to such far off places of spiritual darkness.   How is this discussion relevant to marriage? We must remember that marriage is not an end-all-be-all. Marriage, as well as all aspects of life, is ultimately to be seen as a stewardship—a way to honor and glorify God, and to advance His wonderful kingdom. One may cite, e.g., 1 Corinthians 7:29-33 as speaking about the temporal nature of marriage and exhorting believers to invest in eternity. So husband and wife ought to be mindful of the poor and suffering—"the least of these My brethren" (Mt. 25:40), and husband and wife should come together in Bible study and prayer to see what God would have them do to make a positive and lasting impact in such a lost and needy world.

"Love covers all sins" (Pr. 10:12).

We should not think that because we have positive, sentimental feelings toward God and others that God will forgive a particular sin that we are not willing to forsake. All sin is an affront to God. Jesus said, "If you love Me, keep My commandments" (Jn. 14:15). If we do not obey the Word of God, then we do not love God, which means we are likely not forgiven by God. Also, if we do not love our fellow man, but instead despise them, mistreat them, or ignore those in need when we have the means to help them, then again, we do not love God (1 Jn. 3:17). First John 3:14a says, "We know that we have passed from death to life, because we love the brethren." So if we love God by wholeheartedly obeying His Word and if we love our fellow man—and these are the Bible's two greatest commandments (Mt. 22:36-40), then that indicates Christ is Lord of our lives. Again, 1 John 1:7 says, "But if we walk in the light as He is in the light, we have fellowship with one another, and the blood of Jesus Christ His Son cleanses us from all sin."

Do you stand in need of a fresh touch of God's forgiveness? I encourage you to implement the exhortation of 1 John 1:9 by confessing and forsaking your sins (completely turning away from your sins), and trusting in the atoning blood of Jesus. I also encourage you to go out of your way to demonstrate a significant act of love toward your spouse. Sow love to reap love (Gal. 6:7). How can you show love to your spouse today?

"Overcome evil with good" (Rom. 12:21).

The Associated Press reported the following story. In 1997, in Durham, North Carolina, a Driver's Education teacher had two student drivers in the car with him, one driving. Suddenly, another car pulled in front on them, cutting them off. This infuriated the Driver's Ed teacher. He ordered the fifteen year old student driver to pursue the other car. This piqued the curiosity of the other driver, so he pulled over and rolled down his window to see what the Driver's Ed teacher wanted. The Driver's Ed teacher then punched the other driver in the face, giving him a bloody nose. The other driver quickly drove away. The angry teacher ordered the student to continue pursuing. The police pulled the Driver's Ed car over for speeding. The driver with the bloody nose circled back and reported what had happened. The teacher was arrested, was suspended from his job, and eventually resigned. Driver's Ed teachers are typically known for their patience. But on that particular day, when the circumstances were just so, that teacher allowed rage rather than God's love to flood his heart.

Matthew 5:44-45 says, "love your enemies, bless those who curse you, do good to those who hate you, and pray for those who spitefully use you and persecute you, that you may be sons of your Father in heaven." The Lord Jesus, while dying on the cross, overcame evil with good by forgiving those who were mocking and murdering Him. He came to earth to lay down His life to redeem humanity whom He created but whom had rebelled against Him. We are to emulate Jesus. If others hate us, curse us, do evil to us, spitefully use us, and persecute us, then we are to respond by loving them, blessing them, doing them good, and praying for them. Hopefully, you don't see your spouse as your enemy, but even if your spouse treats you in an ungodly way, you are commanded to respond to your spouse as it says in Matthew 5:44-

45. May the Lord bless you as you sow His love, peace, and patience into your marriage.

"choose for yourselves this day whom you will serve...as for me and my house, we will serve the LORD" (Josh. 24:15).

Joshua, the one who replaced Moses as leader of Israel and led the Israelites into the Promised Land, spoke these words to all the tribes of Israel just before he died. He knew of their evil tendency toward idolatry and he therefore gave them the stern warning to forsake all idols and false gods so they could serve Jehovah God. To give God anything less than one's total devotion would be a violation of the first of the Ten Commandments which Israel had just recently received—"You shall have no other gods before Me" (Dt. 5:7).

Just as Joshua told the people to make a choice as to whom they would serve, each of us is faced with this same choice every day. For instance, do you choose to spend time in the Scriptures and in prayer to start your day? Do you choose to bear the fruit of love when you interact with your spouse throughout the day? Husbands, do you lead your household in Bible study and prayer on a regular basis? In 2002, the American Family Association reported that only twelve percent of America's families pray together.[78] Parents, do you allow your children to be exposed to ungodly influences, whether through TV programs, books, choices of music, or ungodly people? Around 2001, it was reported that the most popular TV show for boys ages twelve to seventeen was *The Simpsons*, and that for girls ages twelve to seventeen, the most popular show was *Temptation Island*. On February 27, 2002, the *Courier Journal* newspaper of Louisville reported the following "sobering" statistics: eighty-one percent of high school students have consumed alcohol, seventy percent have smoked cigarettes, and forty-seven percent have used marijuana. Such behavior is indicative of choices made without any regard for the standards of the Bible.

Joshua indicated that he could not make the people's choice for them, but he let them know he had already made his choice. As head of his household, Joshua declared that his loyalty, and consequently that of his family, was to God. Before Joshua could be the godly, effective leader of Israel, he first needed to be the godly, effective leader of his

---

[78] *On Mission* (magazine), May-June 2002 article: *Family to Family.*

home. Will you, husband / dad, follow the example of Joshua and lead your family in commitment to the Lord? In what areas, if any, could you improve concerning your leadership within your family? Wife, will you commit to being your husband's helpmate in this wonderful endeavor to seek first the kingdom of God and His righteousness (Mt. 6:33)? May the Lord bless you.

"Since you have purified your souls in obeying the truth through the Spirit in sincere *love* of the brethren, *love* one another fervently with a pure heart" (1 Pet. 1:22).

Reverend Jerry Parritt (Assistant District Superintendant for the Kentucky Assemblies of God) shares the following insights from his marriage to Carol. 1) We kiss and tell each other we love each other every day. 2) She has a cup of coffee for me on the sink when I get out of the shower. 3) I stop often and bring her a cappuccino that she loves. 4) We laugh a lot together about the silly things we have done. For example, I dreamt that Carol and I were in a boat together, and it was sinking. I pulled her half out of the bed before she woke me up. We sat on the floor and laughed ourselves silly. 5) We are always touching and hugging. (This makes the kids go crazy. They say it's gross.) 6) Carol is my best friend and supporter. 7) I tell her often how beautiful she is. She says I'm still her handsome prince. 8) We give the best of ourselves to each other. We like each other. We still go on dates. 9) We seldom argue, and we have a deep respect for each other. 10) We live for Christ! We have our (Bible) devotions together. She reads the devotional for the day. Then I pray. Afterward, we discuss the Scriptures that she read.

The Parritts have been married for forty-eight years (they have four children and eight grandchildren), and as you can see, they still fervently love each other. The word "fervent" conveys the idea of heat or burning. A fervent love in marriage includes having passion and a burning desire for one another. The above verse says that fervent love should emanate from a pure heart. Purity of heart comes from the Holy Spirit's utilizing or quickening the Word of God within a person, burning away sinful desires. Being committed to "obeying the truth (God's Word—the Bible) through the Spirit" allows this sanctification process to occur. John the Baptist alluded to such burning away of sin and purifying of one's soul when he said that Jesus would "baptize you with the Holy Spirit and fire" (Mt. 3:11).

The love that the Parritt's had for each other forty-eight years ago at the marriage altar has not diminished, but it has grown. Such fervent love does not come naturally in marriage, but the husband and wife must put forth effort toward that end. Husband and wife should abide in Christ, consistently sacrifice selfish desires for the benefit of the other, and daily invest in one another to guarantee having fervent love for one another. An example of the Parritt's making such effort is their going on dates. Also, the Parritts intentionally give each other the best of each other, instead of giving their best to everyone else to the point that they can only give each other their emotional "leftovers." (Pastors can especially be tempted to allow an imbalance in the distribution of their emotional and physical energy, but they must resist doing that. Rev. Parritt has been able to maintain proper balance in this area, and he has served as pastor of various churches for over forty-one years.) The Parritts daily relate to each other spiritually—through Christ, who is the Source and embodiment of love. Furthermore, the Parritts demonstrate love to one another by serving each other, speaking words of kindness to each other, and enjoying each other's company. Likewise, let each of us who are married diligently seek to cultivate a sincere and fervent love for our spouse.

"Finally, all of you be of one mind, having compassion for one another; *love* as brothers, be tenderhearted, be courteous; not returning evil for evil or reviling for reviling; but on the contrary blessing, knowing that you were called to this, that you may inherit a blessing" (1 Pet. 3:8-9).

This passage contains several godly qualities which ought to be evident within the body of Christ as well as within the Christian marriage. Though Christians may interpret certain passages of Scripture differently and have varying opinions on various topics, still believers are commanded to "be of one mind." And the singular mind that Christians (and married couples) should have is Christ's mind. Philippians 2:5 says, "Have this mind in you which was also in Christ Jesus...." Again, Colossians 3:2 says, "Set your mind on things above, not on things on the earth." It is imperative for husband and wife to regularly study the Word of God together, and speak it to one another—keeping their minds renewed (Rom. 12:2), so that they may walk together in agreement (Amos 3:3).

Webster's defines "compassion" as: "a feeling of deep sympathy and sorrow for someone struck by misfortune, accompanied by a desire to alleviate the suffering; mercy."[79] Matthew 14:14 says: "And when Jesus went out He saw a great multitude; and He was moved with *compassion* for them, and healed their sick." Since we are called to emulate Christ our compassionate Savior, we Christians ought to be known as a caring people—demonstrating compassion for our fellow humans who are struggling with a plethora of difficulties in this fallen world. For example, I visited Haiti about two months before the deadly earthquake that ravaged that country in January 2010, and I personally witnessed the extreme poverty that Haiti already knew. Now, one year after the earthquake, it is estimated that 750,000 Haitians still remain homeless. Many American Christians have reached out in compassion to the people of Haiti, but much compassionate relief is still desperately needed. The body of Christ must continue to care for the least of these our brethren, not only in Haiti, but also throughout all the impoverished third-world countries. Jesus said, "For everyone to whom much is given, from him much will be required" (Lk. 12:48b). Whether we are single or married, we, like Jesus, should look beyond our immediate stations in life in order to minister help and healing to those who are suffering.

"Tenderhearted" means softhearted and kindhearted, as opposed to callous or hardhearted, toward others. When Debbie Clark saw 10,000 children living on the streets in Sierra Leone during the rainy season (they had been orphaned due to West Africa's AIDS epidemic and rebel warfare), she said, "My heart was broken." In other words, her heart was tender, or sensitive, to the needs of others to the point that she was willing to alter her life's direction. As a result, she and her husband, Chris, founded Children of the Nations in 1995, a feeding, housing, and education ministry to needy children around the world.[80] At the core of your being, are you tender toward the leading of God and the needs of others? Psalm 51:17 says: "The sacrifices of God are a broken spirit,

---

[79] *Webster's American Dictionary*, Second College Edition, 163.
[80] "Children of the Nations," *Power for Living*, June 24, 2007, (SP Publications, Colorado Springs, CO).

a broken and a contrite heart—these, O God, You will not despise." Also, are you tender toward the emotional needs of your spouse? Would your spouse see you as kind and caring rather than selfish or irritable?

Webster's defines "courteous" as: "having or showing good manners; polite."[81] Are you polite to your spouse? Do you speak to your spouse with the courtesy and friendliness that you would show toward one of your best friends? Or, do you take your spouse for granted so as sometimes to be rude to your spouse or to speak to your spouse with an unpleasant tone?

Finally, the passage in 1 Peter 3 indicates that if someone commits evil against you, you are to not retaliate, but you are instead to bless that person. This is in emulation of God who also blesses the evildoer—"He makes His sun rise on the evil and on the good, and sends rain on the just and on the unjust" (Mt. 5:45). Furthermore, Jesus, while on the cross, forgave those who were murdering Him (Lk. 23:34). So if your spouse treats you in an ungodly way, respond by blessing your spouse. Make the extra effort to do something kind for your spouse. God will reward you for this, and you will increase the likelihood that your spouse will repent and treat you better in the future.

"Therefore let us pursue the things which make for peace and the things by which one may edify another" (Rom. 14:19).

Toward the end of the nineteenth century, a Swedish chemist named Alfred Nobel read his own obituary in the newspaper. It read, "Alfred Nobel, inventor of dynamite, died yesterday. He devised a way for more people to be killed in a war than ever before." Actually, Alfred's older brother had died; the newspaper reporter had made a mistake. But that obituary got Alfred's attention. He said to himself, "I don't want to be known as the man who got rich by creating something that would be used to kill lots of people." So he instituted a concept that later became known as the Nobel Peace Prize, the annual award given to individuals who significantly foster peace in our world. Alfred Nobel said, "Every man ought to have a chance to correct his epitaph in midstream and write a new one."

The things we ought to pursue in marriage are the things that are conducive to peace and mutual edification. Pursue making your home a

---

[81] *Webster's American Dictionary*, Second College Edition, 186.

place of continual peace where Jesus, the Prince of Peace, reigns. Strife and stress are contrary to God's peace. Worshipping the Lord as a family, speaking Scripture to one another, having family prayer, doing acts of service for each other, and having fun together are vital methods for acquiring peace within the household.

According to Webster, the definition of "edify" is: "to instruct or benefit, especially morally or spiritually; uplift; enlighten."[82] It is good for husband and wife to study the Word of God together, and at other times to share with each other what you have been learning in your private biblical and spiritual devotions so there can be mutual edification in the Lord. Romans 14:19 says we are to pursue such edification. What can you do daily to pursue peace with your spouse and to edify your spouse in the Lord?

---

[82] *Webster's American Dictionary*, Second College Edition, 255.

Chapter 12

Lord, Help Me Tame My Tongue!–Part 2

<u>Proverbs 4:24</u> Put away from you a deceitful mouth, and put perverse lips far from you.

Deceit is trickery, telling lies. The devil is the ultimate deceiver and liar, so if you speak deceitfully then you are being a pawn of the devil. "Perverse lips" refer to speaking in a manner that is unholy and profane. The Lord commands you to refrain from speaking deceitful or perverted words; instead you are to speak the truth in love, and with holiness and grace (Eph. 4:15; 1 Pet. 1:16; Col. 4:6).

<u>Proverbs 6:2</u> You are snared by the words of your mouth.

The words you speak have implications for the condition of your whole being. Speaking the truth in love will bless the hearer and the speaker. Not doing so will snare the speaker. You can also be liberated by the words of your mouth—Proverbs 12:6 says, "the mouth of the upright will deliver them."

Proverbs 6:16-19 These six things the LORD hates, yes, seven are an abomination to Him: A proud look, a lying tongue, hands that shed innocent blood, a heart that devises wicked plans, feet that are swift in running to evil, a false witness who speaks lies, and one who sows discord among the brethren.

This passage refers to several parts of the human body: heart, hands, feet, eyes, and tongue. According to James 3:2, if you tame your tongue, then you can bridle, or tame, all other parts of your body, including your heart, which is the core of your being. Two of the seven "things" listed here that "the LORD hates" pertains to the tongue. God hates "a lying tongue." Revelation 21:8 includes "all liars" in the list of those who will be cast into the lake of fire. God also hates the "one who sows discord among the brethren"—the one who causes division in Christ's body, who opposes the unity that comes through Christian love. This would certainly include the spouse who sows strife within the marriage and family. Instead, you should speak the truth in love. You should speak words conducive to remaining in one accord, not discord.

Notice the text does not say God only "hates" the discord sown, but He hates the one who sows the discord. Objectively, God loves all people in that He sent Jesus to be the propitiation for the sins of the whole world. But unless a person subjectively appropriates God's wonderful salvation through repentance and faith in Christ, then that person is an enemy of God (Jas. 4:4) and a child of wrath (Eph. 2:3), for God hates all workers of iniquity (Ps. 5:5).

Proverbs 10:11 The mouth of the righteous is a well of life, but violence covers the mouth of the wicked.

A person who is righteous is one who, through faith, abides in THE LORD OUR RIGHTEOUSNESS (Jer. 33:16), who is Jesus the Christ (1 Cor. 1:30). We who are believers are "the righteousness of God in Him" (2 Cor. 5:21). His righteousness is imputed, or transferred, to the believer by faith.

As "a well of life" paints the picture of fresh, clean, nourishing, life-sustaining water from a well, so words spoken by the one who abides in Christ our Righteousness should nourish and refresh others, not poison or contaminate them. James 3:9-10 say of the tongue, "With it we bless our God and Father, and with it we curse men, who have been made in the similitude of God. Out of the same mouth proceed blessing and cursing. My brethren, these things ought not to be so." Your mouth should be a well of life only; not also a well of strife (a well of death).

The second half of Proverbs 10:11 indicates that the wicked person hates his neighbor and strikes at him with evil words, and perhaps also with his fists and weapons.

Proverbs 10:12 Hatred stirs up strife, but love covers all sins.

If strife occurs in marriage, it may be caused by one or both spouses harboring hatred in their hearts toward one another, though they may not admit it or even be aware of it. First John 3:15 warns us: "Whoever hates his brother is a murderer, and you know that no murderer has eternal life abiding in him." Conversely, 1 Peter 4:8 says, "And above all things have fervent love for one another, for 'love will cover a multitude of sins.'" Through abiding in Jesus Christ and meditating on verses pertaining to love, grace, and kindness, God can remove hatred from your heart and replace it with His love for your spouse and neighbor. Romans 5:5b says, "the love of God has been poured out in our hearts by the Holy Spirit who was given to us." Hatred must be purged instead of ignored—Proverbs 10:18 says: "Whoever hides hatred has lying lips...." God's love, which is the greatest spiritual quality and is also the fulfillment of God's entire law, covers all sins.

Proverbs 10:13 Wisdom is found on the lips of him who has understanding....

You who are a believer should diligently study God's Word (2 Tim. 2:15), and also rely on the Holy Spirit to teach you all things and give you understanding. Wisdom, which is the chief thing (Pr. 4:7) and a free gift from God (Jas. 1:5), will proceed from the lips of the one who has understanding, the one who humbly embraces God's Word. Wisdom is to know the right choices to make, based on the Bible; ultimately wisdom is Christ (1 Cor 1:30). God's Word offers much wisdom and understanding about the roles of husband and wife, including how they are to treat one another, and how they are to navigate together through the challenges they will face.

Proverbs 10:19 In the multitude of words sin is not lacking, but he who restrains his lips is wise.

Sometimes one's vocation (e.g., a preacher or teacher), or one's circumstances (e.g., a dangerous situation or a sensitive issue) requires one to talk a lot. In such situations, it is even more important to have God's Word hidden within one's heart ahead of time so that one does not sin against God and others, including through his many words.

Generally, it is wise to restrain your lips (Pr. 10:19), to guard your mouth (Pr. 13:3), to spare your words (Pr. 17:27), to not be hasty in your words (Pr. 29:20), and to be slow to speak (Jas. 1:19), because "in the multitude of words sin is not lacking" (Pr. 10:19). This verse does not say, "In the multitude of words, sin is more likely." Instead this verse guarantees you will sin if you talk too much. The more words you speak means more of an opportunity you have to speak idle, corrupt, or prideful words, for which you will have to give an account to God (Mt. 12:36). Ecclesiastes 5:3 says, "A fool's voice is known for his many words." Conversely, "he who has knowledge spares his words (Pr. 17:27).

Proverbs 10: (20) The tongue of the righteous is choice silver.... (21) The lips of the righteous feed many.... (31) The mouth of the righteous brings forth wisdom.... (32) The lips of the righteous knows what is acceptable....

The more that your words reflect Christ's words means the more that your words are valuable to the hearers, even as "choice silver" is valuable. The words of a righteous person (one who, by faith, abides in Christ our Righteousness), should "feed," or nourish, many—bringing them truth, grace, and wisdom. Perhaps God is calling you to "feed many" by preaching and teaching His Word to many people. You who are parents should feed your children the Word of God, in addition to feeding them food at the dinner table. Pertaining to the wisdom of verse 31, Christ is the wisdom of God (1 Cor. 1:30). Our mouths should make the words of Christ known and should magnify Him.

Proverbs 11:9 The hypocrite with his mouth destroys his neighbor, but through knowledge the righteous will be delivered.

If you are not abiding in God's Word, it is easy to allow yourself to develop a critical spirit toward your spouse and others who do not live up to your expectations. Allowing a critical spirit to fester can lead to slander, which can damage another person's reputation, as well as hypocrisy which is insincerity. A hypocrite promotes a standard for others to follow but he willfully fails to live up to that standard himself. Each Christian has fallen short of the glory of God, yet he is saved by God's amazing grace. Regularly reflecting on the depths of this wonderful truth will help you to be appreciative and thankful rather than hypocritical. In the parable of the Prodigal Son, the judgmental older brother was hypocritical, greatly resenting the grace displayed by his father toward his repentant brother. The Lord calls you to love and edify your spouse and your neighbor, not destroy them.

Proverbs 12:6 ...the mouth of the upright will deliver them.

The men of Ephraim were angry with Gideon for not inviting them to help fight the Midianites. But when Gideon spoke wisely, complimenting the Ephraimites, their anger subsided (Jg. 8:1-3).

In addition to deliverance from angry or evil people, deliverance from demons, disease, and sin is available to the man of God, who, in faith, confesses God's relevant promises. In Mark 5, the woman with the issue of blood confessed, "If only I may touch His clothes, I *shall* be made well." Jesus healed her, and her confession of faith was a vital aspect of her being healed.

Proverbs 12:14 A man will be satisfied with good by the fruit of his mouth....

A correlation exists between what you say and what you receive from God. Righteous words spoken in faith by a man of God will cause satisfaction and contentment within the man. Additionally, he will freely receive good gifts from above.

Proverbs 12:18 The tongue of the wise promotes health.

You can speak in a way that promotes healing of the spirit, soul (which includes the mind, will, and emotions), and body in others and in yourself. Speaking words of grace, kindness, and truth can bring healing to your marriage and other relationships, and can even benefit the physical bodies of the hearers. This verse shows that promoting health through your words requires walking in wisdom, recognizing that Christ is the wisdom of God (1 Cor. 1:24; Pr. 8:12-36); thus you should walk in Christ (Col. 2:6). Gracious, healthy speech stands in contrast to Proverbs 11:9: "The hypocrite with his mouth destroys his neighbor...." Daily determine to be an agent of healing and health to your spouse and others through your speech.

Proverbs 13:2 A man will eat well by the fruit of his mouth....

This is similar to Proverbs 12:14, but with a focus on eating. If a man tames his tongue—speaking wisely and righteously—then God will bless him, including with the abundance of good food, which may include spiritual food as well as physical food.

Proverbs 13:3 He who guards his mouth preserves his life, but he who opens wide his lips shall have destruction.

What you say affects your entire life. By guarding your mouth, by restraining your lips (Pr. 10:19), you preserve all aspects of your life, including you marriage. But if you open wide your lips, showing no restraint in your speech but let fleeting feelings dictate what you say, then some level of destruction is coming your way, including damage to your marriage.

Proverbs 14:3 In the mouth of a fool is a rod of pride, but the lips of the wise will preserve them.

As "pride goes before destruction" (Pr. 16:18), what a fool says will facilitate the destruction that he will inevitably experience (Pr. 18:7). By contrast, a wise person remains humble before God; his words deliver him from destruction and preserve him from any snares set against him by the enemies of God (Pr. 12:6b).

In 1 Samuel 25, David sent messengers to Nabal, a rich man, and politely asked him for food for his men. (David's men had treated Nabal's shearers well.) But Nabal, whose name means "fool," spoke very disrespectfully to David's messengers and denied their request. Therefore, David and 400 of his men girded their swords and headed toward Nabal's house with the intention of killing all of the males of his household. But Nabal's wife, Abigail, "a woman of good understanding and beautiful appearance," heard of this development, quickly brought food to David and his men, and spoke wisely and humbly to David. Therefore, David refrained from attacking Nabal's house. Nabal's words almost cost lives, whereas Abigail's words saved lives. About ten days later, the LORD struck Nabal and he died. Then David married Abigail.

Proverbs 15:1 A soft answer turns away wrath, but a harsh word stirs up anger.

In addition to content, tone is an important aspect of communication. Harsh words are likely to create or escalate a problem, but a soft answer can diminish a problem. On the tongue of a virtuous wife is "the law of kindness" (Pr. 31:26). Also, a woman who maintains "a gentle and quiet spirit" is beautiful and very precious to God (1 Pet. 3:4). Such a woman—who is kind, gentle, and quiet—stands in sharp contrast to the immoral woman who is "loud and rebellious" (Pr. 7:11), as well as to the contentious wife (Pr. 19:13b; Pr. 21:19; Pr. 27:15) who is likened to a continual dripping. (Contention means strife, conflict, or dispute.[83]) God also calls husbands to be gentlemen (Gal. 5:22), "peacemakers" (Mt. 5:9), and to love our wives (Eph. 5:25), giving honor (1 Pet. 3:7) and preference (Rom. 12:10) to them. Such positive qualities emulate God: "Your lovingkindness is better than life" (Ps. 63:3); "Your gentleness has made me great" (Ps. 18:35); Jesus is "Prince of Peace" (Isa. 9:6).

When Rehoboam, Solomon's son, began his reign in Israel, all Israel came and told him that if he would lighten the burdensome service Solomon had laid on them, then they would faithfully serve him.

---

[83] Webster's American Dictionary, Second College Edition. Random House, Inc. 2000. p. 175.

Rehoboam told them to return in three days for his answer. Rehoboam asked the advice of the elders, and they said, "If you are kind to these people, and please them, and speak good words to them, they will be your servants forever." But Rehoboam rejected their advice; instead he heeded the advice of the young men with whom he grew up. At the end of three days, Rehoboam answered Israel roughly, saying, "I will add to your yoke…I will chastise you with scourges!" Thus Israel rejected his words and stoned to death one of his staff. Rehoboam had to flee to Jerusalem (2 Chr. 10).

Proverbs 15:4 A wholesome tongue is a tree of life, but perverseness in it breaks the spirit.

In addition to chapters two and three of Genesis, the tree of life is mentioned in Revelation 22:2: "…on either side of the river (that is, the river of water of life, proceeding from God's throne), was the *tree of life*, which *bore twelve fruits*, each tree yielding its *fruit* every month. The leaves of the tree were for the *healing* of the nations." Similarly, a wholesome tongue, which is a tree of life, continually bears the fruit of the Spirit, such as love, joy, peace (Gal. 5:22-23).… As the river of water of life proceeds from God's throne, so rivers of living water should flow of your inmost being, if God is on the throne of your heart and you believe.

A wholesome tongue will also produce healing (Pr. 12:18). If your marriage has wounds and scars, then you can impart love and healing through speaking wholesome words and refraining from speaking unwholesome words.

In tropical Africa and Asia is a large tree, called the upas tree, which secretes a poison used for arrows and blow darts. Upas means poison. James 3:8 says the tongue "is an unruly evil, full of deadly poison." Is your mouth a tree of life or an upas tree? As a tree a life does not produce death, neither should your tongue.

Proverbs 15:23 A man has joy by the answer of his mouth, and a word spoken in due season, how good it is!

This verse does not say that a man has joy based on the way his wife and neighbor treat him. Nor does this verse say that a man has joy based on favorable circumstances. Although how one treats you and having favorable circumstances can contribute to having joy, these factors are external to you. But your joy level should not primarily depend upon external factors.

This verse emphasizes that you can cause joy to rise within you based on what you say. For example, boldly preaching the gospel (and living according to the gospel) will give you joy. For the gospel is joyful news: The angel proclaimed to the shepherds, "I bring you good tidings of *great joy* which will be to all people" (Lk. 2:10). The kingdom of God, which is within the believer, is "...*joy* in the Holy Spirit" (Rom. 14:17). Psalm 43:4 says, "God is my *exceeding joy*"; Ps 16:11 says, "In His presence is the *fullness of joy*." Most people look primarily to external things—pleasure, entertainment, people, or circumstances—to have joy; but true joy comes from God (Gal. 5:22).

Speaking truthfully and graciously to others while refraining from making ungodly and unnecessarily critical comments will give you joy. To a large degree, you are in control of your joy level. Abraham Lincoln said he reckons a fellow is about as happy as he makes up his mind to be. Speaking words of joy will release joy within you. (The same is true of the other fruits of the Spirit, Gal. 5:22-23).

James Grant points out: the reflexive aspect is also important to realize: When you speak faithless or hurtful words, you are not exclusively tearing down the person to whom you are speaking, but you are tearing yourself down also. But when you speak joyful, godly words, you are blessing the hearers and yourself.

Proverbs 15:26b the words of the pure are pleasant.

Pleasant words generally proceed from a pleasant person; that is, one who pleases God. Such a person will attract others to him. One who pleases God is pure of heart (Mt. 5:8); that is, one whose heart has been purified by faith in the blood of Jesus (Acts 15:9). One who is pure of heart makes for pleasant company; one whose heart is full of sin and pride repels those who do the will of God. Do you want your spouse to find you to be pleasant company? Then you should pursue a pure heart and speak gracious, pleasant words.

You can be tempted to take your spouse and children for granted because of the intimate nature of those relationships. You can be tempted to become excessively informal to the point where you think you can "let it all hang out." In other words, you can mistakenly think that in your home it is acceptable to utter anything that pops into your head and that you can speak unedifying words in a reactive way based on any and every emotion you may feel. But such an attitude on your part would violate Ephesians 4:29 and other Scriptural standards and would likely offend your spouse and children. Such an attitude could make your spouse feel like he or she is your dumping grounds for every criticism, every complaint, and every thought you may have. Such behavior would likely constitute verbal abuse. You must resist the temptation to overreact in a negative way on the spur of the moment, to nit-pick, to hastily say whatever negative thoughts come to your mind, especially if they are critical in nature. Instead you should bless your spouse, your children, and your neighbor by speaking words that are wholesome, necessarily edifying, and gracious. Such speech will glorify God, and will make your presence more pleasant.

<u>Proverbs 15:28</u> The heart of the righteous studies how to answer, but the mouth of the wicked pours forth evil.

Unless you are asked a routine or surface-level question, this verse shows that you should consider carefully how you will answer. You should consider what words you could speak that would best glorify God, edify the hearers, and impart grace to them. Can you think of conversations that would have fared much better if you would have first studied how to answer in accordance with God's Word, instead of speaking hastily and being driven by emotions?

<u>Proverbs 16:24</u> Pleasant words are like a honeycomb, sweetness to the soul and health to the bones.

Pleasant words [which proceed from a person who pleases God— one who is pure in heart (see Pr. 15:26)] are a blessing to the inner man (the soul) and the physical man (the bones), potentially imparting physical healing. The speaker and the hearers are both the recipients of these blessings.

In a business setting, you should act professionally. This means you show discretion in your choice of words and tone, you demonstrate respect for others, and you resist the temptation to let your emotions (especially your negative ones) dictate what you say. Do you not think you should demonstrate at least the same level of respect for your spouse whom you pledged to love, and your children, as you should for your work colleagues? It is godly and proper to maintain a level of formality and respect in the home. This is congruent with the Lord's command for each husband to honor his wife (1 Pet. 3:7) and for each wife to respect her husband (Eph. 5:33).[84]

Proverbs 17:9 He who covers a transgression seeks love, but he who repeats a matter separates friends.

Because our holy heavenly Father has graciously forgiven us (those of us who know Christ) of the infinite number of sins we have committed against Him (and He has even forgotten those sins— Isa. 43:25; Jer. 31:34), who are we to bring up the past failures and offenses of others and hold a grudge against them? Christians must forgive each other and not dredge up in conversation past offenses. It is wise to often overlook such offenses (rather than always pointing them out) when doing so would be best for the other person and for the relationship.

Proverbs 17:14 The beginning of strife is like the releasing of water; therefore stop contention before a quarrel starts.

The releasing of water may be difficult to stop. For example, the breaking of the levees and the floodwall failures during Hurricane Katrina caused eighty percent of New Orleans to be flooded. If words of contention (angry, bitter disagreement) are spoken, negative emotions such as anger are likely to escalate within the participants, and could result in a verbal fight, or worse. May we remember the words of Deputy Fife and "nip it (that is, contention) in the bud!" Refuse to participate in contentious dialogue.

---

[84] James Grant, a friend of mine, contributed to the thoughts shared in this section.

Proverbs 18:2 A fool has no delight in understanding, but in expressing his own heart.

James 1:19 exhorts believers to "be swift to hear, slow to speak." Conversely, the fool is slow to hear and swift to speak. Wanting to speak more than to listen can indicate selfishness and pride. Humble, wise believers realize there is much to learn, much understanding to gain, which comes by listening to God's Word and to others and observing their behavior.

Proverbs 18:4 The words of a man's mouth are deep waters; the wellspring of wisdom is a flowing brook.

This emphasizes the gravity of the words you speak, for your words reveal your heart. Jesus said, "Out of the *abundance* of the heart the mouth speaks" (Mt. 12:34b). "Abundance" here is noteworthy because what you talk about on a consistent basis reflects what is the primary, driving concern of your heart. This is in contrast to what may be in your heart only superficially—what you discuss only occasionally.[85] The imagery of clean, refreshing, and nourishing water of "a flowing brook" represents spoken words of wisdom which cleanse, refresh, and nourish the hearers as well as the speaker.

Proverbs 18:6 A fool's lips enter into contention, and his mouth calls for blows.

Because "in the mouth of a fool is a rod of pride" (Pr. 16:18), and "by pride comes nothing by strife" (Pr. 13:10), the prideful words of a fool are conducive to fighting, verbally and physically. Therefore, fighting between husband and wife is indicative of foolishness and pride residing in their hearts.

Several high school students have been disciplined for making threatening statements of violence, either verbally or in writing. In Kentucky, one teen foolishly said he was "going to shoot the school up." He received a felony charge of terroristic threatening and a five-year prison sentence.

---

[85] James Grant assisted me here.

Proverbs 18:7 A fool's mouth is his destruction, and his lips are the snare of his soul.

More than any other aspect of a fool, his mouth (the words he speaks) will bring about his downfall. We see an example of this in 2 Samuel 1. A young Amalekite lied to David, telling him that King Saul commanded the Amalekite to kill him because Saul was severely wounded. He said that he did kill King Saul (even though he did not), thinking to gain David's favor. Instead David killed the Amalekite, saying, "Your own mouth has testified against you, saying, 'I have killed the LORD'S anointed.'" Had the Amalekite not lied, he would not have died. In contrast to the mouth of the fool, and the destruction that inevitably comes upon him, Proverbs 12:6 says, "…the mouth of the upright will deliver them."

Proverbs 18:13 He who answers a matter before he hears *it*, *it is* folly and shame to him.

Listening facilitates learning and requires patience. Answering a matter before hearing it is hasty, presumptuous, prideful, and selfish.

Proverbs 18:20 A man's stomach shall be satisfied from the fruit of his mouth; from the produce of his lips he shall be filled.

In faith, you should confess your victory in Christ, according to God's promises, including being made complete in Him (Col. 2:10). To a large degree, your heart and your circumstances will line up with your confession. Also, this is an effective verse for successful dieting—your stomach's contentment or craving will line up with your confession.

Proverbs 18:21 Death and life are in the power of the tongue, and those who love it will eat its fruit.

What you say will bring varying degrees of death or life to you and your situation, including your marriage. You can sow to your own defeat through speaking faithless, discouraging words, such as "It's going to be a bad day," or "I'm going to get sick," or "You are going to choke," or "You are going to fail," or "I can't be a good husband and father." Proverbs 6:2 says, "You are snared by the words of your mouth…." A friend of mine owned a car lot. He once became so frustrated, he said, "I wish this place would burn down." Within twenty-four hours, a major fire occurred at his car lot, causing over $100,000 worth of damage. He had no insurance. Not that every negative thing you say will come to fruition, but this is a strong warning to guard your tongue. He would have done better to have confessed, "I wish this car lot would prosper, to the glory of God."

You should sow life through speaking in accordance with God's promises, such as, "I can do all things through Christ who strengthens me" (Phil. 4:13), "I will love my wife as Christ loved the church" (Eph. 5:25), and "by His stripes I am healed" (Isa. 53:5). You can say to your spouse, "You are beautiful / handsome," "You are a blessing," and "You are more than a conqueror through Christ who loves you." Jesus said, "By your words you will be justified (life), and by your words you will be condemned (death)" (Mt. 12:37).

The second part of this verse implies: If you love death, you will eat the fruit of death, but if you love life, you will eat the fruit of life. As the wages of sin is death (Rom. 3:23), and the devil had the power of death (Heb. 2:14), you, through faith in Christ who is the Author of life (Jn. 1:4; Jn. 10:10; Jn. 14:6; 1 Jn. 5:11) and has all power, should repent of sin and give no place to the devil (Eph. 4:27).

As death precedes life in Proverbs 18:21, so some form of death preceding life is a theme throughout the Bible: humility precedes exaltation, sowing precedes reaping, and crucifixion precedes resurrection. Therefore, be assured that if you, in faith, humble yourself, crucify your flesh with its passions and desires (Gal. 5:24), and sow God's Word, then God will exalt and reward you greatly.

You who are saved should confess your blessed position in Christ. Many people do not have faith for victorious living, including having a victorious marriage and family life, because they do not know who they are in Christ, or they do not regularly reflect on and confess who they are in Christ. Below is a list of some of the many Biblical confessions you can make, always in Jesus' name. Your spouse, your children, and you can claim these only because of what Christ has done for you. In most or all of the phrases below, you can substitute "my marriage," "my household," or "my spouse" where it says "me" or "I".

- My spouse, my marriage, my children, and I are blessed in the city and blessed in the country (Dt. 28:3).
- The fruit of my body and the produce of my ground are blessed (Dt. 28:4).
- I am blessed when I come in and when I go out (Dt. 28:6. See also Ps. 121:8)
- As I submit to God and resist the devil, then in Jesus' name, any enemies that try to rise against my family and me must flee (Jas. 4:7; Dt. 28:7).
- The LORD will command the blessing on my storehouses and on all to which I set my hand (Dt. 28:8).
- My spouse and I are blessed to not have to borrow because God prospers us (Dt. 28:12; 3 Jn. 2).
- My spouse and I are the head and not the tail, above only and not beneath (Dt. 28:13).
- Because of my faith in Christ, God is for me (Rom. 8:31), with me (Mt. 28:20), in me (1 Cor. 6:19; 1 Jn. 4:4b), and upon me (Acts 1:8).
- God speaks through my spouse and me—"we are ambassadors for Christ, as though God were pleading through us, we implore you on Christ's behalf, be reconciled to God" (2 Cor. 5:20).
- I am redeemed, and by His stripes I was healed (Eph. 1:7-8; Gal. 3:13; 1 Pet. 2:24; Isa. 53:5).
- I am the righteousness of God in Christ (2 Cor. 5:21).
- I am complete in Christ. My spouse and my marriage are complete in Christ (Col. 2:10).
- I am more than a conqueror through Christ who loves me and lives in me (Rom. 8:37; Col. 1:27).
- Whatever my spouse and / or I ask the Father in Jesus' name, if it is in accordance with His will and in faith, He gives us (Mk. 11:23-24; Jn. 14:14; 1 Jn. 3:22; 1 Jn. 5:14-15).
- No weapon formed against my spouse or me shall prosper, including any spirit of strife, sickness, or disease (Isa. 54:17).
- Satan's dominion over my spouse's life, my life, and our marriage, is broken through faith in Christ (Lk. 10:19).
- Thanks be to God who always leads my spouse and me in triumph in Christ (2 Cor. 2:14), who gives us the victory through our Lord Jesus Christ (1 Cor. 15:57).

- My spouse and I prosper in all things and have good health, as our souls prosper (3 Jn. 2; Ps. 1:3; Josh. 1:8).
- No evil shall befall my marriage, my family, or me, nor shall any plague come near our dwelling (Ps. 91:10).
- Nothing shall by any means harm my marriage, my children, or me (Lk. 10:19).
- God has joined my spouse and I together; no one will separate us (Mt. 19:5).
- I am blessed with length of days, long life, peace, and satisfaction, and so is my marriage (Pr. 3:3; Ps. 91:16).
- No grave trouble will overtake my marriage or family, for I trust in Christ, my Righteousness (Pr. 12:21).
- My spouse and I have the mind of Christ (1 Cor. 2:16). We cast down every vain imagination, every high thing that exalts itself against the knowledge of God, and we bring every thought into captivity to the obedience of Christ (2 Cor. 10:5).
- God grants my spouse and me according to our hearts' desire, and fulfills all our purpose (Ps. 20:4).
- The LORD is the shepherd of my family; we shall not want (or lack; Ps. 23:1).
- "Goodness and mercy shall follow me all the days of my life; and I will dwell in the house of the LORD forever" (Ps. 23:6). Goodness and mercy shall also follow my marriage and household.
- The Lord has turned for my spouse and me our mourning into dancing; He has put off our sackcloth and clothed us with gladness (Ps. 30:11).
- The Lord has "set my feet in a wide place" (Ps. 31:8). Also, the Lord has set my marriage in a wide place.
- The Lord is "my hiding place"; He "shall preserve me from trouble"; He "shall surround me with songs of deliverance" (Ps. 32:7). The Lord shall also preserve my marriage and children from trouble.
- As my spouse and I trust in the Lord, mercy surrounds us (Ps. 32:10).
- God gives us drink from the river of His pleasures, and He continues His lovingkindness and righteousness to my spouse, children, and myself (Ps. 36:8, 10).

- As the law of my God is in the hearts of my household, none of our steps shall slide (Ps. 37:31).
- The Lord shall never permit us to be moved, as we abide in Christ who is our righteousness (Ps. 55:22).
- God "performs all things for me" (Ps. 57:2).
- God only is our rock and our salvation; He is our defense; our marriage shall not be moved. In God is our salvation and our glory; the rock of our strength, and our refuge, is in God (Ps. 62:6-7).
- God is merciful to us and blesses us, and causes His face to shine upon us (Ps. 67:1).
- The Lord "daily loads" us with benefits (Ps. 68:19).
- No good thing does God withhold from my household, if we walk uprightly (Ps. 84:11).
- The Lord's mercy is great toward us (Ps. 86:13).
- The Lord brings us out with silver and gold, and we are not feeble (Ps. 105:37).
- The Lord delivers my household and me out of all our distresses (Ps. 107:6).
- As we fear the Lord and delight greatly in His commandments, wealth and riches shall be in our house, and our righteousness (through faith in Christ) endures forever (Ps. 112:1-3).

Praise the Lord for such wonderful benefits on which each of us who know Christ may stand!

Proverbs 25:11 A word fitly spoken is like apples of gold in settings of silver.

There is a proper time as to when certain topics should be discussed and certain words spoken. As Proverbs 15:28 says "the heart of the righteous studies *how* to answer," it is also wise to study, and pray about, *when* to answer, or *when* to address a sensitive topic. This approach takes patience, wisdom, and a willingness to wait on God for the right time.

The gold and silver convey the wealth and beauty that are characteristic of a fitly spoken word. An apple can represent the fruit of the Spirit (Gal. 5:22-23), which should be characteristic of one's speech. An example of a word fitly spoken is seen in Gamaliel's address to the religious council (Acts 6:34-40). His words prevented the council from carrying out of a plot to murder the apostles.

Proverbs 25:11 specifies "a word," instead of words, fitly spoken. Though usually one's speech includes multiple words, "a word" can be seen as emphasizing the Lord's scrutiny of each word one speaks (Mt. 12:36).

Proverbs 29:20 Do you see a man hasty in his words? There is more hope for a fool than for him.

Hasty, or hurried, speech means the speaker has not studied how to answer (Pr. 15:28); he has not taken time to analyze the impact of his words. Not that you can never speak in a hurry; sometimes circumstances require you to speak without having much time for analysis. In such cases, it is even more important that God's Word has been hidden in your heart so that what is spoken in a hurry remains in harmony with God's truth and grace. Generally, however, words spoken in haste are not indicative of the fruit of the Spirit, including the fruit of patience. Proverbs 29:20 shows the Lord has quite a negative view of those who are regularly hasty in their speech. The impetus behind your words should be God's will rather than selfish desires. James 1:19 commands "every man (to) be...slow to speak...."

Ecclesiastes 5:3 a fool's voice is known by his many words.

According to this verse, an indicator in recognizing a fool is that he talks a lot. Certainly, other aspects of a fool's speech help indicate that he is a fool: contentious words (Pr. 18:6), a rod of pride in his mouth (Pr. 16:18), being hasty in his speech (Pr. 29:20), and answering a matter before he hears it (Pr. 18:13). This verse is reminiscent of Proverbs 10:19 "In the multitude of words sin is not lacking." Likewise, in the multitude of words foolishness is not lacking.

Ecclesiastes 5:6-7 Do not let your mouth cause your flesh to sin, nor say before the messenger of God that it was an error. Why should God be angry at your excuse and destroy

the work of your hands? (7) For in the multitude of dreams and many words there is also vanity. But fear God.

What you say can set into motion what you will end up doing. Speaking prideful can cause you to make prideful decisions. Conversely, speaking graciously can cause you to be gracious in your interactions with others. Ecclesiastes 5:3 and 5:7 reiterate the need to be "slow to speak" (Jas. 1:19). Being "zealous for the fear of the LORD all the day" (Pr. 23:17) will help you to tame your tongue all the day.

Ecclesiastes 10:12 The words of a wise man's mouth are gracious, but the lips of a fool shall swallow him up.

Grace is unearned favor; receiving blessings one does not deserve. Each of us is a recipient of God's grace. Consider God's grace toward us on the natural level. Can you cause your heart to beat, your eyes to see, or your digestive system to work? No. We are fearfully and wonderfully made by God (Ps. 139:14), and our physical lives are gifts to us from God. Consider God's grace on the spiritual level. Each of us has sinned infinitely against God, yet through the atoning crucifixion and resurrection of His Son, Jesus, each of us who believe are forgiven (Rom. 5:20; Eph. 2:8; Jn. 1:17). In addition to the divine pardoning of sin of the believer, God freely gives the believer His indwelling Holy Spirit, and richly all things to enjoy (Rom. 8:32; 1 Tim. 6:17). God's grace is amazing!

Because each of us has received God's grace, we should have gratitude toward God instead of an attitude of entitlement and complaining. We should also be gracious in all the words we speak to our neighbor. The Apostle Paul began and ended each of his Scriptural epistles with a salutation of "grace." In contrast to Proverbs 11:9—"The hypocrite with his mouth destroys his neighbor," the sincere believer always speaks grace to his neighbor. Colossians 4:6 says, "Let your speech *always* be with *grace*...." Such is the behavior of a wise person, that is one who abides in Christ—who is the embodiment of the wisdom of God (1 Cor. 1:24).

Chapter 13

Passages from Proverbs on Marriage

"An excellent wife is the crown of her husband" (Pr. 12:4a).

When it comes to the issues of choosing a spouse and marriage, Proverbs has much to say. Though Proverbs contains wisdom for all people, it seems written especially for men in several ways. One, wisdom, a major theme in Proverbs, is described as a female (1:20; 8:2; 9:1). This highlights the beauty and delightfulness of the Lord's wisdom, just as a woman is often described in terms of her beauty.[86] Two, Proverbs does not speak to the wife about finding a husband per se, but it does speak to the husband about finding a wife (18:22). Three, Proverbs does not warn the woman of the immoral man, but it does warn the man of the immoral woman (or woman of folly) and gives insight as to how to recognize her (We see this Proverbs 5, 6, 7, and 9. We will look at these passages in Chapter 7). Finally, in contrast to the immoral woman passages, Proverbs wraps up in Chapter 31 with a description of the virtuous wife and her beautiful

---

[86] James Grant, in conversation with me. Brother Grant assisted me with several of the insights made in this chapter.

qualities that all women should seek to emulate. The virtuous wife, like wisdom, is more valuable than silver or gold, and she enables the man to be all that God has called him to be. Just as there is the aspect of choice in who a person marries, there is also the aspect of choice regarding all of life. Pertaining to marriage, one can choose the virtuous mate or the immoral mate. There will be major consequences associated with his choice. In life, one can choose wisdom or foolishness. Wisdom brings righteousness, prosperity, safety, and various other blessings from God. Foolish living brings various types of destruction, including eternal destruction. Let's now look at Proverbs' treasures of wisdom pertaining to marriage. May you reap her rewards!

"As a ring of gold in a swine's snout, so is a lovely woman who lacks discretion" (Pr. 11:22).

How many farmers would put a valuable gold ring on the pig's nose knowing that pigs wallow in muddy pig troughs? The value and beauty of that gold ring is placed where it does not belong. The pig suggests one who devours. A woman who lacks discretion is one who lacks the ability to distinguish between right and wrong courses of action. The woman is naïve, and lacks the sort of judgment on which the godly life often depends.[87] This stands in contrast to a godly woman who is equipped with biblical knowledge (Hos. 4:6) as well as wisdom that comes from above (Jas. 1:5 and 3:17). A woman who lacks discretion is one who may devour the family's wealth as well as the man's emotional and spiritual resources. Though her physical appearance may be lovely, she is not a good choice of wife for the man of God.

"An excellent wife is the crown of her husband, but she who causes shame is like rottenness to the bones" (Pr. 12:4).

A crown is a mark of high recognition; an honor or an award. An excellent wife is a great asset to the husband; he is proud of her and she can enhance his status. The crown also relates to wisdom in Proverbs 4:8-9. Therefore, the husband will benefit from the wisdom his excellent wife brings to the family.

---

[87] James Grant, in conversation with me.

This passage also points out that as bones make up one's physical structure, or physical foundation, a wife who causes shame brings rottenness to the very foundation of the man. When one's foundation is destroyed, everything else comes tumbling down.

"He who finds a wife finds a good thing, and obtains favor from the LORD" (Pr. 18:22).

Finding does not necessarily mean seeking. In Isaiah 65:1, the LORD says, "I was found by those who did not seek Me." In Chapter 14, you will see that God provides a spouse so that you do not have to strive on your own to attain a spouse. First Corinthians 7:27 says, "Are you loosed from a wife? Do not seek a wife." You ought to seek "first the kingdom of God and His righteousness," and then God will add all things to you (Mt. 6:33). But when the Lord does bring a wife to you, it is a good thing in the Lord's eyes and favor accrues to you.

"Houses and riches are an inheritance from fathers, but a prudent wife is from the LORD" (Pr. 19:14).

Webster's defines "prudent" as "wise, careful in providing for practical matters, discreet, cautious, circumspect."[88] Your natural family can provide you with material things to help you get started in life. But only the Lord knows a person intimately enough to give him or her the best choice of a spouse and at the proper time. A prudent wife can help the man maintain his possessions and increase them rather than squander them.[89] An opposite verse, which is cited above, is Proverbs 11:22.

"Better to dwell in a corner of a housetop, than in a house shared with a contentious woman" (Pr. 21:9).

Contentious means regularly causing strife; argumentative. The opposite of contentiousness is found in Romans 12:18: "If it is possible,

---

[88] *Webster's American Dictionary*, College Edition, Revised and Updated, (Random House, New York, 2000), 635.

[89] James Grant, in conversation with me.

as much as depends on you, live *peaceably* with all men." A contentious woman makes peace within the house a virtual impossibility. No matter what other positive qualities a woman seems to have, if she is contentious, she is not the best choice of wife for the man of God.

Proverbs 31:10–31, an Exposition

Verse 10 introduces the subject of this final section of Proverbs: "the virtuous wife." Verse 28 indicates she has children, so the virtuous wife is also a godly mother. You'd almost expect the name "Linda Carter" to appear in this text as she starred in the television series, *Wonder Woman.* At least twenty-three positive points about the virtuous wife appear in this text.

Her Worth and Trustworthiness:

Verse 10b says: "For her worth is far above rubies." In other words, she is more valuable than riches. A husband should not overwork to get rich and in the meantime neglect his marriage.

Verses 11-12 say, "The heart of her husband safely trusts her; so he will have no lack of gain. She does him good and not evil all the days of her life." This indicates she is trustworthy, a sincere helpmate, and a great asset to her family. She allows her husband to fulfill his potential. It was said of Ruth Graham, the wife of the great evangelist, Dr. Billy Graham, that early in their marriage she gave him her blessing to evangelize the world while she remained at home to raise their four children. She was willing to allow Dr. Graham to be gone for months at a time so that others could hear the gospel and be saved. Had Dr. Graham been married a woman not committed to Christ, then his ministry would have undoubtedly been less effective.

She is Diligent:

Verse 27 says: "(She) does not eat the bread of idleness." Verse 13 says she "willingly works with her hands." The virtuous wife does not work begrudgingly, but she embraces the hard work required of her. Laziness is condemned in Proverbs. Proverbs 13:4 says: "The soul of a lazy man desires, and has nothing; but the soul of the diligent shall be made rich." Again, Proverbs 10:4 says, "He who has a slack hand becomes poor, but the hand of the diligent makes rich."

She is a Businesswoman / Entrepreneur:

Verse 16 says, "She considers a field and buys it; from her profits she plants a vineyard." Verse 18 says, "Her merchandise is good." In verse 24, she makes and sells clothing. This reminds me of Acts 18 where Priscilla was a tent-maker along with her husband Aquila. If the household's finances are adequate, I believe the mother should stay at home with the children, especially during the formative years of the children's lives. Furthermore, I believe homeschooling is best when possible. (Kim and I homeschool our two daughters. Fortunately, my job provides enough income so that Kim does not need to work outside the home. Understandably, not every family is in this financial situation. When this is the case, I admire the mother who excels in wearing both hats: holding down a job as well as holding down the fort.)

She is a Compassionate Mother:

In 1996, at the Brookfield Zoo in Chicago, a group of people were gathered at the gorilla pit watching the gorillas. No one noticed the three year old boy climbing up the railing until he fell over the railing and down inside the gorilla pit. He hit his head on the floor of the pit and lay there unconscious. The crowd began screaming for help. One gorilla, Binti Jua, a mother, quickly ran over and picked up the unconscious boy and began carrying the boy across the pit. This caused the crowd to become more hysterical. Other gorillas came toward the boy, but Binti Jua shielded the boy from them. She laid the boy by the zookeeper's door and guarded the boy until he was quickly rescued. Thankfully, the boy turned out to be relatively unharmed. This story illustrates the caring instincts of a mother as Binti Jua cared for another mother's baby. Verse 20 says, "She extends her hand to the poor, yes, she reaches out her hands to the needy." It is estimated that "30,000 children die every day of hunger and preventable diseases."[90]

---

[90] Oxfam America, *"Fast for a World Harvest: Fighting Hunger Takes More Than Knowing the Facts,"* (Boston: Oxfam America, 2003).

The virtuous wife does not hoard resources with no regard for the plight of the less fortunate. Instead, the virtuous wife has compassion for the children of other mothers. Proverbs 19:17 says, "He who has pity on the poor lends to the LORD, and He will pay back what he has given." Again, 1 John 3:17 says, "But whoever has this world's goods, and sees his brother in need, and shuts up his heart from him, how does the love of God abide in him?" Helping the poor is an aspect of knowing and exemplifying the love of God.

Verse 26 says: "She opens her mouth with wisdom, and on her tongue is the law of kindness." Wisdom is a major theme in Proverbs, a quality that is more valuable than all else, including riches (Pr. 3:13-15). Kindness is an aspect of wisdom; it is the desire to do good to someone. The words of wisdom and kindness that the virtuous wife speaks emanate from her pure heart; Proverbs 4:23 says out of the heart "spring the issues of life."

The Fundamental Key to the Virtuous Wife's Success

Every human being must remain rooted and grounded in the Word of God (the Bible) at all times. Knowing and obeying the Scriptures are mandatory for averting temporal and, more importantly, eternal disaster. Jesus said that if one builds one's life on the Word of God (illustrated by building one's life on a foundation of rock rather than sand), then one will be able to endure the storms of life, including persecutions, temptations, tragedies, etc. (Mt. 7:24-27). The virtuous wife realizes this fundamental truth. Her external accomplishments are only possible because of her inner godly character, which comes from her embracing the Word of God. Verse 30 says that she "fears the LORD." The fear of the LORD is a common theme in Proverbs, and it is a quality of utmost importance. The fear of the LORD means, in part, that because God will justly judge all sin (Ps. 7:11), and because "every transgression and disobedience" will receive "a just reward" (Heb. 2:2), then each of us, realizing these spiritual truths, should fear sinning against God, and we should bend over backwards to live in full obedience to Him. Proverbs 16:6b says, "by the fear of the Lord one departs from evil."

The Bible needs to be the foundation of a young person's life, even beginning when he or she is a child. Paul wrote to Timothy, "I call to remembrance the genuine faith that is in you, which dwelt first in your grandmother Lois and your mother Eunice, and I am persuaded is in you also" (2 Tim. 1:5). Faith was a legacy in Timothy's family—first in Timothy's grandmother, then in his mother, and eventually passed to him. Faith was modeled for Timothy. Likewise, we who are parents need to model faith for our children—we need to genuinely live out the faith we profess. And we need to teach our children the Word of God, as Deuteronomy 6:7 says: "You shall teach them diligently to your children."

"She watches over the ways of her household" (verse 27).

This encompasses a lot. Every situation is different, but in general she provides food, clothing, does laundry, makes sure the kids are doing their homework, and maybe has a job. She is concerned about the well-being and activities of each family member. She says, "How are you doing?", "What are you doing?", "With whom are you keeping company?", and "What's that spot on your shirt?" She strictly monitors all the influences in her children's lives: she monitors their acquaintances, their music, and the television shows they watch. She recognizes that watching over her household is a higher priority than furthering any outside career. And the virtuous wife is a role model. She models responsibility, generosity, compassion for others, respect for elders, a solid work ethic, and the Christian faith.

She is Strong

Some form of the word "strength" is mentioned three times in connection with the virtuous wife—twice in verse 17 and once in verse 25. The virtuous wife is strong in the Lord and perseveres during trials. Philippians 4:13 says: "I can do all things through Christ who *strengthens* me." (See also Ps. 18:32 and Neh. 8:10.)

"She shall rejoice in time to come" (verse 25b).

The virtuous wife is willing to delay gratification. She sacrifices and works hard now, believing that her future will be better as a result. Frugality, thriftiness, and the desire to save money are a few of her qualities. The virtuous wife invests in eternity, storing up treasure in heaven.

"beauty is passing" (verse 30).

Donnie Fritts had a rare cancer that required much of his face to be surgically removed. The surgery removed his nose, upper lip, and much of his forehead. He said he looked like a monster and would not leave his house for a long time after his surgery. But his wife, Sharon, loved and encouraged him through the entire ordeal. Sharon and friends raised money for Donnie to have surgery (as insurance would not cover it) to reconstruct his upper lip and attach a prosthetic nose. Sharon said, "His beauty is he's a giving person, a loving person."

The temporal aspect of physical beauty reminds us that all of this natural earthly realm, including one's mortal life, is temporary. Conversely, the soul of a person (one's mind, will, and emotions) will last forever. So if you are seeking God's wisdom in choosing a prospective spouse, remember that physical beauty should not be the number one determining factor in your choice. Certainly you should be attracted to your prospective spouse, but it is more important that you pay particular attention to the inner qualities of that person. As you can identify the type of tree you see by the fruit the tree bears, so you should look for consistent godly character and the fruit of the Spirit (Gal. 5:22-23) in a prospective spouse. The inside of a person is more important that the outside. If you want to marry someone who will love you, you need to marry someone who loves God. Loving God requires obedience to His Word (Jn. 14:15, 21, 23), as well as loving one's neighbor as oneself. The one who does this will be a good spouse.

"Her children rise up and call her blessed; her husband also, and he praises her" (verse 28).

This shows that the virtuous wife is respected and appreciated by her husband and children. They will praise her because of the love that she has consistently demonstrated toward God and them. She has trained up her children in the way they should go so that when they become older they will not depart from that training (Prov. 22:6). Furthermore, she is a wise, prudent, and excellent wife, the very crown of her husband, so that he can fulfill God's potential for his life (Pr. 19:14; 12:4).

A Difficult Departure and Daring Rescues

Around 1965, Mac Tweed was a forty-five year old Lieutenant Colonel in the Marines. He had just finished a six month tour in Vietnam and was granted leave for rest in Hawaii. At the time, he and his wife, Mary, had two children, both in college. Mary had flown out to Hawaii from their home in Virginia Beach to be with Mac. While she waited on Mac to arrive, she stayed with Elaine Armstrong (a Marine Colonel's wife that Mac had known for years). Colonel Armstrong paid for Mac and Mary to stay at the Royal Hawaiian (a top-rate hotel), and he allowed Mac to borrow his Ford Thunderbird car. Mac and Mary had a wonderful visit. At the end of Mac's leave, Mary accompanied Mac to the airport. As Mac started to tell Mary goodbye, tears came into his eyes, though he tried to hold them back. So many of his comrades were dying in Vietnam that Mac thought he would never see Mary again. Mary shed no tears but was smiling. (Later, she said that Elaine advised her not to be sad because that would not be the best for Mac to see just before his deployment.) Mac arrived in Vietnam twelve hours later. One of Mac's squadron's helicopters awaited him on the runway. As soon as Mac arrived at his base, there was a mission awaiting him. Recon men had been trapped behind enemy lines; one had been killed, and others wounded. At 4:00 a.m., Mac led a flight of four helicopters to make the rescue, which turned out to be dangerous, but was successful. Soon thereafter, Mac led out in another rescue flight. Suddenly, Mac's helicopter came under fifty caliber machine gun fire from the Vietcong. The rotor blades were badly damaged. Mac had to lower the helicopter onto the mountain. A sergeant-major flying with Mac that day was a mechanic! With a hammer, the sergeant-major straightened out the rotor blades, and they successfully flew to safety. For that mission, Mac was awarded the Distinguished Flying Cross. Mac Tweed flew in about two hundred more missions after that, but was never seriously injured. Mac was my grandfather, and he passed away in 2015 at the age of ninety-four. Mary died at the age of eighty-seven; they were married for over sixty-four years.

At the airport, Mary exemplified the strength of the virtuous wife (Pr. 31:17, 25) in the face of Mac's deployment. Furthermore, she single-handedly raised the children and "watched over the ways of her household" during the times that Mac was away flying in World War 2, the Korean War, and the Vietnam War. This story also brings to mind James 4:14: "You do not know what will happen tomorrow. For what is your life? It is even a vapor that appears for a little time and then vanishes away." Each of us needs to cherish our spouse while we can, because we do not know what will happen tomorrow.

Chapter 14

Instructions for Singles Who Are Considering Marriage

"my dove, my perfect one, is the only one" (Song. 6:9).

One Sunday, a pastor told his congregation that the church needed some extra money. He asked the people to consider giving a little extra in the offering plate. He said that whoever gave the most could pick out three hymns. After the offering plate was passed, the pastor noticed a $1000 bill in the offering. He was so excited that he immediately shared his joy with his congregation and said he would like to thank the person who put the money in the plate. An elderly widow raised her hand. The pastor asked her to come forward. He asked her to pick out the next three hymns. Her eyes brightened as she looked over the congregation, pointed to three men, and said, "I'll take him and him and him." A single person could perhaps identify with the elderly lady if the single person has not had a date in a long time. The single person may believe he or she needs to look at multiple prospects with the hope that one will turn out to be a good match. This brings us to a few important questions that I will address in the first part of this chapter. If you are currently single but believe God has called you to marriage, is there one specific person God wants you to marry, or does God's perfect will include there being any number of persons you could marry? Furthermore, does God want you to actively seek a spouse, or should you wait on God to bring His choice of spouse to you? Also in this chapter we will look at singleness verses marriage as well as what it means to be "unequally yoked."

Genesis 2

Read Genesis 2:18-25. In the first two chapters of the Bible, God has created and provided for man the beautiful Garden of Eden, food, gold and other riches, as well as animals. But the crowning culmination of all the blessings that God originally provided for man was his wife. In verse 18, the LORD said, "It is not good that man should be alone; I will make him a *helper comparable* to him." Therefore, one of the roles of the wife is to be the husband's *helpmate*. The word *"comparable"* means suited for, fitted for, or corresponding to. So Eve was the counterpart, or complement, to Adam. She was not identical to him, but rather different. Husband and wife were created to fit together like two pieces of a puzzle. In verses 19-20, God brought all the animals (which were obviously not Adam's counterpart) to Adam for him to name. It was as if God was whetting Adam's appetite for a being that would truly correspond to him after he had seen those who had not corresponded to him.[91]

What is the significance of Adam being asleep when Eve was made from him? Adam did not seek Eve. Adam was completely out of the picture when it came to the selection of a wife. God provided. That is one of the names of God: "Jehovah-Jireh," meaning "The-LORD-Will-Provide" (Gen. 22:14). Adam's wife was a surprise from the LORD! The inference is: if God wants you to marry, then God has one picked out just for you and you will not have to go out looking for that person.

---

[91] James Grant, in conversation with me.

Genesis 24

Genesis 24 contains the story of God providing a wife for Isaac. (Please turn there and follow along.) In verse 7 and verse 40, we see that the LORD would send His angel with Abraham's servant to prosper him in his search for a wife for Isaac. The servant's prayer, found in verses 12-14, indicates that he believed that the LORD had appointed a particular wife for Isaac. We also see this in verses 42-44. Verses 50-51 reveal that the father and brother-in-law do not dispute the servant's view, but agree that the matching of Rebecca with Isaac was done by God. They say, "The thing comes from the LORD...Here is Rebekah before you; take her and go, and let her be your master's son's wife, as the LORD has spoken." In the meantime, we do not see evidence of Isaac striving to find a wife, or actively seeking a wife. Instead, verse 63 shows Isaac meditating in the fields when Rebecca appeared. Isaac was likely meditating on the LORD, maybe praying some. He could have been praying to receive a wife. Again, God provided one specific woman.

Song of Solomon

Song of Solomon focuses on a love relationship between King Solomon and his bride, the Shulamite. Please note, from the following quotations from Song, that the spouse is seen as the best, the one that stands above all others: "O fairest among women" (1:8; 5:9; 6:1); "Like a lily among thorns, so is my love among the daughters" (2:2); "Like an apple tree among the trees of the woods, so is my beloved among the sons" (2:3); "How much better...is your love, and the scent of your perfumes than all spices!" (4:10); "My beloved is chief among ten thousand" (5:10); "my dove, my perfect one, is the only one" (6:9). In this last phrase (6:9), Solomon acknowledges that there is one perfect woman, the only woman, to be his wife. King Solomon penned this under the inspiration of the Holy Spirit, and thus these phrases stand as confirmation that there is one perfect choice of a wife for a particular man. A friend of mine, Kevin Black, said of his wife, Holly, "After fifteen years of marriage, I've come to realize that she is perfect for me." Amen!

The Sovereignty of God

The Biblical doctrine of the sovereignty of God supports that God will provide a specific mate. Jesus said, "Are not two sparrows sold for a copper coin? And not one of them falls to the ground apart from your Father's will. But the very hairs of your head are all numbered" (Mt. 10:29-30). If God designs your whole body and being so intricately so that He knows the number of hairs on your head (also Psalm 139 speaks of God's intimate knowledge of us), then it is reasonable to believe that He is also able to design another human to be perfectly corresponding to you and then bring that person to you at the right time.[92]

Therefore, for singles, the issue is not, "How can I make something happen on my own initiative?" You who are single should not feel a great pressure on yourself to impress a certain young woman or man. Rather, you who are single and desire marriage ought to do two things: 1) Walk with the Lord so the Lord can develop godly character in you. Your character and heart need to be well prepared so that God can entrust one of His children into your care to be your spouse. 2) You need to trust the LORD, that He will bring the one who is His perfect choice into your life at the proper time. If you are not yet married but believe God has marriage in store for you one day, a relevant verse is Psalm 37:23, "The steps of a good man are ordered by the Lord, and He delights in his way." Not that you can be good in and of yourself, but you can be good through walking with Jesus Christ, identifying with His righteousness, and hiding His good Word in your heart. Then you can trust that God will guide and provide. We see this in Matthew 6:33, "But seek first the kingdom of God and His righteousness, and all these things shall be added to you."

Is God Calling You to Singleness or Marriage?

It all comes down to what God wants for you. After all, if you gave God your life, then you gave God the right to make you single or married. Christians regularly pray, "Thy will be done" (Mt. 6:10). As a Christian, you should always want God's perfect will in any and every aspect of your life.

---

[92] James Grant, in conversation with me.

1 Timothy 4:1-3 Now the Spirit expressly says that in latter times some will depart from the faith, giving heed to deceiving spirits and doctrines of demons, (2) speaking lies in hypocrisy, having their own conscience seared with a hot iron, (3) *forbidding to marry*, and commanding to abstain from foods which God created to be received with thanksgiving by those who believe and know the truth.

The decision about whether or not you should marry is between you and the Lord. No religious denomination or hierarchy should tell you what to do. And certainly no religious organization should make singleness a prerequisite for ministry.

Matthew 19:9-12 (Jesus says) "whoever divorces his wife, except for sexual immorality, and marries another, commits adultery; and whoever marries her who is divorced commits adultery." (10) His disciples said to Him, "If such is the case of the man with his wife, it is better not to marry." (11) But He said to them, "All cannot accept this saying, but only those to whom it has been given: (12) For there are eunuchs who were born thus from their mother's womb, and there are eunuchs who were made eunuchs by men, and there are eunuchs who have made themselves eunuchs for the kingdom of heaven's sake. He who is able to accept it, let him accept it."

Verse 11 indicates that God has given some the gift of celibacy. Some have even made themselves eunuchs (a eunuch is someone who has had his testicles removed) for the purpose of advancing God's kingdom without the prospect of any distraction from marriage.

1 Corinthians 7

Part of the message of 1 Corinthians 7 is that singleness is in some sense preferable to marriage. Though this idea is unpopular in churches today, you do not have to be married to be fulfilled or complete. Christ completes you. Singles should not be regarded as second class citizens.

The theme that singleness is recommended appears in six places in this chapter: verses 1, 6-9, 26-27, 32-33, 38, 40. (Please follow along in your Bible to receive the most from this discussion.) Verse 1 says, "It is good for a man not to touch a woman. (The NIV says, "It is good for a man not to marry.") But this could also mean one should avoid unnecessary intimacy or touching in a literal sense before marriage. In verses 6-9, Paul again commends singleness, but admits that each person has his own gift from God: some have the gift of celibacy, and some have the gift of, or calling to, marriage. If one cannot exercise self-control, but instead burns with passion (which is conducive to lust), then it is probably better for that person to marry. Verse 2 reiterates this, indicating one should marry rather than have sexual immorality. In verses 26-27, Paul indicates that if one is single, it is good to stay that way. Verses 32-33 say, "He who is unmarried cares for the things of the Lord—how he may please the Lord. But he who is married cares about the things of the world—how he may please his wife." So the unmarried man has the potential to be single in focus, seeking to please and serve God with no restrictions placed on him or her due to family responsibilities. (This will probably include less financial restrictions as well.) A single person can more quickly uproot and go wherever he or she is called to go. Verse 38 says, "he who does not give her in marriage does better." (Please note that verse 38 contains major differences between the NKJV and the NIV.) So once again, singleness seems preferred. Verse 40 indicates that if a woman is widowed, she may remarry, but Paul thinks she will do better if she does not remarry.

Let's look at 7:29-31.

> But this I say, brethren, the time is short, so that from now on even those who have wives should be as though they had none, (30) those who weep as though they did not weep, those who rejoice as though they did not rejoice, those who buy as though they did not possess, (31) and those who use this world as not misusing it. For the form of this world is passing away.

This earthly life, which includes marriage, jobs, promotions, friendships, materialism, etc., is temporal; verse 29 says, "The time is short." But you are called to live for eternity! Again, Matthew 6:33 says: "seek first the kingdom of God and His righteousness...." So you should not view this temporal earthly life, including marriage, as the end-all-be-all, or the ultimate goal of living. After all, if you are a Christian, then you are an alien and a sojourner on this earth because your citizenship is in heaven (Phil. 3:20). Yes, you should try to meet the expectations of your spouse (that is a definite responsibility of those who are married, as long as those expectations are not sinful), but you must also see marriage as a means to an end. That end is to know, serve, and glorify God; to advance His wonderful kingdom on earth, and to store up treasure in heaven, our eternal home. Certainly married couples can and should do that. They, like others within the body of Christ, should seek to touch and agree in prayer (Mt. 18:19), should be iron sharpening iron (Pr. 27:17), and should spur one another on to love and good works (Heb. 10:24).[93]

2 Corinthians 6:14: "Do not be unequally yoked together with unbelievers."

One of the main devices the devil can use in the life of a new Christian is to try to bring an ungodly person into that new Christian's life, especially through dating and marriage, who could lead that new believer astray. It is possible that God would want to bring about marriage for a relatively new Christian, but a new Christian needs to use discernment in such a prospect. The new Christian should seek God's wisdom and guidance diligently in the matter, and he or she should also seek the council of more mature Christians if such prospects of dating and marriage quickly arise. The new Christian needs to be taught to recognize the tactics of the devil so as to resist whatever or whoever the devil might send. A main factor to be considered in seeking to discern if one should develop a relationship with another is to judge the fruit of the other person (Mt. 7:15-20). Does the person consistently demonstrate a genuine love for Christ, His Word, the advancement of His gospel, and does the person demonstrate humility, a love for others, and a hatred for sin? If you are a serious-minded Christian, I recommend against marrying someone who is backslidden or lukewarm in matters of the Christian faith (Rev. 3:16). However, if a young Christian man has had sex with a young woman to whom he is not married (this is fornication, which I address in Chapter 7), he likely has the moral obligation to remain with her if she desires to remain with him. Certainly God is merciful and can forgive sexual immorality, but do not put yourself in that situation.

The Lord commands believers to be "equally yoked" when it comes to marriage (2 Cor. 6:14). Christians ought to marry Christians. There is no Scriptural violation if a Pentecostal and a Baptist marry, or if a Lutheran and a non-denominational believer marry. Denominational allegiance is not required. The only stipulation for spouse selection is that both be in the body of Christ, knowing and abiding in Christ (Jn. 15:5).

---

[93] James Grant, a friend of mine, contributed to my understanding of this section.

Let's look at some examples of persons in the Bible who were unequally yoked. In 2 Samuel 6, as King David returned the Ark of God to Jerusalem, he was so overcome with joy that he "danced before the LORD with all His might" (verse 14). Now David had married Michal, the daughter of Saul. Indeed they were of the same nationality (Israelites), but spiritually their hearts were quite different. When Michal saw David "leaping and twirling before the LORD, she despised him in her heart" (verse 16). She did not recognize that her attitude, rather than David's attitude, was the problem, and she went a step further and condemned David to his face for his display of righteous zeal for God. At that moment, David realized Michal nowhere close to being a woman of God.

We see an earlier account regarding David and marriage (before he became king, in 1 Samuel 25) where he seems to have fared much better. He and his soldiers were treated shamefully by a rich man named Nabal. His name meant "fool" and he lived up to his name. Abigail was married to Nabal. She may have once called him "my love," but later she called him "scoundrel" (verse 25). That does not sound like a happy marriage. Abigail made a righteous decision to go and ask forgiveness of David on behalf of her husband's folly, and in doing so, she saved many lives. Her act also kept David and his men from shedding much blood. After Nabal's death, which the LORD hastened, David married Abigail. Unlike Michal, she likely contributed righteousness and wisdom to the marriage.

Sampson was another Biblical character who was blessed with a mighty anointing of God on his life, but who chose poorly concerning women. Delilah was an example of one of his poor choices. Her mission was to deceive and betray Sampson by finding out the secret of Sampson's strength (which was his long hair) and then have it removed (she had his hair cut off), in return for money paid to her by the Philistines, Israel's number one foe. Sampson yielded to Delilah's advances, and as a result he lost his anointing for physical strength for a season and he lost his eyes. Furthermore, Sampson was Israel's main weapon of defense. So when Sampson lost his strength, Israel lost a large portion of their national defense. Fortunately, due to God's mercy, Sampson was granted supernatural strength one last time, and he brought destruction to a highly populated Philistine temple, killing three thousand Philistines as well as himself.

When Job, whom the Bible calls blameless and upright, was in his greatest moment of need—beset with sudden, horrible tragedies concerning his family, his finances, and his physical health, his wife was nothing more than a voice-box through which the devil spoke. She said to Job, "Do you still hold fast to your integrity? Curse God and die!" (Job 2:9). Certainly, she had also suffered immense loss—all ten of her children died in one day! Rarely can a person identify with a tragedy so severe. However, due to that tragedy, she was willing to abandon any ounce of submission to God that she perhaps had previously displayed. She was probably bitter toward God. She had likely cursed God herself, and she wanted Job to join her in being bitter toward God and in cursing God. When one spouse is fully committed to God and the other spouse is significantly less committed (perhaps one is saved and the other is lost, or one is spiritually on-fire for the Lord and the other is spiritually luke-warm), then it is likely that the devil will work through the less committed spouse to attack or hinder the more committed spouse concerning that spouse's service unto God. Therefore, it is vital that both spouses be "sold-out," or completely committed, to the Lord. In any case, Job refused to heed the words of his wife. Instead, he rebuked her. We see that Job remained committed to His Creator, the One to whom he knew he would one day have to give an account of his life, when he said in 27:5, "Till I die I will not put away my integrity." (See also Job 13:15).

I do not mean to imply that when husband and wife are equally yoked in Christ, then neither of them will ever stumble into sin or make bad choices. Such faltering happens a lot. Abraham and Sarah are an example of that. Sarah erred when she advised Abraham to father a child by her maidservant, Hagar. Abraham also failed to always keep his mind renewed by God's promise that he would have a son from his own body because he "heeded the voice of Sarai" (Gen. 16:2) and impregnated Hagar. But Sarah advised him well when she later told him to "cast out this bondwoman and her son" (Gen. 21:10). The LORD backed her in this, saying to Abram, "Whatever Sarah has said to you, listen to her voice" (verse 12). Overall, I see Sarah as a woman of faith. Yet she did not always make good decisions or advise her husband according to faith, and negative consequences were the result. Also, Abraham made some bad choices of his own (such as lying—saying to Pharoah that his wife was his sister. He later told the same lie to King Abimelech). But overall Abraham and Sarah were considered faithful servants of God.

Eve was the perfect choice of a wife for Adam. Yet she made a disastrous decision in yielding to temptation and introducing sin to the human race. Adam fared no better, yielding to the word of his wife instead of to the Word of God, and thus he ratified her sin.

Even though some bad decisions are made within marriages where husband and wife are equally yoked by faith in Christ, still there is an infinitely higher level of incompatibility when a Christian is married to someone who is unregenerate at the core of his or her being. If you are a Christian, I urge you not to disobey God by marrying a non-Christian. Seek God first, and wait on His perfect provision of a spouse for you, according to His will. However, if you are already married to a nonbeliever, 1 Corinthians 7:13-16 and 1 Peter 3:1-2 give you instructions to consider, which includes remaining with the one that you have married. Perhaps your godly example, your witness, and your prayers will win your spouse to Christ.

If you are a single person, do you know whether or not God is ultimately calling you to marriage? I encourage you to diligently seek the Lord about this matter. If you are single and do think that you are called to marriage, what are some changes you might need to make in your life so that you can become more of a man or woman of God, and so that God can entrust you with a godly spouse? Also, if you are single and do anticipate getting married one day, I encourage you to educate yourself now about marriage, perhaps utilizing the abundance of marriage and love Scriptures contained in this book. If one studies in preparation to be a lawyer, doctor, minister, pharmacist, etc., then one should also study to be a godly spouse.

Dana Jackson and Bill Stauss recently wedded in Bowling Green, Kentucky, on Dana's hundredth birthday! They were married at a nursing home where they both live, and now they share a room. Dana wore white and Bill, eighty-seven, wore a tux. Several hundred people attended the wedding, which included a cake, flowers, candles, and ribbons and was held in the dining room of the nursing home. They had known each other for two years. Dana had been married three times, and Bill had been married once (for fifty-five years), but their former spouses are deceased. Both Dana and Bill admitted they were nervous before the ceremony, but they were also excited to be getting married to each other. Bill shed tears as he faced Dana during the ceremony. He later said, "When I saw her close up, I saw how beautiful she was." So perhaps one is never too old to get married.[94]

Marriage Is Like a Marathon

Molly and David were engaged to each other, and both loved to run. So in January 2011, the couple decided to incorporate their brief wedding ceremony into the 26.2 mile Houston Chevron Marathon they ran together. The bride wore all white running attire and included a wedding veil, and the groom ran in a black tuxedo shirt. The couple paused at the sixteen mile mark, exchanged vows, and then ran the remaining 10.2 miles of the marathon.[95] In a sense, marriage has some similarities to running a marathon. As Molly and David likely had trained with diligence for their marathon and had persevered by completing the marathon, hopefully they had also prepared themselves spiritually for their anticipated life-long journey together in marriage and would apply the godly quality of perseverance to deal with the trials that are an inherent part of marriage. If you commit to running a marathon, then you likely need to have counted the cost ahead of time. Typically, you need to train in advance in order to build up your endurance for the big event rather than simply to show up and see what you can do. Similarly, you should only approach the prospect of marriage with the gut level determination that the marriage will last for the rest of your natural life. Furthermore, you should prepare for the prospect of marriage by cultivating godly character (Gal. 5:22-23) and by studying the Word of God pertaining to love and marriage so that you will remain spiritually and emotionally "in shape" for marriage and family life. Anyone who successfully completes a marathon not only enjoys the satisfaction of having reached that lofty goal, but also enjoys the benefits of having achieved relatively good physical fitness through the process. Similarly, any spouse in a Christ-abiding marriage will benefit from having developed the Christ-like qualities of patience and enduring love which pleases our heavenly Father and reflects the infinite love embodied by our divine Bridegroom, the

---

[94] *Pair Marry On Bride's 100th Birthday*, Associated Press, Feb. 7, 2012.

[95] *Couple tie the knot while running marathon*, by Brian Gillie, Examiner.com. February 1, 2011.

Lord Jesus Christ. As "he who endures to the end shall be saved" (Mt. 24:13); likewise, you who endure in marriage to the end, with Christ remaining central to your marriage, will be greatly rewarded, and you will be a blessing to your family, church, and society.

Printed in the United States
By Bookmasters